JIM MANTHORPE wrote the first edition of this book. He has trekked in many of the world's mountainous regions from Patagonia to the Himalaya and Scandinavia to the Canadian Rockies. He is the author of three other Trailblazer guidebooks: *Pembrokeshire Coast Path, Tour du Mont Blanc* and *Scottish Highlands Hillwalking Guide*. He has also researched and updated numerous other Trailblazer titles.

Jim lives on the west coast of the Scottish Highlands and now works as a wildlife cameraman and film-maker. He has filmed eagles, otters and orcas for various BBC programmes including *Springwatch*. See 🖥 www.jimmanthorpe.com.

This **sixth edition** of *South Downs Way* was updated by **DANIEL MCCROHAN**. He was joined, as ever, by his trusty sidekick, Yoyo, his seven-year-old daughter who has now hiked her way along four of Britain's national trails.

Daniel is
author and flu
has spent the
updating more
both Trailbla
covering dest
Boscastle to l
his adventure
🖥 danielmccr

Authors

South Downs Way

First edition: 2004, this sixth edition 2018

Publisher Trailblazer Publications
The Old Manse, Tower Rd, Hindhead, Surrey, GU26 6SU, UK
info@trailblazer-guides.com, www.trailblazer-guides.com

British Library Cataloguing in Publication Data
A catalogue record for this book is available from the British Library

ISBN 978-1-905864-93-5

© **Trailblazer** 2004, 2007, 2009, 2012, 2015, 2018: Text and maps

Editor and layout: Anna Jacomb-Hood
Cartography: Nick Hill **Proofreaders**: Nicky Slade and Jane Thomas
Index: Anna Jacomb-Hood **Photographs (flora)**: C3 Bottom right, © Jane Thomas
All other photographs: © Bryn Thomas unless otherwise indicated

The maps in this guide were prepared from out-of-Crown-
copyright Ordnance Survey maps amended and updated by Trailblazer.

Acknowledgements

From Daniel Special thanks goes to my daughter, Yoyo McCrohan, for once again proving to
be the most effervescent of walking partners – the Seven Sisters were no match for this seven-
year-old! I'm also grateful to Bryn Thomas for commissioning me for this project. Thanks too
to Fraser C Addecott for his local expertise, and to Mum, Sam and Heidi, for holding the fort
back home. I'd also like to thank all those readers who wrote in with comments and suggestions, in particular, Stuart Blackburne, Gerald Cleaver, David Cocovini, Anne Conchie, Susan
Corbett, Bea Delannoy & Olivier, Rodney Duggua, Rachel & Karl-Peter Hammer, Richard
Marshall, Keith McKenna, Nick Price, Trudi & Andy Rintoul, Paloma Sainsbury and Sue
Wood. Finally, thanks as always, to everyone at Trailblazer: Anna Jacomb-Hood for editing,
layout and index; Nick Hill for the maps and Nicky Slade and Jane Thomas for proofreading.

A request

The author and publisher have tried to ensure that this guide is as accurate and up to date
as possible. Nevertheless, things change. If you notice any changes or omissions that should
be included in the next edition of this book, please write to Trailblazer (address above) or
email us at 💻 info@trailblazer-guides.com. A free copy of the next edition will be sent to
persons making a significant contribution.

Warning: coastal walking and long-distance walking can be dangerous

Please read the notes on when to go (pp12-16) and outdoor safety (pp66-8). Every effort
has been made by the author and publisher to ensure that the information contained herein
is as accurate and up to date as possible. However, they are unable to accept responsibility
for any inconvenience, loss or injury sustained by anyone as a result of the advice and information given in this guide.

Updated information will be available on: 💻 www.trailblazer-guides.com

Photos – Front cover and **this page**: The view along the Seven Sisters cliffs. (Photo © Yoyo
McCrohan). **Previous page**: The classic chalky line of the Way, stretching up Beeding Hill.
Overleaf: Yellow rape-seed flowers bring Iford Hill to life. (Photos © Daniel McCrohan).

Printed in China; print production by D'Print (☎ +65-6581 3832), Singapore

South Downs
WAY

WINCHESTER TO EASTBOURNE

60 large-scale maps & guides to 49 towns and villages

PLANNING – PLACES TO STAY – PLACES TO EAT

JIM MANTHORPE

SIXTH EDITION RESEARCHED AND UPDATED BY
DANIEL McCROHAN

TRAILBLAZER PUBLICATIONS

Contents

INTRODUCTION

PART 1: PLANNING YOUR WALK

PART 2: THE ENVIRONMENT & NATURE

PART 3: MINIMUM IMPACT WALKING & OUTDOOR SAFETY

PART 4: ROUTE GUIDE AND MAPS

Contents

ABOUT THIS BOOK

This guidebook contains all the information you need. The hard work has been done for you so you can plan your trip from home without the usual pile of books, maps, guides and internet research.

When you're all packed and ready to go, there's comprehensive public transport information to get you to and from the trail and 60 detailed maps and town plans to help you find your way along it.

The guide includes:

- All standards of accommodation with reviews of campsites, camping barns, hostels, B&Bs, pubs/inns, guesthouses and hotels
- Walking companies if you want an organised tour, and baggage-transfer services if you just want your luggage carried
- Itineraries for all types of walkers
- Answers to all your questions: when to go, degree of difficulty, what to pack, and how much the whole walking holiday will cost
- Walking times in both directions and GPS waypoints
- Cafés, pubs, tearooms, takeaways, restaurants and food shops
- Rail, bus & taxi information for all villages and towns on the path
- Street plans of the main towns both on and off the path
- Historical, cultural and geographical background information

---

❏ MINIMUM IMPACT FOR MAXIMUM INSIGHT

Nature's peace will flow into you as the sunshine flows into trees. The winds will blow their freshness into you and storms their energy, while cares will drop off like autumn leaves. **John Muir** (one of the world's earliest and most influential environmentalists, born in 1838)

Why is walking in wild and solitary places so satisfying? Partly it is the sheer physical pleasure: sometimes pitting one's strength against the elements and the lie of the land. The beauty and wonder of the natural world and the fresh air restore our sense of proportion and the stresses and strains of everyday life slip away. Whatever the character of the countryside, walking in it benefits us mentally and physically, inducing a sense of well-being, an enrichment of life and an enhanced awareness of what lies around us.

All this the countryside gives us and the least we can do is to safeguard it by supporting rural economies, local businesses, and low-impact methods of farming and land-management, and by using environmentally sensitive forms of transport – walking being pre-eminent.

In this book there is a detailed and illustrated chapter on the wildlife and conservation of the region and a chapter on minimum-impact walking, with ideas on how to tread lightly in this fragile environment; by following its principles we can help to preserve our natural heritage for future generations.

Break clear away, once in awhile, and climb a mountain or spend a week in the woods. Wash your spirit clean. (**John Muir**).

INTRODUCTION

The South Downs are a 100-mile (160km) line of chalk hills stretching from the historic city of Winchester, in Hampshire, across Sussex to the Pevensey Levels by Eastbourne. For centuries travellers and traders have used the spine of the Downs as a route from one village to the next.

> **For centuries travellers and traders have used the spine of the Downs as a route from one village to the next.**

Today that route is still used by walkers, outdoor enthusiasts and others who simply need to escape from box-like offices in congested towns and cities. London, Brighton, Southampton and other urban areas are all within an hour or two of the South Downs, making these beautiful windswept hills an important recreational area for the millions who live in the region.

A traverse from one end to the other following the South Downs Way national trail is a great way of experiencing this beautiful landscape with its mixture of rolling hills, steep hanging woodland and windswept fields of corn. Add to this the incredible number of pretty Sussex and Hampshire villages with their friendly old pubs, thatched cottages and gardens bursting with blooms of roses, foxgloves and hollyhocks and one begins to understand the appeal of the Downs as a walking destination.

The South Downs Way begins in the cathedral city of Winchester from where it heads across rolling hills and the Meon Valley with its

The official start of the South Downs Way is now the City Mill in Winchester, marked by a wooden sign (**right**) with a trail profile cut into the top of it. Until 2017, the trail began from Winchester Cathedral, (**left**, © Daniel McCrohan) which is well worth visiting before you start your walk.

INTRODUCTION

The Way ends on the outskirts of Eastbourne but most walkers will want to continue into this seaside town with its impressive Victorian pier.

lazy, reed-fringed chalk-bed river and charming villages. At Butser Hill the Way reaches the highest point of the Downs with views as far as the Isle of Wight and, in the other direction, the North Downs. Continuing along the top of the ridge the Way passes through ancient stands of mixed woodland, past the Roman villa at Bignor and on towards the sandstone cottages of Amberley. Close by is the fascinating town of Arundel with its grand cathedral and even grander castle rising above the trees on the banks of the River Arun. Then it is on to Chanctonbury Ring with its fine views across the Weald of Sussex. The next stretch climbs past the deep valley of Devil's Dyke and over Ditchling Beacon to Lewes with its crooked old timber-framed buildings and the famous Harvey's Brewery. Finally, the path reaches the narrow little lanes of Alfriston with more historic pubs than one has any right to expect in such a small village. The walk's grand finale includes the meandering Cuckmere River and the roller-coaster Seven Sisters chalk cliffs – before reaching the final great viewpoint of Beachy Head, overlooking the seaside town of Eastbourne.

Walking the Way can easily be fitted into a week's holiday but you should allow more time to be able to explore the many places of interest such as Arundel, Lewes and Winchester itself ... not to mention the lure of all those enchanting village pubs that are bound to make the trip longer than intended!

(**Below**): The chalk cliffs between Cuckmere and Birling Gap are known as the Seven Sisters. If it's a warm day, you can go down to the beach at Birling Gap and have a swim. (Photo © Daniel McCrohan)

INTRODUCTION

History

There has been a long-distance route running along the top of the South Downs for far longer than walking has been considered a leisure activity. The well-drained chalk hilltops high above the densely forested boggy clay below were perfect for human habitation and were certainly in use as far back as the Stone Age.

From this time onwards a complex series of trackways and paths developed across the land and it is believed that by the Bronze Age there was an established trade route along the South Downs. All along the crest of the Downs escarpment there is evidence of Iron Age hill-forts and tumuli (ancient burial grounds), many of them very well preserved, particularly the Old Winchester hill-fort site in Hampshire.

In more recent times the land was cleared and enclosed, and the flat hilltops were put under the plough. Although this process erased many of the lesser tracks the most significant remained; the one which ran east–west along the edge of the escarpment.

It was not until 1972, amid rapidly growing public interest in walking, that the then Countryside Commission designated the 80 miles from Eastbourne to the Sussex–Hampshire border the first long-distance bridleway in the UK. Later, the final section through

Arundel Castle rises above Arundel town which is five minutes by train from Houghton Bridge.

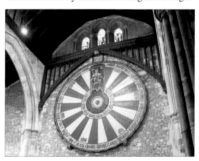

Hanging on the wall in the Great Hall in Winchester is the table top said to be from King Arthur's Round Table. As it dates only from the 13th century it's too young to be genuine but still impressive at about 800 years old.

St Peter's Church in Southease (see p158) has an unusual round tower dating from the middle of the 12th century.

(Photos above © Daniel McCrohan)

Hampshire was added bringing the length of the South Downs Way to 100 miles and giving it a spectacular start in the historic city of Winchester. Today the route is growing in popularity with walkers, cyclists and horse-riders alike, all of whom tend to mingle with ease.

How difficult is the path?

The South Downs Way is one of the most accessible and easiest of Britain's long-distance paths. Those on foot will find the route usually follows wide, well-drained tracks in keeping with its designation as a long-distance bridleway, catering for cyclists, horse-riders and more recently pony-cart wheelchair users, as well as walkers. If anything walkers may, on occasion, crave a few more lightly trodden paths since the route always sticks to the well-beaten track.

The South Downs Way is one of the most accessible and easiest of Britain's long-distance paths.

This 100-mile walk can be conveniently divided into sections starting and stopping at any of the numerous little villages that sit at the foot of the escarpment or in a fold in the hills.

One thing to note, though, is that because the Way generally follows the high ground along the top of the South Downs, to reach the villages offering accommodation, pubs and shops you usually have to descend steeply off the Downs and climb back onto them to continue, which can make pub lunches less attractive! When calculating the day's timings you need to bear in mind this extra walking time involved.

INTRODUCTION

Above: A typically quaint thatched cottage in the village of Amberley (see p118). The Way takes you through, or close by, numerous pretty English villages such as this one, with their little cottages, cosy pubs, village greens and ancient churches. **Below**: Sweeping views of the Arun Valley on the approach into Amberley. (Photos © Daniel McCrohan)

How long do you need?

The whole route can be tackled over the course of a week worth taking a couple of extra days to enjoy the beautiful downland villages that are passed along the Way. It is also worth taking time to explore the former capital of Saxon England, Winchester, a historic town with a beautiful cathedral. At the other end of the walk Eastbourne is, to be polite, perhaps a little less interesting but will keep those who like to sit on a windy seafront happy for hours.

Walkers will find that the whole route can be tackled over the course of a week but it is well

See pp32-3 for suggested itineraries covering different walking speeds The practical information in this section will help you plan your walk and design an itinerary to meet your particular preferences.

When to go

The south-east of England has probably the best climate in a country maligned for its fickle weather. It doesn't suffer from too much rain and enjoys more hours of sunshine than other parts of the UK. The route can be followed at any time of year but the chances of enjoying good weather do depend on the season.

(**Below**): Lewes Castle was built shortly after the Battle of Hastings in 1066.
(Photo © Daniel McCrohan)

SEASONS

Spring

A typical spring is one of sunshine and showers. From March to May a day walking on the Downs may involve getting drenched in a short sudden shower only to be dried off by warm sunshine a few minutes later. However, the weather can vary enormously from year to year, sometimes with weeks of pleasantly warm sunny weather and in other years days of grey drizzle.

Alfriston's village store – a good place to stock up for a picnic. (Photo © Daniel McCrohan)

In general this is a great time to be on the Downs. Walker numbers are low and the snowdrops, bluebells and primroses decorate the bare woodland floors.

Summer

It can get surprisingly hot and sunny from June to September but again the weather can vary from one year to the next. Always be prepared for wet weather but also be confident of enjoying some balmy summer days too. Occasionally it can be a touch too hot for walking. This can be a problem as there is not much water on the Downs so fill up your water bottles whenever you can. Visitor numbers are high at this time of year, as you might expect, so it can be a little difficult to enjoy a solitary day on the Way. The hills are colourful in summer with wild flowers in bloom in the meadows, red poppies among the corn and fields of bright yellow oil-seed rape. Hay-fever sufferers may not agree that this is such a good thing. However, everyone seems to be in a good mood and the pubs are brimming with all sorts of folk, from fellow walkers to country gents. The big advantage of summer walking is that it remains light until well after nine in the evening so there is never any rush to finish a day's walk.

Autumn

Autumn is probably the season when you can reliably expect to be rained on. The weather from September to November tends to be characterised by low-pressure systems rolling in from the Atlantic one after another, bringing with them prolonged spells of rain, mist and strong winds. On the positive side those who enjoy a bit of peace and quiet will find very few fellow walkers out and about at this time of year. Furthermore, it is not all rain and

Famous local landmarks, the two windmills above Clayton are known as Jack and Jill (see p142); this is Jill.

❏ MAIN FESTIVALS & EVENTS

May/June

● **Charleston Festival** (🖥 charleston.org.uk) Held in Charleston (see p158) in the last week or two of May. Arts and literature abound.

● **Goodwood Race Course** (🖥 goodwood.com) Horse-racing takes place here **between May and October**; booking accommodation in the area can be tricky when meetings are being held, so check the website for schedules.

● **Goodwood Festival of Speed** (🖥 goodwood.com) Held over three days in late June on the Goodwood Estate a few miles south of Cocking; see box p102.

● **Aegon International** (🖥 lta.org.uk/major-events/Aegon-International-Eastbourne) tennis championship is held in Eastbourne at the end of June.

July/August

● **Qatar Goodwood Festival** (🖥 goodwood.com) Known in horse-racing circles as 'Glorious Goodwood', this is one of the highlights of the flat-racing season and is held over five days at the start of August.

● **Winchester Hat Fair** (🖥 hatfair.co.uk) Originally a buskers' festival, now a cele-bration of street arts and community; all events are free but contributions are wel-come – just put your money in the hat. First weekend of July.

● **Winchester Festival** (🖥 winchesterfestival.co.uk) A 10-day festival in early July which includes classical and choir music in the cathedral, folk music in the pubs, dancing in the street, art exhibitions, comedy events and plenty more.

For details of other festivals throughout the year in Winchester visit 🖥 festivals inwinchester.co.uk.

● **Airbourne: Eastbourne International Airshow** (🖥 eastbourneairshow.com) Held in Eastbourne mid to late August.

● **Arundel Festival** (🖥 arundelfestival.co.uk) takes place over the last 10 days of August in the castle's grounds and features folk, rock and classical music as well as plays (Shakespeare) and comedy.

September

● **Goodwood Revival** (🖥 goodwood.com) A festival of motor racing involving rare and unusual racing cars held at Goodwood over three days in mid September.

November

● **Lewes Bonfire Night Celebrations** (🖥 lewesbonfirecelebrations.com) Largest bonfire-night celebration in the country, held on 5 November unless it's a Sunday.

wind. Sometimes the weather can surprise you with a day of frost and cold sun-shine that can make a day on the Way a real treat. It's important to remember that some businesses reduce their opening hours at this time of year or even close all together.

Winter

Southern England doesn't experience as many cold snowy winters as it used to some ten to twenty years ago. From December to February these days it's usu-ally relatively mild with wet weather and occasional spells of colder, dry weath-er. Any snow that does fall is usually during January and February. It is more likely the further east you go since it is the south-east corner that gets caught by

(Opposite): The chalk cliffs rise high above Beachy Head Lighthouse.

INTRODUCTION

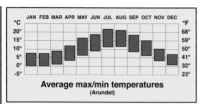

Average max/min temperatures
(Arundel)

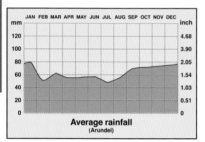

Average rainfall
(Arundel)

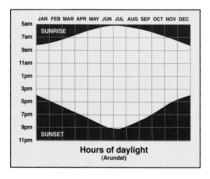

Hours of daylight
(Arundel)

the snow showers that roll in from the North Sea, when the wind is from the north or east. Many walkers will appreciate winter walking for the wilder weather it offers and the days of solitary sauntering along the high windswept crest of the Downs. The best days are the cold, frosty ones when the air is clear and the views stretch for miles. Bear in mind that in winter some businesses, particularly in the more remote villages, are closed. It is always wise, for example, to call a pub before turning up expecting dinner.

TEMPERATURE

Generally, temperatures are comfortable year-round. In winter, warmer clothes will be needed as the temperature drops towards and, on occasion, just below freezing. Summer is usually pleasantly warm with temperatures around 16°C to 23°C but temperatures as high as the low 30s Celsius do occur on at least a few days during July or August which can make walking on exposed sections of the Way uncomfortable.

RAINFALL

The weather in England is affected mostly by the weather systems that come from the south-west. These are usually low-pressure systems that contain a lot of rain. Rain can and does fall in any month of the year but dry weather is usually more likely in the early summer.

DAYLIGHT HOURS

If walking in autumn, winter and early spring, you must take account of how far you can walk in the available light. Also bear in mind that, depending on the weather, you may get a further 30-45 minutes of usable light before sunrise and after sunset.

PLANNING YOUR WALK

Practical information for the walker

ROUTE FINDING

There is very little opportunity to get lost along the Way. It would be an easy route to follow even without the waymark posts, which are usually marked with the National Trail 'acorn' symbol. An acorn on a **yellow** chevron indicates that this route is a footpath, ie exclusively for pedestrians. A **blue** background indicates that the trail is a bridleway and can therefore also be used by horses and cyclists. A **purple** background quaintly adds a pony and trap. A **red** or **white** background

The Way is very well marked. If in doubt, follow the acorn.

warns that the route can also be used by motorbikes. Bear in mind that other footpaths may be indicated on the waymark posts so **follow the acorn**.

Nevertheless, it is hard to go astray. Should you find yourself erring from the path the chances are a fence on one side or the steep Downs escarpment on the other will deflect you back in the right direction. In addition there are usually other walkers around who you can ask for directions.

Using GPS with this book

Particularly given the above, modern Wainwrights will scoff at the idea of using GPS technology for navigation on this trail but, now built into most smartphones, it's an easily accessible if non-essential aid. In no time at all a GPS receiver with a clear view of the sky will establish your position and altitude.

The maps in the route guide include numbered waypoints; these correlate to the list on p183 and pp186-8, which gives the latitude/longitude position in a decimal minute format as well as a description. Where the path is vague, or there are several options, you will find more waypoints. You can download the complete list of these waypoints for free as a GPS-readable file (that doesn't include the text descriptions) from the Trailblazer website: ☐ trailblazer-guides.com (click on **GPS waypoints**).

It's also possible to buy state-of-the-art digital mapping to import into your GPS unit, assuming that you have sufficient memory capacity, but it's not the most reliable way of navigating and the small screen on your pocket-sized unit will invariably fail to put places into context or give you the 'big picture'.

Bear in mind that the vast majority of people who walk the Way do so perfectly well without a GPS unit. Instead of rushing out to invest in one, consider putting the money towards good-quality waterproofs or footwear instead.

South Downs Way app

A Trailblazer South Downs Way app is now available. For more information see the Trailblazer website 🖳 www.trailblazer-guides.com.

ACCOMMODATION

The South Downs lie in a populous area so there are plenty of villages and towns within easy reach of the Way, most of which offer accommodation for the walker. However, the Way generally follows the high ground along the top of the South Downs escarpment while the villages lie at the foot of the hills. This tends to leave the walker with a small detour to reach a bed at the end of each day. Bear this in mind when calculating times and distances from the maps in Part 4. As a general rule it is a good idea to allow an extra hour each day for the walk to and from your accommodation.

Camping

With the exception of the High Titten wild camping site (p116), there is little to no opportunity for wild camping on the South Downs so campers have to rely on organised campsites. Fortunately, there are quite a few, so it is feasible to camp your way along the entire trail, providing you leave yourself enough time to catch a train home from Eastbourne after your final day, as there are no campsites after Alfriston.

Refer to the itinerary chart for campers on p33 to help organise a schedule, and pay particular attention to the 'Camping on the Way' box (see below), which lists all camping options that are right on the trail, rather than in more distant downland villages, which are a pain to get to and from with a heavy rucksack.

❏ Camping on the Way

Especially for walkers carrying heavy camping gear, here is a complete list of campsites that are right on the trail (or very close to it), rather than at the end of a steep descent into a downland village.

Map 4 Holden Farm Camping (p83)	**Map 29** YHA Truleigh Hill (p137)
Map 8 Meon Springs (p86 & p88)	**Map 31** Saddlescombe Farm (p137)
Map 9 Sustainability Centre (p89)	**Map 32** The White House (p140)
Map 16 Hilltop Cottages (Manor Farm; p102 & p104)	**Map 35** Housedean Farm (p152)
	Map 38 YHA South Downs (p158)
Map 22 Foxleigh Barn & High Titten wild camping site (both p116)	**Map 42** Alfriston Camping Park (p162)

Campsites charge between £5 and £15 per camper. Some of the more organised sites have showers and washing facilities while others are merely a place to pitch a tent in the grass. You can also camp at two of the three YHA hostels.

Those who have the urge to camp in greater isolation where there is no recognised site may find it worthwhile asking a landowner for permission to set up camp; see p63.

Those who do camp will certainly appreciate the experience: the pampered comforts of a bed and breakfast are outweighed by the chance to sleep under the stars and be woken by the sun, should it happen to be showing.

Hostels and bunkhouses

There are three **YHA hostels** on the Way but all are located on the last third of the trail. However, there's an **independent hostel** called Wetherdown Lodge (p89), which is part of the Sustainability Centre near East Meon.

Despite the name, anyone of any age can join the YHA. This can be done at any hostel or by contacting the **Youth Hostels Association of England and Wales** (YHA; ☎ 0800-0191 700 or ☎ 01629-592700, 🖳 www.yha.org.uk). A year's membership costs £15/20 if paid by direct debit/credit card (£5/10 for under 26s), or £25/30 for household membership. YHA hostels are easy to book, either online or by phone and you can stay even if you aren't a member though expect to pay £3pp per night more. It is now possible to pay by credit card at all the hostels. All the hostels on this trail have showers, shared living space, a drying room and a fully equipped kitchen, and all except the Eastbourne one have a café-restaurant offering meals. Bedding is provided but not towels, though they can be rented.

Other cheap lodgings include: **bunkhouses** (in Cocking, Houghton Bridge and Pyecombe), **camping barns** (Gumber Bothy, near Bignor Hill, and in Houghton Bridge), **shepherd's huts** (in Chilcomb, Butser Hill, Pyecombe, Bury and near Lewes) and **camping pods** and **bell tents** (at YHA South Downs).

Bed and breakfast

Some B&Bs can be quite luxurious and come at a price, but generally speaking, all the Downs walker really wants is a warm bed and a hot bath. For this reason

---

❑ **Booking accommodation**

You should always **book your accommodation in advance** because of the competition for beds in summer and during events such as those held at Goodwood (see box p14). It is often possible to book online but if not phone the establishment; many are now linked to online agencies, but you will get the best rate overall if you book direct. When booking **check the rate and facilities** and if walking with your children or your dog, check this won't be a problem (some hostels do not allow children to stay in dormitories, for example). You may be asked to pay a **deposit**, usually 25-50%. Always let the owner know if you need to cancel so that they can free the bed for someone else.

If you are having problems finding accommodation, **tourist information centres** (see p40) usually have a list of places and some provide a booking service for which they may make a charge. The majority take a 10% deposit towards the cost of the first night's accommodation, though this is then deducted from the bill.

most of the B&Bs listed in this guide are recommended because of their usefulness to the walker and convenience to the Way, not for how many stars the tourist board has awarded them.

Bed and breakfast owners are often proud to boast that all rooms are **en suite**. This enthusiasm for private facilities has led proprietors to squeeze a cramped shower and loo cubicle into the last spare corner of the bedroom. Not having an en suite room is sometimes preferable as you may get sole use of a bathroom across the corridor and a hot bath is just what you need after a day's walking – and you will also probably save a few pounds each night.

You may find it hard to find establishments with **single** rooms. **Twin** rooms and **double** rooms are often confused but a twin room usually comprises two single beds which can either be pushed together for a couple or kept separate. A double room has one double bed. **Triple/quad** rooms are for three/four people and usually consist of a double bed and one or two single beds or bunk beds, but occasionally three/four single beds.

B&Bs do of course provide **breakfast** (see opposite). Some also provide a packed lunch or an evening meal but you will need to request this in advance and there will be an extra charge. Most B&Bs, however, are close enough to a pub or restaurant and if not the owner may give you a lift to one.

B&Bs in this guide vary from £30 per person (pp) for two sharing in the most basic accommodation to £60pp (or more) for the most luxurious places with en suite facilities; most charge £35-45pp. See also box below.

Guesthouses, hotels, pubs and inns
(See also box below) **Guesthouses** are usually more sophisticated than B&Bs, offering evening meals and a lounge for guests; rates are around £40-70 per person (pp) for two sharing.

Pubs and inns offer bed and breakfast of a medium to high standard and have the added advantage, of course, of having a bar downstairs and also generally offer food, so it's not far to stagger back to bed. However, the noise from tipsy punters below your room might prove a nuisance if you want an early night. Prices usually range from £30 to £60pp per night for two sharing. Generally, **hotels** tend to be more expensive, ranging from £35 to £100pp (or more) for two sharing. There are now also a few **restaurants with rooms** which are great for a treat. Expect to pay £35 to £75pp for two sharing.

Airbnb
The rise and rise of Airbnb (🖳 airbnb.co.uk) has seen private homes and apartments opened up to overnight travellers on an informal basis. While

---

❏ **Rates for B&B-style accommodation**
Note that all per person (pp) rates are based on two people sharing a room. Many places do not have a single room so they generally add a supplement (£20-30) for single occupancy of a room. Prices can drop during the winter months and also for three or more people sharing a room. If you are on a budget you could always ask to have a room-only rate (ie no breakfast) which will usually be about £10 less.

accommodation is primarily based in cities, the concept is spreading to tourist hotspots in more rural areas, but do check thoroughly what you are getting and the precise location. While the first couple of options listed may be in the area you're after, others may be far too far afield for walkers. At its best, this is a great way to meet local people in a relatively unstructured environment, but do be aware that these places are not registered B&Bs, so standards may vary, yet prices may not necessarily be any lower than the norm.

FOOD AND DRINK

Breakfast and lunch

If staying in a B&B, guesthouse or hotel you'll usually be served a full cooked breakfast which may be more than you are used to. However, some places offer a lighter continental breakfast which you may prefer first thing in the morning and some also are happy to provide vegetarian/vegan breakfasts if requested in advance; alternatively, ask to have a packed lunch instead of breakfast, particularly if you are planning an early start. If requested in advance, and for an additional cost, many places can also provide you with a packed lunch.

Alternatively, breakfast and packed lunches can be bought and made yourself; there are some great cafés and bakeries along the Way which can supply both. Remember that certain stretches of the walk are devoid of places to eat so check the information in Part 4 to ensure you don't go hungry.

Evening meals

The **pubs** that grace the pretty flint villages of the Downs rank as some of the most authentic country inns in England. Many of them date from the 14th or 15th centuries and have fascinating histories. Food can vary from cheap traditional pub grub to high-quality cuisine served in a pub restaurant. For the serious

PLANNING YOUR WALK

❏ **Food**

Food in Hampshire and Sussex is varied and tasty. Local farm produce concentrates on beef and pork but there is also a variety of local cheeses and other dairy products. Look out for traditional dishes such as steak and ale pie, shepherd's pie and ploughman's lunch which can all be found on pub menus.

Fruit farms are a common sight in the south. Most of them invite people to '**pick your own**'; an invitation to help yourself to their strawberries, raspberries, blueberries and other fruit growing in the fields. Once you have picked enough, you take the fruit to be weighed and paid for.

Hampshire has also long been well-known for its **watercress** beds, particularly around Warnford, Overton and Hurstbourne Priors. The large-scale propagation of watercress in these areas dates back to the 19th century and is much aided by alkaline water provided by the chalky streams of Hampshire. Some of the original watercress beds are still used today.

Cream teas can be ordered in many of the cafés along the South Downs Way. Partaking in this quintessentially English activity is usually done in the mid afternoon and involves a pot of tea accompanied by scones, clotted cream and jam.

❏ **Real ale**
There's a plethora of local breweries for the real-ale connoisseur to get excited about. Probably the most famous Sussex brewery, and certainly the oldest, is **Harvey's** (🖥 harveys.org.uk) of Lewes (p147) which dates from 1790. Beers to look out for include their Sussex Best and Armada Ales, while in September they release their seasonal Southdown Harvest Ale which they proudly describe as the 'taste of the South Downs'.

There are also several newer local breweries. **Rectory Ales** of Plumpton Green, for example, is a tiny brewery set up in 1996 by the rector of Plumpton to raise funds for the local parish, a once-common tradition. Their most popular brews are Rector's Pleasure (4%) and Rector's Revenge (5%).

On tap at the The Five Bells in Buriton (p93), meanwhile, is real ale from **Ballard's Brewery** (🖥 ballards-brewery.co.uk), which was founded on a farm near Petersfield in 1980.

It's also worth seeking out ales from **Long Man Brewery** (🖥 longmanbrewery .com), in Litlington. You'll find their beers in Ye Olde Smugglers Inne, in Alfriston (p164), and in the Plough & Harrow, in Litlington (p165) itself. Then there's **Riverside Brewery** (🖥 riversidebreweryltd.co.uk) in Upper Beeding who do a Beeding Best Bitter (4.2%), with a hint of liquorice, and a hoppy Sneaky Steamer (5.1%). You'll find them in the Jack & Jill Inn in Clayton (see p142), and in the Castle Inn in Bramber (see p134).

You can try **Flowerpots Bitter** (🖥 flowerpotscheriton.co.uk) right where it's brewed, at the Flower Pots Inn in Cheriton (p83). And finally, look out for beers from **Gribble Brewery** (🖥 gribbleinn.co.uk), based in Oving near Chichester, whose ales deserve awards not just for flavour but for decorating beer pumps with some of the quirkiest names. There's Pig's Ear, and the dangerously named Plucking Pheasant, but go steady on the Winter Wobbler (7.2%).

'connoisseur' drinker the best thing about the downland pub is the range of real ales on offer (see box above).

While evening meals in the villages are often limited to whatever the local pub is serving, some of the larger towns such as Winchester, Eastbourne, Lewes and Petersfield are home to some quality **restaurants** with specialities ranging from fish to Italian fare.

Those on a budget, or walkers who stumble into town late in the evening, will find a number of late-night **takeaway** joints offering everything from kebabs and pizzas to Indian and Chinese and, of course, traditional fish & chips.

Self-catering supplies

If you are camping, fuel for the stove and other equipment is an important consideration. Supplies can be found at any of the outdoor shops in Winchester and Eastbourne, whilst en route there are outdoor shops in Lewes as well as hardware stores, which stock some camping-stove fuel, in the villages of Storrington and Steyning.

Some of the bigger campsites also sell camping-stove fuel, while some provide fire pits and sell bundles of kindling. Check Part 4 for more detailed information about these shops.

❏ Farmers' markets

Farmers' markets are held in a number of towns and villages throughout Hampshire and Sussex. These give local farmers a chance to showcase their produce and give consumers the opportunity to purchase locally grown stuff in the knowledge that they are helping not just the local economy but the environment too. Buying local produce helps cut down on the wasteful long-distance carriage of food – both nationally and internationally – plus, of course, the food is much fresher.

To find out more about farmers' markets near the South Downs Way check out the websites 🖳 hampshirefarmersmarkets.co.uk, or 🖳 www.westsussex.info/farmers-markets.shtml. Also try 🖳 localfoodbritain.com, or 🖳 farma.org.uk.

Drinking water

Depending on the weather you may need to drink as much as 3-4 litres of water a day. If you're feeling lethargic it may well be that you haven't drunk enough, even if you're not feeling particularly thirsty.

Although drinking directly from streams and rivers can be tempting, it is not a good idea. Streams that cross the path tend to have flowed across farmland where you can be pretty sure any number of farm animals have relieved themselves. Combined with the probable presence of farm pesticides and other delights, it is best to avoid drinking from these streams. Fortunately, there are quite a few drinking-water taps along the Way; we've marked them on our route maps. They are also marked on the South Downs Way trail map on the National Trails website (🖳 nationaltrail.co.uk/south-downs-way/plan). Also remember that, unless otherwise specified, all tap water in the UK, even that from the taps in public toilets, is safe to drink.

Where drinking-water taps are thin on the ground, remember that you can always ask staff in shops, cafés or pubs to fill your bottle or pouch from the tap. In England, licensed premises (ie places that serve alcohol) are required by law to provide customers with free tap water, but kind staff will sometimes be happy to help fill up your bottle even if you're not buying anything from them.

MONEY

While Eastbourne and Winchester at each end of the Way have plenty of banks and **ATMs** (cashpoints/cash dispensers), the villages in between do not. Bear in mind that some of these ATMs (albeit a decreasing number) charge up to £1.75 per withdrawal. However, if you find yourself without a penny on the Way it is only a short detour to some of the larger towns; banks and/or ATMs can be found in Petersfield, Midhurst, Arundel, Storrington, Steyning, Lewes and Meads.

Nevertheless, it is worth having more **cash** than you think you might need since some small local shops will require you to pay in cash, as will most B&Bs, camping barns and campsites.

PLANNING YOUR WALK

Shops that do take cards, such as supermarkets, will sometimes advance cash against a debit card (a transaction known as '**cashback**') as long as you buy something for at least £5 at the same time. Pubs sometimes do the same.

Getting cash from a post office

Several banks in Britain have an agreement with the post office allowing customers with a debit card and PIN to make cash withdrawals at post office counters throughout the country. For a full list of banks that are part of this scheme contact the Post Office (🖥 www.postoffice.co.uk/branch-finder). This is a useful service particularly if no ATM is available.

❏ Information for foreign visitors

● **Currency** The British pound (£) comes in notes of £50, £20, £10 and £5, and coins of £2 and £1. The pound is divided into 100 pence (usually referred to as 'p', pronounced 'pee') which come in silver coins of 50p, 20p, 10p and 5p, and copper coins of 2p and 1p.

● **Money** Up-to-date **rates of exchange** can be found on 🖥 xe.com/ucc, at some post offices, or at any bank or travel agent.

● **Business hours** Most **shops and supermarkets** are open Monday to Saturday 8am-8pm (sometimes up to 15 hours a day) and on Sunday from about 9am to 5 or 6pm, though main branches of supermarkets generally open 10am-4pm or 11am-5pm. Occasionally, especially in rural areas, you'll come across a local shop that closes at lunchtime on one day during the week, usually a Wednesday or Thursday; this is a throwback to the days when all towns and villages had an 'early closing day'.

Main **post offices** are open at least from Monday to Friday 9am-5pm and Saturday 9am-12.30pm; branches in villages stores are often now open the same hours as the store. **Banks** typically open at 9.30am Monday to Friday and close at 3.30pm or 4pm though in some places they may open only two or three days a week and/or in the morning only; **ATMs** (**cash machines**) though are open all the time as long as they are outside; any inside a shop or pub will only be accessible when that place is open. Note that ATMs that charge (see p23), such as Link machines, may not accept foreign-issued cards.

Pub hours are less predictable; although many open daily 11am-11pm, often in rural areas opening hours are Monday to Saturday 11am-3pm & 5 or 6-11pm, Sunday 11am/noon-3pm & 6 or 7-10.30pm. Last entry to most **museums and galleries** is half an hour, or an hour, before the official closing time.

● **National (bank) holidays** Most businesses are shut on 1 January, Good Friday (March/April), Easter Monday (March/April), first and last Monday in May, last Monday in August, 25 December and 26 December.

● **School holidays** State-school holidays in England are generally as follows: a one-week break late October, two weeks over Christmas and the New Year, a week mid February, two weeks around Easter, one week at the end of May/early June (to coincide with the bank holiday at the end of May) and five to six weeks from late July to early September. Private-school holidays fall at the same time, but tend to be slightly longer.

● **Documents** If you are a member of a National Trust organisation in your country bring your membership card as you should be entitled to free entry to National Trust properties and sites in the UK; see also p58.

● **EHICs and travel insurance** Although Britain's National Health Service (NHS) is free at the point of use, that is only the case for residents. All visitors to Britain should be properly insured, including comprehensive health coverage.

OTHER SERVICES

Many villages and all the towns have at least one **public telephone** (although some of the infrequently used ones are now being taken out of service), a small **food shop** and a **post office**. Post offices can be useful for sending unnecessary equipment home which may be weighing you down. In Part 4 mention is given to services that may be of use to the walker such as **banks**, **cash machines**, **outdoor equipment shops**, **launderettes**, **internet access**, **pharmacies** and **tourist information centres**, some of which can be used for finding and booking accommodation among other things.

The European Health Insurance Card (EHIC) entitles EU nationals (on production of the EHIC card so ensure you bring it with you) to necessary medical treatment under the NHS while on a temporary visit here. Note, this may change once Britain has left the EU. For details, contact your national social security institution. Also note that this is not a substitute for proper medical cover on your travel insurance for unforeseen bills and for getting you home should that be necessary.

Also consider cover for loss and theft of personal belongings, especially if you are camping or staying in hostels, as there may be times when you'll have to leave your luggage unattended.

● **Weights and measures** In Britain, milk can be sold in pints (1 pint = 568ml), as can beer in pubs, though most other liquid including petrol (gasoline) and diesel is sold in litres. Distances on road and path signs is given in miles (1 mile = 1.6km) rather than kilometres, and yards (1yd = 0.9m) rather than metres.

The population remains divided between those who still use inches (1 inch = 2.5cm), feet (1ft = 0.3m) and yards and those who are happy with millimetres, centimetres and metres; you'll often be told that 'it's only a hundred yards or so' to somewhere, rather than a hundred metres or so.

Most food is sold in metric weights (g and kg) but the imperial weights of pounds (lb: 1lb = 453g) and ounces (oz: 1oz = 28g) are frequently displayed too. The weather – a frequent topic of conversation – is also an issue: while most forecasts predict temperatures in Celsius (C), some older people continue to think in terms of Fahrenheit (F; see the temperature chart on p16 for conversions).

● **Smoking** The ban on smoking in public places relates not only to pubs and restaurants, but also to B&Bs, hostels and hotels. These latter have the right to designate one or more bedrooms where the occupants can smoke, but the ban is in force in all enclosed areas open to the public – even if they are in a private home such as a B&B. Should you be foolhardy enough to light up in a no-smoking area, which includes pretty well any indoor public place, you could be fined £50, but it's the owners of the premises who carry the can if they fail to stop you, with a potential fine of £2500.

● **Time** During the winter, the whole of Britain is on Greenwich Meantime (GMT). The clocks move one hour forward on the last Sunday in March, remaining on British Summer Time (BST) until the last Sunday in October.

● **Telephone** The international country access code for Britain is ☎ 44 followed by the area code minus the first 0, and then the number you require. Within Britain, to call a landline number with the same code as the landline phone you are calling from, the code can be omitted: dial the number only. If you're using a mobile phone that is registered overseas, consider buying a local SIM card to keep costs down.

● **Emergency services** For police, ambulance, fire or coastguard dial ☎ 999 or ☎ 112.

PLANNING YOUR WALK

WALKING COMPANIES AND BAGGAGE TRANSFER

Several companies provide 'self-guided holidays' which include detailed advice and notes on itineraries, maps, accommodation booking, daily baggage transfer and transport at the start and end of your walk. Most can also tailor make a holiday for you. If the thought of carrying a heavy rucksack doesn't appeal there is a company which will transfer your luggage to your next B&B or campsite and another which will book your accommodation if that is what you prefer.

Baggage transfer and accommodation booking

● **South Downs Discovery** (☎ 01925-564475, 🖥 southdownsdiscovery.com, Cheshire) Maximum weight 20kg.

For an agreed charge some **B&B owners** may be prepared to take your luggage on to your next accommodation; it's always worth enquiring. Some **taxi companies** are also prepared to transfer your luggage on an ad hoc basis.

● **Sherpa Van Project** (☎ 01609-883731, 🖥 sherpavan.com, North Yorkshire) offers an **accommodation-booking service** for the South Downs Way.

Self-guided holidays

Note: most companies listed below can also tailor make a holiday.

● **Absolute Escapes** (☎ 0131-240 1210, 🖥 absoluteescapes.com, Edinburgh) Itineraries of 6-9 days.

● **British & Irish Walks** (☎ 01242-254353, 🖥 britishandirishwalks.com, Gloucestershire) Itineraries along the whole and parts of the Way.

● **Celtic Trails** (☎ 01291-689774, 🖥 celtictrailswalkingholidays.co.uk, Monmouthshire) The whole Way in 10- to 13-day itineraries.

● **Contours Walking Holidays** (☎ 01629-821900, 🖥 contours.co.uk, Derbyshire) Has a variety of South Downs packages from 2-day tasters to the whole walk.

● **Explore Britain** (☎ 01740-650900, 🖥 explorebritain.com, County Durham) The whole walk from Eastbourne to Winchester, plus a 4-day walk, using Eastbourne as your base each night.

● **Footpath Holidays** (☎ 01985-840049, 🖥 footpath-holidays.com, Wiltshire) Has been organising walking holidays for 35 years. A 9-night full walk, or parts of the Way using Alfriston as a base.

● **Footprints of Sussex** (☎ 01903-813381, 🖥 footprintsofsussex.co.uk, West Sussex) Has been organising SDW walks for 25 years. Offers the full Way as well as sections. Also organises an annual, supported rather than guided, walk each June (🖥 southdownsway.com) and walks with dogs (see Paw Prints, opposite).

● **Freedom Walking Holidays** (☎ 07733-885390, 🖥 freedomwalkingholidays .co.uk, Oxfordshire) A 7- to 8-day full-walk itinerary.

● **Let's Go Walking** (☎ 01837-880075, 🖥 www.letsgowalking.com, Devon) The whole path in 9 days' walking/10 nights.

● **Load Off Your Back** (☎ 01707-386726, 🖥 loadoffyourback.co.uk, Hertfordshire) Offers 4- to 10-day packages.

● **Macs Adventure** (☎ 0141-5303628, 🖥 macsadventure.com, Glasgow) The full Way in 6-8 days.

PLANNING YOUR WALK

● **Mickledore** (☎ 01768-772335, 🖳 mickledore.co.uk, Cumbria) Have itineraries offering the whole route in 6-10 days, or each half of the Way, and a short break 2-day circular walk.

● **PawPrints of Sussex** (🖳 pawprintsofsussex.co.uk), a subsidiary of Footprints (see opposite), offer weekend breaks or 7/9-night treks along the full trail for dog owners and their pets, with dog-friendly B&B accommodation.

● **Responsible Travel** (☎ 01273-823700, 🖳 responsibletravel.com, East Sussex) The whole Way in 9 days' walking/10 nights.

● **Sherpa Expeditions** (☎ 020-8875 5070, 🖳 sherpaexpeditions.com, London) An 8-day and a 10-day itinerary.

● **South Downs Discovery** (see opposite) South Downs Way specialists offering itineraries for 2-10 days.

● **The Walking Holiday Company** (☎ 01600-713008, 🖳 thewalkingholiday company.co.uk, Wales) Itineraries with 2-10 walking days.

Guided holidays

● **HF Holidays** (☎ 0345-470 7558, 🖳 hfholidays.co.uk, Herts) This long-established company covers the whole Way in 10 days' walking/11 nights based at Abingworth Hall, nr Thakeham, West Sussex.

❏ MOUNTAIN BIKING THE SOUTH DOWNS WAY

The South Downs Way is perfect for mountain bikers. As Britain's first long-distance bridleway it was specifically geared to horse-riders, cyclists and walkers. The entire route can be followed on two wheels on wide tracks which are, on the whole, well drained, with only a few very steep sections either side of the major river valleys. There are some sections where walkers and cyclists must follow different routes but these are well marked with blue chevrons indicating byways and yellow chevrons for footpaths.

   Extreme MTB (☎ 0844-870 8648, 🖳 extrememtb.co.uk, Hampshire) offers 2-, 3- and 4-day **cycling itineraries** incorporating the whole Way.

Tips for cycling the Way

● **Camp rather than stay in B&Bs** Cycling gives you the perfect opportunity to experience the joys of camping without having to carry any of your gear on your back. Strap a tent, sleeping bag and roll mat onto your bike, and off you go! See the box on p18 for a list of campsites that are on the Way itself, rather than in the surrounding countryside far below.

● **Stick to the Way** Most of the downland villages are some distance below the Way itself, and whilst it's a joy to freewheel down to them for a pub lunch, it can be tough pulling your bike back up onto the trail afterwards. Plan accordingly; it's far better to stay on the Way at all times, if at all possible.

● **Be prepared for punctures** It hardly needs saying but don't forget your puncture repair kit (and know how to use it!) as well as your pump. Though famed for its chalk, much of the South Downs Way also contains super-sharp fragments of flint, which can cause havoc for even the sturdiest mountain-bike tyres.

● **Wet-weather gear** Chances are it will rain at some stage, and when it does the Way gets muddy; sometimes very muddy. Come prepared with wet-weather gear, including waterproof panniers, mudguards and a rag to wipe down any dirty gear.

PLANNING YOUR WALK

TAKING DOGS ALONG THE WAY

Dogs are allowed on the South Downs but should be kept on a lead whenever there are sheep around. Considering the Downs is a prime sheep-farming area this is most of the time and it is worth remembering that farmers are perfectly within their rights to shoot any dog they believe to be worrying their sheep.

See pp188-90 for detailed information on long-distance walking with dogs and Paw Prints (p27) for self-guided holidays with dogs.

DISABLED ACCESS

In the summer of 2016 the South Downs Way became the first fully inclusive National Trail when it was completed in its entirety by a wheelchair user using a state-of-the-art pony cart, specially developed by PonyAxeS (☎ 07510 736518, 🖥 ponyaxes.com/south-downs-way). Unfortunately, for those without access to such carriages, some parts of the South Downs Way are still quite inaccessible to disabled people, despite many of the councils taking steps to improve access to the Sussex and Hampshire countryside.

Nevertheless, there are stretches of the Way that can be followed quite easily, particularly where roads provide direct access to the top of the hills such as at **Ditchling Beacon** (see p140). Here there are gates designed for wheelchair users and there are also plenty of benches at intervals along the path to the west of Ditchling Beacon. **Devil's Dyke** (see p134) is another good spot where access is relatively easy and the path not too rough. **Seven Sisters Country Park** (see box p166) has good facilities for the disabled both in the park and at the visitor centre and access to the beach at Cuckmere Haven is quite straightforward.

Further west the easiest stretches of the Way can be found to the west of **Bignor Hill** (see p113), where there's a car park near the top, and on **Harting Down** (p102) which has a relatively long stretch of gentle, level pathways. **Queen Elizabeth Country Park** (p93) has wide, level tracks and easy access.

For more information see 🖥 accessiblecountryside.org.uk/southeast.

Budgeting

CAMPING

Campsites generally charge £5-15 per person (pp) so if camping and cooking all your own food expect to need £10-20pp per day. However, it is always best to allow for more than you think necessary, to cover those occasional luxuries such as a warm bed after a day walking in the pouring rain. If you like a pint at the end of the day remember that one costing less than £4 is a rare thing in the south of England. Bearing this in mind it is worth counting on at least £20 per day.

HOSTELS AND BUNKHOUSES

There are very few hostels and camping barns on the Way, so you won't be able to use this type of accommodation exclusively. Combined with camping, or one or two nights in B&Bs, it can still be very cost-effective, though.

The only true **camping barn** on the Way, called Gumber Bothy (see p113), will set you back £12pp per night. Dorm beds in **hostels** along the route cost around £13-21pp (less £3 if you're a YHA member). The YHA charges for beds in its hostels following the modern online model with lowest prices during quieter periods and rates increasing with popularity of location and date. Rooms (around £15-30pp) are surprisingly good for such a budget price. Hostels usually have a self-catering kitchen allowing you to survive on cheap food from the supermarket or local shop. However, if you want to make use of their meals, expect to pay around £5 for breakfast, around the same for a packed lunch and £6.50-10 for an evening meal. Note YHAs sometimes have a kids-eat-for-free deal.

To cover the cost of a night in a hostel and the occasional bar meal and drink, count on at least £25-30 per person per day. If you eat out most nights this figure is likely to be £35pp per day or more.

B&B-STYLE ACCOMMODATION

Rates for bed and breakfast in a B&B, pub or guesthouse are usually £30-70pp (hotels are likely to be more) for two sharing a room (most places add a single occupancy supplement of at least £10 but some charge the full room rate). Breakfast is, of course, almost always included in the rate but you will need to allow about £5 for a packed lunch (more if eating in a pub or café) and about £10-15 for an evening meal. If you decide to treat yourself to quite a few meals in pubs or restaurants, drink beer and have other goodies you will probably need around £50-80pp per day.

EXTRAS

Don't forget all those little things that push up your daily bill – laundry, souvenirs, beer, ice-cream, buses here, buses there, more beer and getting to and from the Way. All these will probably add up to between £50 and £100.

Itineraries

This guidebook has been divided into daily stages but these are not rigid. Instead, it's structured to make it easy for you to plan your own itinerary. The South Downs Way can be tackled in any number of ways, the most challenging of which is to do it all in one go; this requires about one week. Others may prefer to walk it over a series of short breaks, coming back year after year to do a bit more. Some choose to walk only the best bits. *(cont'd on p32)*

PLANNING YOUR WALK

	TOWN AND				
Place name (Places in brackets are a short walk off the SDW)	**Distance from previous place** approx miles/km (+) = miles from SDW		**ATM/ (cash machine) Bank**	**Post Office**	**Tourist Information Centre/Point (TIC)/(TIP)**
Winchester	0		✔	✔	TIC
Chilcomb	2	3.5			
(Cheriton)	4½	7	(+1.5)		✔
Exton & Corhampton	5½	9			✔
(East Meon)	5	8	(+1)		✔
(Buriton)	7½	12	(+0.5)		
(Petersfield)			(+2)	✔	✔	TIC
(South Harting)	3½	5.5	(+0.5)		✔
(Cocking)	7	11	(+0.5)		✔
(Heyshott)	2	3	(+0.5)		
(Graffham)	1½	2.5	(+1)		mobile
(Sutton & Bignor)	4	6.5	(+1)		
(Bury)	2½	4	(+1)		mobile
Houghton Bridge & Amberley	1	1.5		✔		
(Arundel)			(+4)	✔	✔	TIP
(Storrington)	3	4.5	(+1.5)	✔	✔	TIP
(Washington)	3	4.5	(+0.5)			
(Steyning, Bramber & Upper Beeding)	4	6	(+1)	✔	✔	TIP
(Fulking)	6½	11	(+0.5)			
(Poynings)	2	3	(+0.5)			
Pyecombe	2	3				
(Clayton)	1	2	(+0.5)			
(Ditchling)	1½	2	(+1.5)		✔	
(Plumpton)	2	3	(+0.5)			
(Lewes)	1	1.5	(+3)	✔	✔	TIC
(Kingston-nr-Lewes)	5	8	(+1)			
Rodmell & Southease	4	6				
(West Firle)	3½	5.5	(+1)		✔	
(Alciston & Berwick)	2½	4	(+1)			
Alfriston	2	3			✔	
Litlington	1	2				
Exceat/Westdean	1½	2.5				
Birling Gap	4	6				
Beachy Head	3	4.5				
Meads	1½	2.5		✔	✔	
Alternative (inland) route from Alfriston						
(Milton Street)	1	2	(+0.5)			
(Wilmington)			(+1)			
Jevington	2½	4				
Eastbourne	4	6		✔	✔	TIC

Total distance 100 miles/162km (via Seven Sisters), 97½ miles/158km (via Jevington)

VILLAGE FACILITIES

Eating Place ✔ = one; ✔✔ = two; ✔✔✔ = three+	Food store	Campsite* H (Ind hostel) (B) bunkhouse (CB) camping barn	Hostel*	B&B-style accommodation ✔ = one, ✔✔ = two ✔✔✔ = three+	Place name (Places in brackets are a short walk off the SDW)
✔✔✔	✔	✔ (2¼)		✔✔✔	**Winchester**
		✔ (2)		✔	**Chilcomb**
✔	✔	✔ (2)		✔	**(Cheriton)**
✔✔	✔	✔ (¾)		✔✔✔	**Exton & Corhampton**
✔	✔	✔	H	✔✔	**(East Meon)**
✔✔				✔✔	**(Buriton)**
✔✔✔	✔	✔ (1¼)		✔✔✔	**(Petersfield)**
✔	✔			✔✔✔	**(South Harting)**
✔	✔	✔✔	B	✔✔✔	**(Cocking)**
✔				✔	**(Heyshott)**
✔	✔	✔		✔✔	**(Graffham)**
✔			CB	✔✔✔	**(Sutton & Bignor)**
✔				✔✔	**(Bury)**
✔✔✔	✔	✔✔	B/CB	✔✔✔	**Houghton Bridge & Amberley**
✔✔	✔	✔		✔✔✔	**(Arundel)**
✔✔✔	✔			✔	**(Storrington)**
✔		✔		✔	**(Washington)**
✔✔✔	✔	✔	YHA (2½)	✔✔✔	**(Steyning, Bramber & Upper Beeding)**
✔					**(Fulking)**
✔✔✔		✔ (Newtimber Hill)		✔	**(Poynings)**
✔	✔	✔✔		✔✔	**Pyecombe**
✔				✔	**(Clayton)**
✔✔✔	✔	✔ (½)		✔✔✔	**(Ditchling)**
✔					**(Plumpton)**
✔✔✔	✔			✔✔✔	**(Lewes)**
✔		✔		✔	**(Kingston-nr-Lewes)**
✔✔		✔	YHA	✔✔	**Rodmell & Southease**
✔	✔			✔	**(West Firle)**
✔✔				✔	**(Alciston & Berwick)**
✔✔✔	✔	✔		✔✔✔	**Alfriston**
✔✔					**Litlington**
✔✔				✔	**Exceat/Westdean**
✔				✔	**Birling Gap**
✔					**Beachy Head**
✔	✔			✔✔	**Meads**
					Alternative (inland) route from Alfriston
✔					**(Milton Street)**
✔				✔	**(Wilmington)**
✔				✔	**Jevington**
✔✔✔	✔		YHA	✔✔✔	**Eastbourne**

PLANNING YOUR WALK

* The distances in brackets show how far the campsite, or YHA, is from the Way.

(cont'd from p29) To help plan your walk the **colour maps and gradient profiles** (see the end of the book) and the **table of town and village facilities** (pp30-1) give a rundown on the essential information you will need regarding accommodation possibilities and services. Alternatively, you could follow one of the **suggested itineraries** (see below and opposite). See box p18 for details of campsites that are closest to the trail.

There is also a list of recommended **day and weekend walks** (see pp34-5) which cover the best of the path, most of which are well served by public transport. The **public transport map** is on p45.

Once you have an idea of your approach turn to **Part 4** for detailed information on accommodation, places to eat, and other services in each place on the route. Also in Part 4 you will find route descriptions to accompany the trail maps.

WHICH DIRECTION?

There are many criteria that will determine in which direction to tackle the Way. It always seems a good idea to finish a walk with something that is worth walking towards. With this in mind Winchester is a far more attractive place to finish in than Eastbourne. Thus, east to west seems a good choice of direction. However, the scenery improves towards the eastern end and what finer place to conclude the walk than by the sea and on top of the white cliffs of the Seven Sisters and Beachy Head. Another factor is the prevailing wind which normally comes from the south-west. Having the wind at your back is a great help so this would also suggest starting at Winchester and finishing at Eastbourne.

Although the maps in Part 4 are arranged in a west to east direction, times are given for walking in both directions so that the book can be used back to front.

PLANNING YOUR WALK

STAYING IN B&B-STYLE ACCOMMODATION

Night	Relaxed pace Place	Approx distance mls	km	Medium pace Place	Approx distance mls	km	Fast pace Place	Approx distance mls	km
0	Winchester			Winchester			Winchester		
1	Cheriton	8	13	Cheriton	8	13	Exton	12	19.5
2	Exton	7	11	East Meon	13	20	South Harting	16½	26.5
3	East Meon	6	9.5	South Harting	12½	20	Amberley	20	32
4	Buriton	8½	13.5	Graffham	10½	17	Pyecombe	20½	33
5	Cocking	11	18	Amberley	9	14.5	Kingston-nr-Lewes	11	17.5
6	Amberley	13½	21.5	Steyning	13	21	Alfriston	13	21
7	Steyning	13	21	Kingston	20	32	Eastbourne	12½	20
8	Pyecombe	9½	15	Alfriston	13	21			
9	Kingston-nr-Lewes	11½	18.5	Eastbourne	12½	20			
10	Rodmell	5	8						
11	Alfriston	8	13						
12	Eastbourne	12½	20						

mls = miles & **km** = kilometres

SUGGESTED ITINERARIES

The itineraries are based on different accommodation types – B&B-style accommodation (opposite), campsites and hostels/bunkhouses (both below) – with

CAMPING

Night	Relaxed pace Place	mls	km	Medium pace Place	mls	km	Fast pace Place	mls	km
0	Winchester*			Winchester*			Winchester*		
1	Holden Farm	7	11	Holden Farm	7	11	Meon Springs	17	27
2	Meon Springs	10	16	Sustainbty Ctr	13	21	Manor Farm	18	29
3	Butser Hill	6	9.5	Manor Farm	16	26	Amberley	12	19.5
4	Manor Farm	13	21	Amberley	12	19.5	Saddlescmb Fm	18	29
5	Gumber Bthy	7	11	Truleigh Hill	14	22.5	Alfriston	24	39
6	Amberley	7	11	Ditchling	9	14.5	Eastbourne*	12½	20
7	Washington	7	11	Southease	11	18			
8	Truleigh Hill	8	13	Alfriston	8	13			
9	Pyecombe	6	9.5	Eastbourne*	12½	20			
10	Housedean Fm	8	13						
11	Southease	7	11						
12	Alfriston	8	13						
13	Eastbourne*	12½	20						

mls = miles & **km** = kilometres

(also see 'Camping on the Way' box, p18)

Note: In some cases it is necessary to walk up to a mile for the campsite.
* There are no campsites at places marked with an asterisk. For Winchester consider Morn Hill Caravan Club Campsite, 2¼ miles away but accessible by bus from Winchester bus station. For Eastbourne stay in the YHA, or catch the last train home.

STAYING IN HOSTELS/BUNKHOUSES

Night	Relaxed pace Place	mls	km	Medium pace Place	mls	km	Fast pace Place	mls	km
0	Winchester*			Winchester*			Winchester*		
1	Cheriton*	8	13	Cheriton*	8	13	East Meon	18	29
2	East Meon	13	20	East Meon	13	20	Buriton*	9	14.5
3	Buriton*	9	14.5	Sth Harting*	12½	20	Bignor	19½	31.5
4	Cocking	11½	18.5	Bignor	16	25.5	Truleigh Hill	20	32
5	Bignor	9	14.5	Truleigh Hill	20	32	Rodmell	21	33.5
6	Washington*	12½	20	Ditchling*	10½	17	Eastbourne	20½	33
7	Truleigh Hill	8½	13.5	Rodmell	13½	21.5			
8	Ditchling*	10½	17	Alfriston*	8	13			
9	Kingston*	10	16	Eastbourne	12½	20			
10	Rodmell	5	8						
11	Alfriston*	8	13						
12	Eastbourne	12½	20						

mls = miles & **km** = kilometres

* No hostels/camping barns at places marked; alternative accommodation available

PLANNING YOUR WALK

each divided into three categories of walking speed. They really are only suggestions and all of them can be easily adapted by using the more detailed information on accommodation found in Part 4; the distance chart on pp184-5 will also help you plan your itinerary.

Don't forget to add your travelling time from/to your accommodation both before and after the walk.

PLANNING YOUR WALK

❏ HIGHLIGHTS – THE BEST DAY WALKS

There is nothing quite like taking on a long-distance path in one go but sometimes the time needed is just not available.

The following list suggests a number of day and weekend walks covering the best of the South Downs Way, which are accessible using public transport (see pp44-7) unless specified, though Sunday services may be limited or non existent. Fitter walkers will find that the weekend walks suggested opposite can be completed in a day.

DAY WALKS

Exton to Buriton   **12 miles/19.5km (see pp86-93)**
The best of the East Hampshire downland, passing over Old Winchester Hill and its magnificent hill-fort remains and Butser Hill, the highest hill on the Downs, with magnificent views over the Meon Valley and Queen Elizabeth Country Park.

There are no bus services at Exton but there are to East Meon so if you need to use public transport it is easiest to start there.

Amberley to Steyning   **13 miles/21km (see pp123-32)**
Starting in one of the prettiest villages on the Way and ending in one of the most beautiful towns, this walk provides extensive views from the spine of the Downs, taking in the famous local landmark of Chanctonbury Ring.

Devil's Dyke to Ditchling Beacon   **5 miles/8km (see pp134-43)**
Possibly the most spectacular dry valley on the Downs, Devil's Dyke is the magnificent starting point of this short section that continues by climbing over the isolated Newtimber Hill before ending at the beauty spot of Ditchling Beacon. There are seasonal bus services (Sat, Sun and bank holidays only) to both Devil's Dyke and Ditchling Beacon.

Kingston-near-Lewes to Southease   **5 miles/8km (see pp152-8)**
One of the quieter stretches of the Downs with fine views of Mount Caburn on the other side of the Ouse Valley and a little bit of literary history to be had at Rodmell, once the home of Virginia Woolf.

Exceat to Eastbourne via Cuckmere Haven **9 miles/14.5km (see pp166-72)**
Arguably the finest day of walking anywhere between Winchester and Eastbourne, following the rollercoaster tops of the Seven Sisters chalk cliffs to the high point of Beachy Head high above Eastbourne.

Alfriston to Eastbourne via Jevington   **10 miles/16km (see pp172-7)**
This inland route is not as spectacular as the coastal route to Eastbourne but equally enjoyable, encompassing the beautiful Cuckmere Valley, the ramshackle timber-framed houses of Alfriston and the curious Long Man of Wilmington chalk figure.

❏ HIGHLIGHTS – THE BEST WEEKEND WALKS

Buriton to Amberley   **23½ miles/38km (see pp93-119)**
Stopping off in either Cocking or Midhurst for the night, this section takes in the fine
wooded sections close to Buriton and the airy Harting Down on the first day, followed
by Bignor Hill with its Roman road, Stane Street, on the second day.

Amberley to Pyecombe   **20½ miles/33km (see pp119-40)**
Extensive views and the curious, enchanted Chanctonbury Ring are the highlights of
the first day with a wide choice of places to stay in historic Steyning, or Bramber with
its castle. The second day follows the open top of the Downs all the way to the
impressive valley of Devil's Dyke.

Circular walk including Eastbourne, Alfriston and Cuckmere Haven
                  19 miles/30.5km
The Exceat to Eastbourne and Alfriston to Eastbourne walks (see opposite) can be
combined to make a wonderful circular walk and can be started and finished any-
where on the circuit. You'll pass through the beautiful villages of Jevington, Alfriston,
Litlington and Westdean as well as walking the entire coastal section from Cuckmere
Haven to Eastbourne.

What to take

Deciding how much to take with you can be difficult. Experienced walkers
know that you really should take only the bare essentials but at the same time
you need to ensure you have all the equipment necessary to make the trip safe
and comfortable.

KEEP YOUR LUGGAGE LIGHT

Carrying a heavy rucksack really can ruin your enjoyment of a good walk and
can also slow you down a great deal, turning an easy seven-mile day into an
interminable slog. Be ruthless when you pack and leave behind all those little
home comforts that you tell yourself don't weigh that much really. Always pack
the essentials, of course, but try to leave behind anything that you think might
'come in handy' but probably won't. This advice is even more pertinent to
campers who have the added weight of camping equipment to carry.

HOW TO CARRY IT

The size of the **rucksack** you should take depends on where you are planning
to stay and how you are planning to eat. If you are camping and cooking for
yourself you will probably need a 65- to 75-litre rucksack which can hold the
tent, sleeping bag, cooking equipment and food. All the hostels on the Way

provide bedding (though not towels) and have cooking facilities, so if staying in these a 40- to 60-litre rucksack should be sufficient. If you have gone for the B&B option you will probably find a 30- to 40-litre daypack is more than enough to carry your lunch, clothes, camera and guidebook. If you've booked a self-guided holiday, or are using a baggage-transfer service (see p26), you could even just take a suitcase, although a backpack is still probably better for the beginning and end of your trip where you may have to carry your luggage.

Whatever size your rucksack is, ensure it has a stiffened back and can be adjusted to fit your back comfortably; this will make carrying the weight much easier. Rucksacks are decorated with seemingly pointless straps but if you adjust them correctly it can make a big difference to your personal comfort while walking. Make sure the hip belt and chest belt (if there is one) are fastened tightly as this helps distribute the weight; most of it should be carried on your hips.

When packing the rucksack make sure you have all the things you are likely to need during the day – this guidebook (of course!), a map, a water bottle, waterproofs, packed lunch – near the top or in the side pockets. A good habit to get into is always to put things in the same place and memorise where they are. There is nothing more annoying than pulling everything out of your pack to find that lost banana when you're starving or that camera when there is a butterfly basking briefly on a nearby rock.

Even though most rucksacks come with their own rain cover, it is still a good idea to keep everything inside it in **canoe bags**, **waterproof rucksack liners** or strong plastic bags (or binliners). If you don't it's bound to rain.

If you are using a baggage-transfer service you will need a small **bum bag** or **day pack** for the essentials for the day.

FOOTWEAR

Boots versus trainers

Your footwear is arguably the most important item of gear that can affect the enjoyment of your hike. In summer you can get by with a light pair of running trainers or trail shoes, especially if you're carrying only a small pack, although this is an invitation for wet, cold feet if there is any rain and they don't offer support for your ankles. On the plus side, lightweight running trainers dry off after a rainstorm much more quickly than big heavy hiking boots. Some of the terrain can be quite rough and wet, though, so many people prefer a pair of good walking boots. If going down this route, remember they must fit well and be properly broken in: it is no good discovering that your boots are slowly murdering your feet two days into a one-week walk.

Socks

The traditional wearing of a thin liner sock under a thicker wool sock is no longer necessary if you choose a high-quality sock specially designed for walking. A high proportion of natural fibres makes them much more comfortable. Three pairs are ample, although you may need more if it rains a lot.

Extra footwear

Some walkers like to have a second pair of shoes to wear when not on the trail. Trainers, sport sandals, or flip flops are all suitable as long as they are light. Flip flops are certainly useful for wearing in the shower blocks at campsites.

CLOTHES

Experienced walkers will know the importance of wearing the right clothes. Always expect the worst weather even if the forecast is good. Modern technology in outdoor attire can seem baffling but it basically comes down to the old multi-layer system: a base layer to transport sweat away from your skin; a mid-layer to keep you warm; and an outer layer or 'shell' to protect you from the rain.

Underwear and base layer

As with socks, two or three changes of whatever your normal **underwear** is fine. Cotton absorbs sweat, trapping it next to the skin which will chill you rapidly when you stop exercising. A thin lightweight **thermal top** made from a synthetic material is better as it draws moisture away, keeping you dry. It will be cool if worn on its own in hot weather and warm when worn under other clothes in cooler conditions. A spare would be sensible. Also bring a **shirt** or top for wearing in the evening.

Mid layers

In the summer a woollen jumper or mid-weight polyester **fleece** will suffice. For the rest of the year you will need an extra layer to keep you warm. Both wool and fleece, unlike cotton, have the ability to stay reasonably warm when wet.

Outer layer

A decent **waterproof jacket** is essential year-round and will be much more comfortable (but also more expensive) if it's also 'breathable' to prevent the build up of condensation on the inside. This layer can also be worn to keep the wind off.

Leg wear

Whatever you wear on your legs it should be light, quick-drying and not restricting. Many British walkers find **polyester tracksuit bottoms** comfortable. Poly-cotton or microfibre trousers are excellent. Denim jeans should never be worn; if they get wet they become heavy, cold and bind to your legs. A pair of **shorts** is nice to have on sunny days. Thermal **longjohns** or thick tights are cosy if you're camping but are probably unnecessary even in winter.

Waterproof trousers are necessary most of the year. In summer a pair of windproof and quick-drying trousers is useful in showery weather.

Gaiters are not really necessary but may come in useful in wet weather, when the vegetation around your legs is dripping wet.

Other clothes

A **warm hat** and **gloves** should always be kept in your rucksack; you never know when you might need them. In summer you should also carry a **sun hat** with you, preferably one which covers the back of your neck. For cooling off on beaches, or in local swimming pools, take a **swimsuit**.

TOILETRIES

Take only the minimum: unless staying in B&Bs, you'll need a small bar of **soap** or small bottle of **shower gel**, either of which can also be used instead of shaving cream and for washing clothes; a tiny tube of **toothpaste** and a **toothbrush**; and one roll of **loo paper** in a plastic bag. If you are planning to defecate outdoors you will also need a **lighter** for burning the paper and a lightweight **trowel** for burying the evidence (see pp62-3 for further tips). You'll also need a **towel** (if camping or staying in a hostel), **razor**, **deodorant**, **tampons/sanitary towels** and a high-factor **sunscreen** and/or **lip balm**.

FIRST-AID KIT

Medical facilities in Britain are excellent so you need only take a small kit to cover common problems and emergencies. A basic kit will contain a pack of **aspirin** or **paracetamol** for treating mild to moderate pain and fever; **plasters/Band Aids** for minor cuts; 'moleskin', 'Compeed' or 'Second skin' for blisters; a **bandage** for holding dressings, splints or limbs in place and for supporting a sprained ankle; an **elastic knee support** for a weak knee; a small selection of different-sized **sterile dressings** for wounds; **porous adhesive tape**; **antiseptic wipes**; **antiseptic cream**; **safety pins**; **tweezers** and a small pair of **scissors**. Pack the kit in a waterproof container.

GENERAL ITEMS

Essential

The following should be in everyone's rucksack: a **water bottle/pouch** (holding at least one litre); a **torch** (flashlight) with spare bulb and batteries in case you end up walking after dark; **emergency food** which your body can quickly convert into energy; a **penknife**; a **watch** with an alarm; and a **bag** for packing out any rubbish you accumulate. A **whistle** is also worth taking. It can fit in a pocket and although you are very unlikely to need it you may be grateful of it in the unlikely event of an emergency (see p68).

Reception on the Way is generally good for **mobile phones**. Even so, make sure you always have a card (credit, debit, BT or prepaid), or cash, to call from a public phone box in case you have no signal at the crucial moment. Calls to the emergency services (☎ 999, or ☎ 112 from a mobile) are free of charge. Other calls from a phone box cost a minimum of 60p (including a 40p connection charge; thereafter 10p a minute).

Useful

Many would list a **camera/camera phone** as essential but it can be liberating to travel without one once in a while; a **notebook** can be a more accurate way of recording your impressions (but remember to take some pens). Other items include a **book** to pass the time on train journeys; a pair of **sunglasses**; **binoculars** for observing wildlife; **walking poles** to take the strain off your knees and a **vacuum flask** for carrying hot drinks. Although the path is easy to follow a 'Silva' type **compass** could be a good idea.

CAMPING GEAR

Campers need a decent **tent** (or bivvy bag if you enjoy travelling light) that's able to withstand wet and windy weather; a two- to three-season **sleeping bag** (but obviously in winter a warmer one is a good idea and on hot summer nights you could get away with a one-season bag); a **sleeping mat**; a **stove** and **fuel** (there is special mention in Part 4 of which shops stock fuel); a **mug**; a **spoon**; a wire/plastic **scrubber** for washing up; and a pan or **cooking pot**. One pot is fine for two people; some pots come with a lid that can be used as a plate or frying pan. You can also buy camping pot sets that pack away neatly into one pot.

MONEY

There are not many banks along the Way so you will have to carry most of your money as **cash**. A **debit card** is the easiest way to withdraw money either from banks or cash machines and a debit or **credit card** can be used to pay in most larger shops, restaurants and hotels. A **cheque book** is useful for walkers with accounts in British banks as many B&Bs do not accept payment by card, though you should also have a debit card to act as a guarantee.

MAPS

The **hand-drawn maps** in this book cover the trail at a scale of 1:20,000 – plenty of detail and information to keep you on the right track; the **colour maps** at the back of the book are at a smaller scale covering the surrounding area.

PLANNING YOUR WALK

❑ **Digital mapping**

There are several software packages on the market today that provide Ordnance Survey maps for a PC or smartphone. The two best known are Memory Map and Anquet. Maps are supplied electronically, on DVD, USB media, or by direct download over the internet. The maps are then loaded into an application, also available by download, from where you can view them, print them and create routes on them.

The real value of digital maps, though, is the ability to draw a route directly onto the map from your computer or smartphone. The map, or the appropriate sections of it, can then be printed with the route marked on it, so you no longer need the full versions of the OS maps (though the SDW AZ Adventure Series map, see p40, provides the same thing). Additionally, the route can be viewed directly on the smartphone or uploaded to a GPS device. Most modern smartphones have a GPS chip so you will be able to see your position overlaid onto the digital map on your phone. Almost every device with built-in GPS functionality now has some mapping software available for it. One of the most popular manufacturers of dedicated handheld GPS devices is Garmin, who have an extensive range. Prices vary from around £100 to £600.

Smartphones and GPS devices should complement, not replace, the traditional method of navigation (a map and compass) as any electronic device can break or, if nothing else, run out of battery. Remember that the battery life of your phone will be significantly reduced, compared to normal usage, when you are using the built-in GPS and running the screen for long periods. **Stuart Greig**

To explore even further afield you might be interested in Ordnance Survey maps (☎ 0845-605 0505, 🖳 ordnancesurvey.co.uk for map sales and digital downloads). Relevant sheets include OS Landranger maps (pink cover) at a scale of 1:50,000, Nos 185, 197, 198 and 199, or OS Explorer Maps (orange cover) at 1:25,000 Nos 119, 120, 121, 122, 123 and 132 (all are £8.99 each). OS also offers **digital maps** (see box p39).

The *AZ Adventure Series South Downs Way map* (🖳 az.co.uk) includes the relevant section of the OS maps at a scale of 1:25,000 and also has an index.

There's also a single-sheet Harvey's *South Downs Way Map* (Harvey Maps, £13.95, 🖳 harveymaps.co.uk) at a scale of 1:40,000.

A Trailblazer **South Downs Way app** is now available; for more information see the Trailblazer website 🖳 www.trailblazer-guides.com.

Sections of the South Downs Way are now available on **Google Street View**.

❑ **SOURCES OF FURTHER INFORMATION**

Tourist information

Tourist/Visitor Information Centres (TICs) are based in towns throughout Britain; they provide all manner of locally specific information and most provide accommodation booking (see box p19). However, some are staffed by volunteers who can provide information but not book accommodation; they also generally have limited opening hours. The following TICs lie on or near the Way: **Winchester** (see p72); **Petersfield** (see p94); **Lewes** (see p147); **Eastbourne** (see p179).

Tourist information points (TIPs) are not staffed, but brochures about places of interest in the area are available; there are TIPs in **Arundel** (see p120), **Storrington** (p125) and **Steyning** (p131). In addition there are some **visitor centres** such as the ones at Queen Elizabeth Country Park (see p93) and Seven Sisters Country Park (see box p166). Visitor centres generally only have information about the actual attraction.

● **Tourism South East** This regional tourist board (🖳 visitsoutheastengland.com) is responsible for the official tourist information centres. Their website has a wealth of information regarding accommodation, things to see and do, and they can keep you informed about upcoming festivals and events.

● **South Downs Society** See p59.

Organisations for walkers

● **Backpackers' Club** (🖳 backpackersclub.co.uk) A club aimed at people who are involved or interested in lightweight camping through walking, cycling, skiing and canoeing. They produce a quarterly magazine, provide members with a comprehensive advisory and information service on all aspects of backpacking, organise weekend trips and also publish a farm-pitch directory. Membership costs £15/20/8.50/12 per year for an individual/family/anyone under 18 or over 65/retired couple.

● **The Long Distance Walkers' Association** (🖳 ldwa.org.uk) Membership includes a journal (*Strider*) three times per year with details of challenge events and local group walks as well as articles on the subject. Information on over 730 paths is presented in their *UK Trailwalkers' Handbook*. Membership costs £13 a year.

● **Ramblers** (🖳 ramblers.org.uk) A charity that looks after the interests of walkers throughout Britain and promotes walking for health. Annual membership costs £34.50 (concessionary £20.50), and includes their quarterly *Walk* magazine as well as access to their library of walking routes and access to walks arranged by the various groups.

RECOMMENDED READING

Many bookshops and most of the tourist information centres along the South Downs Way stock many of the following books.

An excellent read recounting **one person's experience** of his walk is *The South Downs Way* (Mainstream, 2000) by Martin King. Other books worth considering are: *Alone on the South Downs Way: one woman's solo journey from Winchester to Eastbourne* by Holly Worton (Tribal, 2016); *The South Downs Way* by Belinda Knox (Frances Lincoln, 2008), a photographic based guide, or *Whan That Aprille: For the Curious: An Exploration of the South Downs Way in Hampshire*, Heather Lacey (Redback Publishing; 2016).

For **birds** there are plenty of books to choose from including the *Collins Bird Guide* by Lars Svensson et al and the *New Birdwatcher's Pocket Guide to Britain and Europe* by Peter Hayman and Rob Hume. The RSPB's *Pocket Guide to British Birds* (Simon Harrap and David Nurney) is also recommended; birds are identified by their plumage and song.

One of the best field guides to **flora** is *The Wildflowers of Britain and Ireland* by Marjorie Blamey et al. Now sadly out of print, but used copies may be available online, the best guidebook specifically aimed at the **wildlife of the region** is *Downland Wildlife – A Naturalist's Year in the North & South Downs* by John S Burton, published by Phillips.

The Field Studies Council (☎ 01952-208910, ⌨ field-studies-council.org) publishes a series of **fold-out charts** in the form of laminated sheets (£3.80 each) showing commonly found birds, trees, flowers etc. The series includes *Features of the South Downs Way*.

There are also several **field guide apps** for smartphones, including those that can aid in identifying birds from their song as well as by their appearance.

Getting to and from the South Downs Way

It could not be easier to reach the South Downs from London as there are numerous road and rail links not just to Winchester and Eastbourne, the start and finish of the walk, but to many other points along the Way. Most parts of the South Downs Way are no more than 1½-2 hours from the capital. Access from other parts of Britain often involves going via London but there are rail services to Winchester and Southampton via Reading. The rail line running across the south coast goes from Dover to Ashford International, then to Hastings and along the coast to Eastbourne and Brighton; from Brighton there are services to Portsmouth and Southampton.

See box p42 for routes from continental Europe to the south coast of England.

❏ **Getting to Britain**

● **By air** The nearest international airport to Winchester is Southampton Airport (🖥 southamptonairport.com) on the south coast. The alternative would be to fly to London's Gatwick (🖥 gatwickairport.com) or Heathrow airports (🖥 heathrow.com), both of which serve destinations worldwide. Further away but with a direct rail connection to Brighton is Luton Airport (🖥 london-luton.co.uk). Another option is London City Airport (🖥 londoncityairport.com); the Docklands Light Railway is connected to the airport terminal and from there it is easy to access Waterloo station.

● **From Europe by train** Eurostar (🖥 eurostar.com) operates a high-speed passenger service via the Channel Tunnel between Paris/Brussels and London. The Eurostar terminal in London is at St Pancras International station: some services also stop at Ashford International. For information about the various rail services to Britain from the continent contact your national rail service provider, or visit 🖥 railteam.eu.

● **From Europe by coach** Eurolines (🖥 eurolines.com) have a huge network of long-distance coach services connecting over 500 cities in 25 European countries to London. However, these tickets often don't work out that much cheaper than flying the same route with a budget airline which is also far quicker (although less environmentally friendly, of course). **Megabus** (🖥 megabus.com) is part of the Stagecoach group and it operates low-cost coach services from a number of destinations in Europe to London and other cities.

● **From Europe by car** Eurotunnel ('le shuttle'; 🖥 eurotunnel.com) operates a shuttle **train** service for vehicles via the Channel Tunnel between Calais and Folkestone, taking an hour between the motorway in France and the motorway in England.

There are many **ferry** routes between France (Caen, Calais, Cherbourg, Dieppe, Dunkerque, Le Havre and St Malo) and the south coast ports of England such as Dover, Newhaven, Poole and Portsmouth. There are also services from Spain (Bilbao and Santander) to Portsmouth. Look at 🖥 ferrysavers.com or 🖥 directferries.com for a full list of companies and services.

NATIONAL TRANSPORT

By rail

The two main rail operators for services to locations along the South Downs are Southern (from London Victoria to the south coast) and SouthWest Trains (from London Waterloo stopping at Winchester and Petersfield). Other providers are: Thameslink (from Bedford to Brighton via Luton Airport and St Pancras International) and Cross Country (from Manchester/Birmingham to Bournemouth and calling at Winchester). See the box opposite and map on p45 for contact and service details.

Timetables, ticket and fare information can be found on the rail operators' websites or through **National Rail Enquiries** (☎ 03457-484950, 🖥 nationalrail .co.uk); you can purchase tickets through the relevant rail operator's website. Note, it is much cheaper if you book tickets in advance and especially if you can travel on trains at a specific time. It may also be worth looking at 🖥 thetrainline .com to see if you can get an even cheaper fare.

If you think you may want to book a taxi for when you arrive, visit 🖥 train taxi.co.uk for details of taxi companies operating at rail stations throughout

❏ **USEFUL RAIL SERVICES** [see map p45]

Note: not all stops are listed here, nor are all shown on the map. Check the relevant operator's website for full details.

Southern Trains (☎ 0345-127 2920, 🖥 southernrailway.com)
(**Note**: services from London Victoria usually also stop at Clapham Junction, East Croydon and Gatwick Airport)
● London Victoria to Horsham via Three Bridges & Crawley, Mon-Sat 2/hr, Sun 1/hr
   At Horsham the trains divide:
      to **Bognor Regis** via Christ's Hospital (1/hr), Billingshurst, Pulborough, Amberley (1/hr) & Arundel, Mon-Sat 2/hr, Sun 1/hr
      to **Portsmouth Harbour** via Barnham, Chichester & Havant, daily 1/hr
      to **Southampton Central** via Barnham, Chichester & Havant, Mon-Sat 1/hr
● London Victoria to Brighton (fast service), daily 2/hr
● London Victoria to Haywards Heath, daily 2/hr
   At Haywards Heath the trains divide:
      to **Brighton** via Burgess Hill & Hassocks, daily 1/hr
      to **Littlehampton** via Hove, Shoreham-by-Sea & Worthing, daily 1/hr
         (note: the train divides again at Worthing and the other half goes to **Portsmouth Harbour** via Chichester & Havant, daily 1/hr)
      to **Eastbourne** via Wivelsfield, Lewes, Polegate & Hampden Park, daily 1/hr
      to **Ore** via Plumpton, Lewes, Polegate, Eastbourne & Hastings, daily 1/hr
● Ashford International to Brighton via Hastings, Eastbourne & Lewes, daily 1/hr
   (note: Sunday services also call at Berwick & Glynde)
● Ore to Brighton via Eastbourne, Berwick, Glynde, Lewes & Falmer, daily 1/hr
● Portsmouth to Brighton via Havant, Chichester, Barnham & Shoreham, daily 1/hr
● Southampton to Brighton via Havant, Chichester, Barnham & Shoreham, daily 1/hr
● Brighton to Seaford via Lewes, Southease (1/hr) & Newhaven, daily 2/hr

SouthWest Trains (☎ 0345-600 0650, 🖥 southwesttrains.co.uk)
● London Waterloo to Weymouth via Clapham Junction, Winchester, Southampton Airport, Southampton & Bournemouth, Mon-Sat 2/hr, Sun 1/hr
● London Waterloo to Portsmouth via Petersfield, Mon-Sat 2/hr, Sun 1/hr
● London Waterloo to Portsmouth via Woking, Basingstoke & Winchester, daily 1/hr

Thameslink (🖥 thameslinkrailway.com)
● Bedford to Brighton via Luton/Luton Airport, London St Pancras International, East Croydon, Gatwick Airport, Three Bridges, Haywards Heath & Burgess Hill, daily 2/hr plus 2/hr to Three Bridges

Cross Country Trains (☎ 0844 811 0124, 🖥 crosscountrytrains.co.uk)
● Manchester to Bournemouth via Birmingham, Winchester & Southampton, daily 1/hr

England. It is also often possible to book train tickets that include (discounted) bus travel to your ultimate destination; enquire when you book your train ticket or look at Plus Bus's website (🖥 plusbus.info).

By coach
Coach travel is generally cheaper but takes longer than the train. **National Express** is the principal coach (long-distance bus) operator in Britain and has services to a number of destinations on or near the Way; see box p44.

❏ **USEFUL COACH SERVICES**

National Express (☎ 0871-781 8181, 🖳 nationalexpress.com)
Note: not all stops are listed – contact National Express for full details.

024	London Victoria Coach Station (VCS) to **Eastbourne** via Gatwick Airport South Terminal, East Grinstead, Uckfield & Polegate, 1/day
025	London VCS to Brighton via Gatwick Airport South Terminal, 10-11/day
031	London VCS to **Petersfield**, 1/day
032	London VCS to Southampton via **Winchester**, 7/day
203	Heathrow Airport to Portsmouth via **Winchester** & Southampton, 10/day
310	Leeds to Poole via Birmingham, Reading, **Winchester** & Southampton, 1/day
315	Helston to **Eastbourne** via Bournemouth, Southampton, Portsmouth, Chichester, **Arundel**, Worthing, Brighton, Newhaven & Seaford, 1/day
539	Edinburgh to Bournemouth via Birmingham, Oxford & **Winchester**, 1/day
727	Norwich to Brighton via Stansted, Heathrow & Gatwick airports, 7/day
747	Heathrow Airport to Brighton via Gatwick Airport, 1/day

By car

The south of England is overrun with dual carriageways and bypasses so there is no shortage of 'A' roads to follow down to the Downs. On holiday weekends, however, be prepared for long tailbacks as everyone heads for the coast. There are main roads from London passing through Winchester, Petersfield, Cocking, Amberley, Arundel, Washington, Pyecombe, Lewes, Brighton and Eastbourne.

By air

Although there are local airports, such as the one at Shoreham, the easiest way to fly to the South-East from other corners of England is to get a flight to Gatwick or Southampton; see box p42.

Do always bear in mind the environmental cost of flying, details of which can be found here: 🖳 chooseclimate.org.

LOCAL TRANSPORT

Hampshire, West Sussex and East Sussex have good local transport networks which make getting to and from the Way and planning linear day and weekend walks fairly easy.

The public transport map opposite summarises all the useful routes; see the box on pp46-7 for details (though not all stops are listed). For more information contact **traveline** (🖳 travelinesoutheast.org.uk). Where school bus services may be of use to walkers they are mentioned in the relevant place in the route guide. The tourist information centres along the Downs can provide, free of charge, a comprehensive local transport timetable for their particular region.

Most bus companies (apart from Emsworth & District) permit up to two **dogs** on a bus but it is also up to the discretion of the driver and dogs must be on a lead, well behaved and sitting under the seat or on their owner's lap; definitely not actually on a seat.

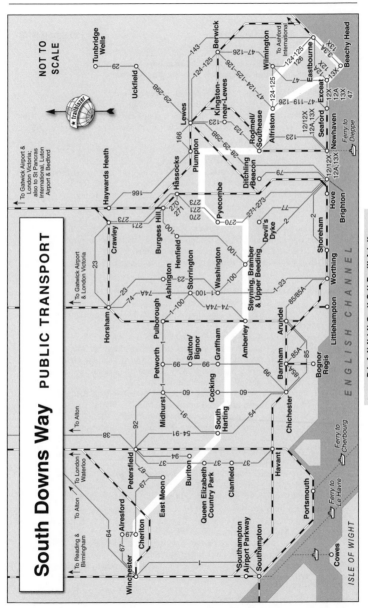

PLANNING YOUR WALK

❏ LOCAL BUS SERVICES   [see map p45]

Note: not all stops are listed for all routes.

bluestar (☎ 01202-338421, 🖳 bluestarbus.co.uk)
1   Southampton to **Winchester**, Mon-Sat 4/hr, Sun 2/hr

Brighton & Hove Buses (☎ 01273-886200, 🖳 buses.co.uk)
2   Rottingdean to Shoreham via Brighton, Mon-Sat 2/hr, Sun 1/hr
       Rottingdean to **Steyning** via Brighton, **Upper Beeding** & **Bramber**, daily 1/hr
12   (Coaster) Brighton to Seaford via Rottingdean & Newhaven, Mon-Sat 3/hr
       Sun 2/hr
12A   Brighton to Eastbourne: same route as No 12 to Seaford then to **Exceat** (Seven
       Sisters Park Centre) & East Dean, daily 2/hr
12X   (Coaster) Brighton to **Eastbourne** as for No 12A but fewer stops, Mon-Sat 3/hr
13X   Brighton to **Eastbourne** via Newhaven, Seaford, **Exceat** (Seven Sisters Park
       Centre), **Birling Gap** & **Beachy Head**, Sat, Sun & bank holidays 3/day
28   Brighton to Ringmer via **Lewes**, Mon-Sat 2/hr, Sun 4/day (to Uckfield)
29   Brighton to Tunbridge Wells via **Lewes** & Uckfield, Mon-Sat 2/hr, Sun 1/hr
29B   Brighton to Uckfield via **Lewes**, Mon-Sat 2/hr
77   Brighton to **Devil's Dyke**, mid June to mid Sep daily 2/hr, late Apr to mid June
       Sat, Sun & Bank hols 12/day (every 45 mins)
79   Brighton (station) to **Ditchling Beacon**, late Apr to mid Sep Sat, Sun & bank
       holidays 1/hr

Compass Travel (☎ 01903-690025, 🖳 www.compass-travel.co.uk)
74/74A Horsham to **Storrington**, Mon-Sat 2/day plus 2/day to Amberley (one
        afternoon service continues to Amberley Railway station and Houghton on
        school days)
85   Worthing to Chichester via **Arundel**, Mon-Sat 3/day
85A   Worthing to Chichester via **Arundel** & Barnham, Mon-Sat 2/day
99   Chichester to Petworth via Goodwood, East Dean, Charlton, **Graffham**,
       Sutton & Bignor, Mon-Sat 4-6/day but only stops between Chichester and
       Petworth if prebooked (☎ 01903-264776)
100   Burgess Hill to Pulborough via Henfield, **Upper Beeding**, **Bramber**,
       Steyning, Washington & **Storrington**, Mon-Sat 9-10/day plus 2/day to
       Storrington
123   Newhaven to **Lewes** via **Southease**, **Rodmell** & **Kingston-near-Lewes**,
       Mon-Fri 7/day, Sat 5/day
119   Seaford to **Alfriston**, Mon-Sat 1/day
126   Seaford to **Alfriston**, Mon-Sat 2/day (see also CCB opposite)
143   **Eastbourne** to Lewes via Polegate, Hailsham & Ringmer, Mon-Fri 3/day
       plus 2/day Hailsham to Lewes
166   **Lewes** to Haywards Heath via **Plumpton** & Wivelsfield, Mon-Fri 6/day

Cuckmere Community Bus (CCB; ☎ 01323-870920, 🖳 cuckmerebuses.org.uk)
Note: Everybody involved in Cuckmere Community Bus (CCB) is a volunteer.
47   Cuckmere Valley Rambler: **Berwick** Station circular route via **Alfriston**,
       Seaford, **Exceat**, **Seven Sisters Country Park**, **Litlington**, **Lullington** &
       Wilmington, late Mar to late Oct Sat, Sun & public hols 1/hr
125   **Lewes** to **Eastbourne** via **Glynde**, **Charleston**, **Berwick**, **Alfriston**,
       Wilmington & Willingdon, Sat 3/day plus 1/day Alfriston to Eastbourne
       (Mon-Fri service operated by Seaford & District)

Cuckmere Community Bus *(cont'd)*
126   Seaford to **Berwick** via **Alfriston**, Mon-Sat 1-2/day,
         Seaford to **Eastbourne** via **Alfriston, Berwick** (Drusillas), **Wilmington**,
         Polegate & Willingdon, Sun & bank hols 4/day plus 1/day to Berwick
         (see also Compass Travel opposite)
CCB also operate some **limited-frequency services** which stop where it is safe.
  These include: **40** Seaford to Berwick via Exceat, Westdean, Charleston,
  Litlington, Lullington, Wilmington & Alciston, Tue & Fri 1/day; **41** Eastbourne
  circular route via Jevington, Tue & Thur 2/day; **42** Hailsham to Berwick circular
  route via Alciston & Alfriston Wed 1/day, Hailsham to Berwick only Mon/Wed/Fri
  1/day; **44** Berwick to Eastbourne via Polegate, Mon 1/day, Tue 2-3/day (also via
  Wilmington), Thur 2-3/day (services also call at Alciston & Wilmington)

Emsworth & District (☎ 01243-372025, 🖳 emsworthanddistrict.co.uk)
54   **Petersfield** to Chichester via **South Harting** & **Uppark**, Mon-Sat 5/day
91   **Midhurst** to **Petersfield** via **South Harting**, Mon-Sat 1/day
92   **Midhurst** to **Petersfield**, Mon-Sat 5/day (see Stagecoach for Sun service)

Metrobus (☎ 01293-449191, 🖳 metrobus.co.uk)
23   Crawley to Worthing via Horsham, Ashington & **Washington**,
         Mon-Sat approx 1/hr, Sun & bank hols 5/day
270   East Grinstead to Brighton via Burgess Hill, Hassocks & **Pyecombe**,
         Mon-Sat approx 1/hr, Sun & Bank hols 3/day
271   Crawley to Brighton via Burgess Hill, Hassocks & **Pyecombe**,
         Mon-Fri 9/day, Sat 5/day, Sun 3/day
273   Crawley to Brighton via Hickstead, Hassocks & **Pyecombe**,
         Mon-Fri 8/day, Sat 6/day

Seaford & District (☎ 01273-510181, 🖳 seafordanddistrict.co.uk)
124   **Lewes** to **Eastbourne** via **Glynde**, Firle, **Charleston, Berwick, Alfriston,**
         Wilmington & Polegate, mid June to Aug Sat, Sun & Bank Hol Mons 3/day
125   **Lewes** to **Eastbourne** via **Glynde, Charleston, Berwick, Alfriston,**
         Wilmington & Willingdon, Mon-Fri 4/day (see also Cuckmere Buses)

Stagecoach (🖳 stagecoachbus.com)
Note that Stagecoach services are operated by different regions so when searching for
timetables on their website you need to check the correct region is set
1   **Midhurst** to Worthing via Petworth, Pulborough, **Storrington, Washington**
         & Findon, Mon-Sat 1/hr, Sun 6/day
3/3A   **Foot of Beachy Head** to **Eastbourne** via **Meads**, Mon-Sat 2/hr, Sun
         10/day, plus Meads to Eastbourne, Mon-Sat 3/hr
37   Havant to **Petersfield** via Waterlooville, Clanfield, **Queen Elizabeth Country**
         Park (request stop), Mon-Fri 9/day, Sat 6/day (services connect with No 38)
38   Alton to **Petersfield**, Mon-Fri 6/day (connects with No 37)
60   Chichester to **Midhurst** via West Dean, Singleton & **Cocking**, Mon-Sat 2/hr,
         Sun 1/hr
64   Alton to **Winchester**, Mon-Sat 2/hr, Sun & Bank Hols 6/day
67   **Winchester** to Petersfield via Alresford, **Cheriton**, Bramdean, West Meon &
         East Meon, Mon-Fri 6/day, Sat 4/day

Wheel Drive (☎ 01730-892052)
94   **Petersfield** to **Buriton**, Mon-Fri 4-5/day

PLANNING YOUR WALK

2

THE ENVIRONMENT & NATURE

Flora and fauna

The South Downs region is essentially a man-made landscape. Centuries of farming have shaped these rolling hills and left a unique habitat for a variety of common and not-so-common species. Left alone the South Downs would revert to scrub and woodland. This may not appear to be a great tragedy. However, the habitat that would be lost is a much scarcer one that provides sanctuary to a variety of endangered species which rely on the unique chalk grassland environment. The Downs are not free of trees either. The plough never reached the steep scarp slope that runs along the northern edge of the Downs. Indeed there is a healthy balance between the open grassland of the high ground and the deciduous beech woodland which can claim to be some of the oldest and most undisturbed woodland in Britain.

BUTTERFLIES

The Downs are famous for their butterflies. Many of the national nature reserves in the area were set up specifically because of the variety and number of butterflies. One of the most prevalent is the **meadow brown** (*Maniola jurtina*), a very common species, dusty brown in colour with a rusty orange streak and dark, false eyes. They can be seen in meadows all across the Downs. The small **gatekeeper** (*Pyronia tithonus*) likes similar habitat and is also widespread throughout the Downs. They are identified by their deep orange and chocolate-brown markings.

The **peacock** (*Inachis io*) is surely Britain's most beautiful butterfly; it's quite common in this area. The markings on the wings are said to mimic the eyes of an animal to frighten off predators. Also common is the impressive **red admiral** (*Vanessa atalanta*). Owing to climate change it is now starting to overwinter in Britain and appears to be thriving. The **brimstone** (*Gonepteryx rhamni*) is also widespread, though well camouflaged as its wings look very like leaves; the **white admiral** (*Limenitis camilla*), however, is declining in numbers but may still be seen in some woodland sites. Although it has also recently been in decline in other parts of the country, the **small tortoiseshell** (*Aglais urticae*) is still widespread here and also in towns and villages. Other very common butterflies include the **small**

Peacock
Inachis io

Small Tortoiseshell
Aglais urticae

Brimstone
Gonepteryx rhamni

Common Blue
Polyommatus icarus

Chalkhill Blue
Polyommatus/Lysandra coridon

Painted Lady
Cynthia cadui

Small Garden/Cabbage White
Pieris/Artogeia rapae

Meadow brown
Maniola jurtina

Red Admiral
Vanessa atalanta

Large Garden/
Cabbage White
Pieris brassicae

White Admiral
Limenitis camilla

Common Dog Violet
Viola riviniana

Common Centaury
Centaurium erythraea

Honeysuckle
Lonicera periclymemum

Wild marjoram
Origanum vulgare

Germander Speedwell
Veronica chamaedrys

Herb-Robert
Geranium robertianum

Lousewort
Pedicularis sylvatica

Self-heal
Prunella vulgaris

Scarlet Pimpernel
Anagallis arvensis

Viper's Bugloss
Echium vulgare

Ramsons (Wild Garlic)
Allium ursinum

Bluebell
Hyacinthoides non-scripta

Dog Rose
Rosa canina

Meadow Buttercup
Ranunculis acris

Gorse
Ulex europaeus

Tormentil
Potentilla erecta

Birdsfoot-trefoil
Lotus corniculatus

Ox-eye Daisy
Leucanthemum vulgare

St John's Wort
Hypericum perforatum

Primrose
Primula vulgaris

Cowslip
Primula veris

Common Ragwort
Senecio jacobaea

Red Admiral butterfly (*Vanessa atalanta*) on
Hemp Agrimony (*Eupatorium cannabinum*)

Foxglove
Digitalis purpurea

Early Purple Orchid
Orchis mascula

Pyramidal Orchid
Anacamptis pyramidalis

Bell Heather
Erica cinerea

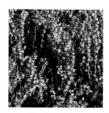

Heather (Ling)
Calluna vulgaris

Common Poppy
Papaver rhoeas

Rosebay Willowherb
Epilobium angustifolium

Common Vetch
Vicia sativa

Forget-me-not
Myosotis arvensis

Rowan (tree)
Sorbus aucuparia

Old Man's Beard
Clematis vitalba

Red Campion
Silene dioica

white (*Pieris/Artogeia rapae*) and the **large white** (*Pieris brassicae*); both can travel large distances, some migrating from continental Europe each year.

Along many of the country lanes and tracks the **speckled wood** (*Pararge aegeria*) can be seen basking on hedgerows. It is a small dark butterfly with a few white spots and six small false eyes at the rear.

There are several butterflies that are synonymous with chalk downland, notably the butterflies known as blues. The **holly blue** (*Celastrina argiolus*) and **chalkhill blue** (*Polyommatus/Lysandra coridon*) are both similar in appearance, being very small and pale blue in colour, although the chalkhill blue has a dark strip on the edge of each wing. The **common blue** (*Polyommatus icarus*) is even smaller and as the name suggests is the most common of the blues. The underside of its wings is a dusty brown colour with small orange and white spots.

A rare downland butterfly is the **Duke of Burgundy fritillary** (*Hamearis lucina*) which you may be lucky enough to see on Beacon Hill or Old Winchester Hill. It has pale orange spots on small dark wings. Another rarity that relies on chalk grassland is the **silver spotted skipper** (*Hesperia comma*), a diminutive yellow butterfly with small white flashes on the undersides of the wings.

Finally, the **brown argus** (*Aricia agestis*), a small dark butterfly with distinctive orange spots along the edges of each wing, is another that is restricted to chalk grassland; it can sometimes be seen flying close to the ground.

FLOWERS

Many of the flowering meadows that once covered large stretches of downland farmland have been destroyed by modern farming techniques. However, in places, efforts are being made to revive these by encouraging farmers to employ more flower-friendly methods.

Meadows

The dominant grass found in fields all over the Downs is the appropriately named **sheep's fescue** (*Festuca ovina*) which was cultivated specifically for pastureland and is the grass of choice for downland sheep.

Of far greater interest are the likes of the **common poppy** (*Papaver rhoeas*) with its spectacular deep red petals. They often colonise arable fields and path edges, preferring well-disturbed soil. Entire fields turn red in the flowering season in late summer.

Earlier in the season walkers are likely to come across the **cowslip** (*Primula veris*) and its head of pale yellow flowers. The flowers flop down in small bunches earning the plant the old nickname 'bunch of keys'.

Perhaps one of the most beautiful of the downland flowers is the **round headed rampion** (*Phyteuma orbiculare*). Its striking dark blue flowers have earned it the local name 'The Pride of Sussex'.

The tiny yellow flower of **tormentil** (*Potentilla tormentilla*) can be seen hugging the ground in short grassland. It gets its name from an age when it was used as a medicinal remedy for diarrhoea and haemorrhoids: the taste is so foul that it tormented whoever took it.

Another tiny flower that can also be found close to the ground is the **scarlet pimpernel** (*Anagallis avensis*), a member of the primrose family. The flowers are just 5mm in diameter but stand out from their grassy background thanks to their light red colour.

Many people assume orchids to be so rare as to be nearly impossible to find. In truth there are several fairly common species that may readily be seen flowering on the Downs, usually around mid-summer. These include the **early purple orchid** (*Orchis mascula*) which can be seen in rough grassland. It stands about 10-15cm tall and has an elongated head of pinky-purple flowers.

There are of course some species that do fit the rare orchid label including the **fly orchid** (*Ophrys insectifera*) with flowers resembling small insects. These cleverly designed flowers attract wasps which pick up the pollen and take it on to the next insect-shaped flower they see. Another orchid with the same tactic is the **bee orchid** (*Ophrys apifera*) whose flowers are shaped like, well, bees.

Apart from the orchids, one of the most endangered and also one of the most striking flowering plants that may be seen, particularly on the Downs above Eastbourne, is **pheasant's-eye** (*Adonis annua*) with its blood red petals and large seed head.

In overgrown areas thorny **gorse** (*Ulex europeous*) bushes brighten up the summer with their small yellow flowers that burst open from February until June, filling the air with a coconut-like scent.

Woodland and hedgerows

There are several flowering plants associated with open woods and woodland edges. In May the pink flowers of the slightly inaccurately named **red campion** (*Silene dioica*) come into view along woodland edges and at the foot of hedgerows while deeper into the woods the floor becomes covered with **bluebells** (*Hyacinthoides non-scripta*) in the early spring. Other common woodland flowering plants include the **wood anemone** (*Anemone nemorosa*) with its round white flowers which cover forest floors in a similar way to bluebells. A more isolated flower, although sometimes seen growing in small groups, is the cheerful yellow **primrose** (*Primula vulgaris*).

Bramble (*Rubus fruticosus*) is a common woodland and hedgerow species with small sharp thorns. It spreads rapidly, engulfing everything in its path. In its favour, blackberries appear on the branches in the autumn to provide sustenance for hungry birds and peckish walkers. In hedgerows and along woodland edges you'll see the distinctive feathery climber, **old man's beard** (*Clematis vitalba*), also known as traveller's joy. The feathery part of the plant is actually the fruit.

The **foxglove** (*Digitalis purpurea*) is a very tall and graceful plant with white or purple trumpet-like flowers. It is commonly spotted along hedgerows, roadside verges and in shady woodland. Other fairly common woodland species that are just as comfortable on hedgebanks include the **forget-me-not** (*Myosotis arvensis*) which has very small blue flowers and **cow parsley** (*Anthriscus sylvestris*), a tall plant with a head of white flowers.

Perhaps the most unusual and to some eyes the ugliest of plants, found in dark corners of beech woodland, is the pale yellow **bird's nest orchid** (*Neottia*

THE ENVIRONMENT & NATURE

nidus-avis), so-called because of its nest-like root system that intertwines across the ground.

TREES

Over the last few hundred years the once-extensive forest cover in southern England has been fragmented into a patchwork of copses and coppiced woodland. Trees were felled for fuel and for shipbuilding and, in the case of the South Downs, to clear land for agricultural needs. In more recent times many of the hedgerows that helped create the familiar patchwork landscape have been grubbed up to create much larger fields.

Nevertheless, there are parts of the Downs that have survived the threat from axe and chainsaw. The north-facing scarp slope was, and still is, too steep for clearing and too inaccessible for ploughing. Consequently, this is where most of the trees are found. Although there are still areas of semi-natural or ancient mixed woodland, much of the remaining woodland has been coppiced, an old method of promoting growth of more numerous and narrower trunks by cutting a tree at its base. Coppicing was common in hazel stands and the resulting product used in constructing fences and making furniture. Although coppicing is no longer widespread it is still practised in some parts by enthusiasts of old woodland crafts and also by conservationists who recognise that coppiced woodland can be beneficial to certain species.

Most of the woodland the walker will encounter on the Downs is mixed deciduous, made up largely of beech and ash but there are many other species to look out for.

Tree species

The **beech** (*Fagus sylvatica*) with its thick, silvery trunk is one of the most attractive native trees. It can grow to a height of 40 metres with the high canopies blocking out much of the light. As a result the floors of beech woodlands tend to be fairly bare of vegetation. They favour well-drained soil, hence their liking for the steep scarp slope. In autumn the colours of the turning leaves can be quite spectacular. One species that does survive the shady floor of beech woodland is the distinctive **common holly** (*Ilex aquifolium*) with its dark waxy leaves which have sharp points. Holly varies in size, usually growing as a sprawling bush on the woodland floor or in hedgerows but also as a tree when established in more isolated locations.

Famous for its longevity, lasting for well over a thousand years in some cases, the **common yew** (*Taxus baccata*) is abundant in churchyards but there are also natural stands on the scarp slope and among beech woodland. The dark glossy needles are quite distinctive as is the flaky red bark of the often gnarled and twisted old trunks and branches. Do not be tempted to eat the bright red berries; they're poisonous. Another tree with red berries is the **hawthorn** (*Crataegus monogyna*). It has small leaves and is usually found in hedgerows but can also grow as a small tree. In early autumn the berries provide food for woodland birds and are particularly popular with blackbirds.

THE ENVIRONMENT & NATURE

MAMMALS

The well-drained soil of chalk downland is ideal habitat for the **badger** (*Meles meles*), a sociable animal with a distinctive black-and-white-striped muzzle. Badgers live in family groups in large underground 'setts'. They are rarely spotted since they tend to emerge after dark to hunt for worms in the fields. Sadly, they are more commonly seen dead on the road: after hedgehogs they are the most inept at crossing roads. The **fox** (*Vulpes vulpes*) is another common mammal on the Downs. Although they prefer to come out at night they are not exclusively nocturnal; particularly in summer they may be out in broad daylight in some of the quieter corners of the hills though the best time to spot a fox is at dusk when you might see one trotting along a field or woodland edge.

The **rabbit** (*Oryctolagus cuniculus*) is seemingly everywhere on the Downs. The well-drained, steep grassland is ideal for their warrens.

The **grey squirrel** (*Sciurus carolinensis*) was introduced from North America at the end of the 19th century. Its outstanding success in colonising Britain is very much to the detriment of other native species including the red squirrel. Greys are bigger and stockier than reds and to many people the reds, with their tufted ears, bushy tails and small beady eyes, are the far more attractive of the two. Sadly there are no red squirrels anywhere on the Downs.

The **roe deer** (*Capreolus capreolus*) is a small, native species of deer that tends to hide in woodland. They can sometimes be seen, alone or in pairs, on field edges or clearings in the forest but you are more likely to hear the sharp dog-like bark made when they smell you coming.

At dusk **bats** can be seen hunting for moths and flying insects along hedgerows, over rivers and around street lamps. All 17 species in Britain are protected by law. The commonest, and smallest, species is the **pipistrelle** (*Pipistrellus pipistrellus*). Although it is only about 4cm long it can eat up to 3000 insects in one night. You may also be lucky enough to see the slighter larger **Daubenton's** bat (*Myotis daubentonii*) hunting for mosquitoes over rivers and ponds.

If the Downs were made for any one species it is probably the **brown hare** (*Lepus europaeus*) which, if you are observant, can be seen racing across the fields on the hilltops. Hares are bigger than rabbits, with longer hind legs and ears, and are far more graceful than their prolific little cousins. Some other small but fairly common species to keep an eye out for include the carnivorous **stoat** (*Mustela erminea*), its smaller cousin the **weasel** (*Mustela nivalis*), the **hedgehog** (*Erinaceus europaeus*) and a number of species of **voles**, **mice** and **shrews**.

REPTILES

The **adder** (*Vipera berus*) is the only poisonous snake in Britain. It is easily recognised by the distinctive zigzag markings down its back and a diamond shape on the back of its head. On summer days adders bask in sunny spots, such as on a warm rock or in the middle of a path so watch your step. Adders tend to move out of the way quickly but should you be unlucky enough to inadvertently step on one and get bitten sit still and send someone else for help. Their venom is designed to kill small mammals, not humans. A bite is unlikely to be fatal to an adult but *is* serious enough to warrant immediate medical attention, especially in the case of children. Nevertheless, the likelihood of being bitten is minuscule. Walkers are far more likely to frighten the adder away once it senses your footsteps.

The **grass snake** (*Natrix natrix*), an adept swimmer, is a much longer, slimmer snake with a yellow collar around its neck. It's non-venomous but does emit a foul stench should you attempt to pick one up. It's much better for you and the snake to leave it in peace.

The **common lizard** (*Lacerta/Zootoca vivipara*) is a harmless creature which can often be seen basking in the sun on rocks and stone walls. About 15cm long, it is generally brown with patterns of spots or stripes. However, you are far more likely to hear them scuttling away through the undergrowth as you approach.

A curious beast, looking like a slippery eel or small snake, is the **slow worm** (*Anguis fragilis*) which, despite the name, is neither a worm nor indeed an eel or snake but a legless lizard. Usually a glossy grey or copper colour, they can be seen on woodland floors and in grassland. They are completely harmless and usually slip away into the leaf litter when they hear footsteps.

BIRDS

The chalk grassland of the Downs is ideal for a variety of bird species but the grassy hillsides are not the only habitat on the Downs. There are many woodland species in the beech forests on the steep scarp slope, freshwater species on the rivers and sea birds by Cuckmere Haven and the Seven Sisters' cliffs. The following list gives just a few of the birds that may be seen while walking on the Downs.

Scrubland and chalk grassland

LAPWING/PEEWIT
L: 320MM/12.5"

One of the most attractive birds the Downs walker might spot, usually seen feeding on open arable farmland, is the **lapwing** (*Vanellus vanellus*), also known as the peewit. It has long legs, a short bill and a distinctive long head crest. Sadly, this attractive bird is declining in numbers. The name comes from its lilting flight, frequently changing direction with its large rounded wings. It is also identified by a white belly, black and white head, black throat patch and distinctive dark green wings.

Towards dusk **barn owls** (*Tyto alba*) hunt for voles along field and woodland edges. To see a barn owl, with its ghostly white plumage, is a real treat but their dwindling numbers make such a sighting increasingly rare.

The colourful little **stonechat** (*Saxicola rubicola*) with its deep orange breast and black head is among the more commonly sighted of Downland birds.

THE ENVIRONMENT & NATURE

STONECHAT
L: 135MM/5.25"

They are easily identified by their habit of flitting from the top of one bush to another, only pausing to call out across the fields. The stonechat's call sounds much like two stones being struck together, hence the name.

The **yellowhammer** (*Emberiza citrinella*), also known as the yellow bunting, can sometimes be seen perched on the top of gorse bushes. Most field guides to birds along with some old romantic country folk claim that the distinctive song of the yellowhammer sounds like the bird is saying the phrase: 'a little bit

❑ GEOLOGY OF THE DOWNS

How the chalk Downs were formed

It helps to examine the geology of the region as a whole in order to understand how the South Downs reached their present-day form. South-East England is made up of three bands of rock and sediment, the deepest layer being sandstone, the one above clay and the top layer chalk. Over time these three layers were pushed up, probably due to tectonic plate movements, with Africa nudging into Europe. Through the ensuing millennia the soft chalk was eroded through weathering, exposing first the clay and then the more resistant sandstone. The North and South Downs are all that remains of the chalk that lies over the deeper clay and sandstone layers. They are still being eroded today.

One interesting feature of the Downs is the lack of streams. Chalk is highly permeable so streams flow only very briefly during periods of very heavy rainfall. It is worth remembering this when walking on a hot day.

Flint

Flint is a mineral found in bands within chalk and has played a big part in the history of the Downs. When man first found the ability to make tools the folk who lived on the Downs used flakes of flint to make arrowheads and knives. It was also found to be a very useful stone for starting fires. Today flint can be seen in local village architecture, being a very versatile building brick. The traditional Sussex Downs house and barn would not be the same if it were not for flint.

Dew ponds

The chalk soil of the Downs is highly permeable so there is rarely any standing or free-flowing water available for livestock. To combat the problem farmers have, since prehistoric times, constructed dew ponds. These small, circular ponds are designed to collect and retain water for the sheep and cattle that graze the dry hilltops. Despite their name, dew accounts for very little of the moisture that collects in these man-made bowls; most of it is rainwater. The water is prevented from filtering through the chalk thanks to a base layer of straw and clay, although modern-day dew ponds usually have a layer of concrete instead.

Many dew ponds are hundreds of years old and in a state of disrepair, being overgrown and barely recognisable as ponds. However, in recent years many have been restored, either because of their historic interest or simply to be used again for their original purpose. Good examples of dew ponds can be seen near Chanctonbury Ring and also between Southease and Alfriston.

THE ENVIRONMENT & NATURE

of bread and no cheese'. At a push they are right, but the yellowhammer is certainly no talking parrot.

The call of the **skylark** (*Alauda arvensis*) can probably be considered the sound of the Downs. This small, buff-coloured, ground-nesting lark is usually heard but not often seen. The characteristic flight pattern, rising steadily upwards on rapid wingbeats whilst twittering relentlessly, is what makes the skylark such a distinctive little bird. However, the skylark is difficult to see against the blue sky but if you look carefully you might just spot one way up high.

SKYLARK
L: 185MM/7.25"

Woodland

A common raptor that is often heard before it's seen is the **buzzard** (*Buteo buteo*), a large broad-winged bird of prey which looks much like a small eagle. It is dark brown in appearance but slightly paler on the underside of its wings. It has a distinctive mewing call and can be spotted soaring ever higher on the air thermals or sometimes perched on the top of fenceposts. Buzzards are less common towards the eastern end of the Downs where the woodland cover is not so great. They are far easier to spot above the dense woodland on the West Sussex Downs and around the Meon Valley in Hampshire.

The **kestrel** (*Falco tinnunculus*), a small falcon, is much smaller than the buzzard and is far more prevalent. It hovers expertly in a fixed spot above grassland and roadside verges, even in the strongest of winds, hunting for mice and voles.

Similar in size and appearance but rarely seen is the **hobby** (*Falco subbuteo*) which appears in the summer months, often on the margins of woodlands.

The **green woodpecker** (*Picus viridis*) is not all green, sporting a bright red and black head. They are sometimes spotted clinging to a vertical tree trunk or feeding on the ground in open fields. The most common view, however, is as the bird flies away when disturbed. The undulating flight pattern is characterised by rapid wing beats as the bird rises followed by a pause when the bird slowly drops. This is accompanied by a loud laughing call that has earned the bird its old English name of 'yaffle'.

WOODCOCK
L: 330MM/13"

The **woodcock** (*Scolopax rusticola*), with its long straight beak and plump body, is common in damp woodland where it can lie hidden thanks to its leafy brown plumage. It is most easily sighted in spring at dusk and dawn. This is when the males perform their courtship flight, known as 'roding', which involves two distinct calls, one a low grunting noise, the other a sharp 'k-wik k-wik' call.

THE ENVIRONMENT & NATURE

Conservation of the South Downs

Ever since the Industrial Revolution and the rapid development over the last 200 years the English countryside has been put under a great deal of strain. The South Downs were once wooded hills, home to wolves, wild boar and other species that have long since departed. The need to feed an increasing population led to much of the countryside being cleared and ploughed. The result of this is the landscape we see today, although the traditional patchwork pattern of fields and hedgerows has been replaced in some parts of the Downs by much larger fields, the hedgerows having been torn out.

The South Downs is, then, a man-made landscape; even the woodland has been coppiced and the meadows ploughed at one time or another. This is not necessarily a bad thing, however. The resulting habitat is a rare one that provides an essential niche for endangered species, most notably the butterflies for which the Downs are famous.

Although the Downs, positioned in a populous corner of England, continue to be put under pressure from road and housing projects, the increasing awareness of the value of our natural (or perhaps semi-natural) heritage has resulted in greater efforts in the conservation of the Downs. There are several groups, on both a local and national scale and on both a voluntary and government basis,

---

❑ How the South Downs became a National Park

The South Downs almost became one of the first designated national parks back in the 1950s but the proposal was rejected on the grounds that the area did not offer sufficient recreational possibilities for the public. This seems rather surprising today when you consider the number of walkers, cyclists, horse-riders and paragliders who use the hills. National Park status is not just about providing an area of fun for outdoor enthusiasts, however. It is about protecting the area from harmful development such as road building, a real problem in the South-East, and preserving the natural and cultural heritage of the area.

In 1999 the Department of the Environment, now Department for Environment, Food and Rural Affairs, proposed that the Countryside Agency, now part of Natural England, designate the South Downs a National Park. A Designation Order was published in late 2002 and in November 2003 a public inquiry began, to hear the views of those likely to be affected by the change. In 2006 a report was passed to the Secretary of State. After several more delays and legal wrangles, in 2009 it finally was announced that the South Downs would receive National Park status, and the newly appointed **South Downs National Park Authority** (⌨ southdowns.gov.uk) officially assumed responsibility for it on 1st April 2011.

Although at 1648 sq km it is not the largest in area (that distinction going to the Lake District National Park at 2292 sq km), being only an hour from London it encompasses several large towns including Petersfield and Lewes, and is by far the most densely populated of all the National Parks, with over 110,000 residents.

❏ **National Trails**
The South Downs Way is one of 15 National Trails (🖳 nationaltrail.co.uk) in England and Wales. These are Britain's flagship long-distance paths which grew out of the post-war desire to protect the country's special places, a movement which also gave birth to National Parks and AONBs. The Pennine Way was the first to be created.
  National Trails in England are designated and largely funded by Natural England and are managed on the ground by a National Trail Officer. They co-ordinate the maintenance work undertaken by the local highway authority and landowners to ensure that the trail is kept to nationally agreed standards.

who help protect the species, habitats and buildings of the Downs. They also help visitors to get the most out of their trip to the countryside whilst at the same time trying to ease the pressure brought by the increase in tourist numbers.

Now that the South Downs have National Park status (see box opposite) the effort to conserve the area should become less of a struggle owing to the increased environmental protection and financial benefits that the designation brings.

GOVERNMENT AGENCIES AND SCHEMES

Natural England
Natural England (🖳 gov.uk/government/organisations/natural-england; regional offices) is the single government body responsible for identifying, establishing and managing National Parks, Areas of Outstanding Natural Beauty, National Nature Reserves, Sites of Special Scientific Interest, and Special Areas of Conservation.

The highest level of landscape protection is the designation of land as a **National Park** which recognises the national importance of an area in terms of landscape, biodiversity and as a recreational resource. This designation does not signify national ownership and they are not uninhabited wildernesses, making conservation a knife-edged balance between protecting the environment and the rights and livelihoods of those living in the park. In April 2011 the South Downs became England's ninth National Park, and its most densely populated (see box opposite). Some 85% of the land within the South Downs National Park is agricultural, so this balancing act is particularly critical here.

The next level of protection within the National Park includes **National Nature Reserves (NNRs)** and **Sites of Special Scientific Interest (SSSIs)**. The NNRs along the course of the South Downs Way (SDW) include: Beacon Hill (see p83), just before the village of Exton; Old Winchester Hill (see p86), just after Exton; Butser Hill (see p90) several miles further along the path and Lullington Heath (p174).

SSSIs range in size from little pockets protecting wild flower meadows, important nesting sites or special geological features, to vast swathes of upland, moorland and wetland. They are a particularly important designation as they have some legal standing. They are managed in partnership with the owners and

THE ENVIRONMENT & NATURE

❏ **Other statutory bodies**
● **Department for Environment, Food and Rural Affairs** (🖥 gov.uk) Government ministry responsible for sustainable development in the countryside.
● **Historic England** (🖥 historicengland.org.uk) Created in April 2015 as a result of dividing the work previously done by English Heritage (see below). Historic England is now the name for the government department responsible for looking after and promoting England's historic environment and is in charge of the listing system, giving grants and dealing with planning matters.
● **County Councils: Hampshire** (🖥 hants.gov.uk); **East Sussex** (🖥 eastsussex.gov .uk); **West Sussex** (🖥 www.westsussex.gov.uk)

occupiers of the land who must give written notice before initiating any operations likely to damage the site and who cannot proceed without consent from Natural England. SSSIs along the SDW include: Cheesefoot Head (see p78), Butser Hill (see p90), Heyshott Down (see p106), Chanctonbury Hill (see p128) and Seaford to Beachy Head.

Special Areas of Conservation (SACs) are designated by the European Union's Habitats Directive and provide an extra tier of protection to the areas that they cover. Along the SDW Butser Hill NNR and SSSI is also a SAC.

See Natural England's website for further information about all of these.

CAMPAIGNING AND CONSERVATION ORGANISATIONS

The **National Trust** (NT; 🖥 nationaltrust.org.uk) is a charity which aims to protect, through ownership, threatened coastline, countryside, historic houses, castles, gardens and archaeological remains for everyone to enjoy. It manages large sections of the Downs including an area of chalk grassland on the Seven Sisters between the hamlet of Crowlink and Birling Gap (see p169), Harting Down (see p101), Devil's Dyke and Newtimber Hill (see p139 for both). It also owns various properties on the Way, such as Monk's House (see p155) in Rodmell and Alfriston Clergy House (see box p161), its first-ever property, bought in 1896; both are open to the public.

English Heritage (🖥 www.english-heritage.org.uk) has been a charitable trust since April 2015 (see Historic England, box above). It cares for over 400 historic buildings, monuments and sites in England; Bramber Castle (see p132) is one of the properties it manages.

❏ **International Dark Sky Reserve (IDSR)**
In May 2016 the South Downs National Park became an IDSR, with 66% of the park being recognised as having Bronze Level Skies. Not only are such dark skies great for star-gazing, they also help nocturnal wildlife such as moths and bats thrive.
    Areas with the darkest skies on the South Downs include Old Winchester Hill (p86), Butser Hill (p90), Devil's Dyke (p139), Ditchling Beacon (p143) and Birling Gap (p169).

THE ENVIRONMENT & NATURE

The **Wildfowl & Wetlands Trust** (WWT; 🖥 wwt.org.uk) is the biggest conservation organisation for wetlands in the UK; their centre at Arundel (see p120) is well-known and very popular with visitors year-round.

The Wildlife Trusts (🖥 wildlifetrusts.org) undertake projects to improve conditions for wildlife and promote public awareness of it as well as acquiring land for nature reserves to protect particular species and habitats. The Sussex Wildlife Trust (🖥 sussexwildlifetrust.org.uk) manages: the Amberley Wild Brooks network of ponds and marshland; Ditchling Beacon; and Malling Down, Lewes. The Hampshire and Isle of Wight Wildlife Trust (🖥 hiwwt.org .uk) manages St Catherine's Hill, Winchester.

The **Royal Society for the Protection of Birds** (RSPB; 🖥 rspb.org.uk) was the pioneer of voluntary conservation bodies and although it doesn't have any reserves directly on the South Downs Way, there is one near Pulborough, a couple of miles north of Storrington. The wet grassy meadows here attract ducks, geese, swans and wading birds.

Butterfly Conservation (🖥 butterfly-conservation.org) was formed to prevent the decline in the number of butterflies and moths. The two branches relevant to the SDW are Hampshire and the Isle of Wight (🖥 hantsiow-butterflies .org.uk) and Sussex (🖥 sussex-butterflies.org.uk). Sites along the SDW where butterflies are likely to be found include Beachy Head and Malling Down.

There are also smaller conservation groups such as **Murray Downland Trust** (🖥 murraydownlandtrust.blogspot.co.uk) which manages five reserves (Heyshott Escarpment, Heyshott Down, Buriton, Under Beacon, and The Devil's Jumps) in West Sussex and East Hampshire. The Trust's main objective is to 'rescue and enhance neglected areas of unimproved chalk downland' but it also looks after some ancient monuments in the area such as the Bronze Age archaeological site (see p106). Access to the Trust's sites is permitted except when the area should be left undisturbed for conservation reasons. The trust relies on volunteers to help clear the land in its care and sheep are often brought in during the winter months to eat the scrub that threatens the grassland.

The **South Downs Society** (🖥 southdownssociety.org.uk) campaigns specifically for the conservation and enhancement of the landscape of the South Downs. It was formed in 1923 and is supported entirely by donations and subscriptions (membership costs £25/35 individual/joint members). The Society describes itself as operating as a 'critical friend' of the South Downs National Park Authority and has divided the Downs from Winchester to Eastbourne into 12 distinct areas. Each area is looked after by a volunteer District Officer whose main task is to peruse all planning applications that may affect the Downs. In 2017 they successfully campaigned against Eastbourne Borough Council's plans to sell off four downland farms located in the South Downs National Park behind Beachy Head, stating that 'there is no substitute for benign ownership if landscape, wildlife, recreation and cultural heritage are to be conserved and enhanced'. They also arrange a programme of strolls and walks, on and around the Downs, throughout the year.

THE ENVIRONMENT & NATURE

3

MINIMUM IMPACT & OUTDOOR SAFETY

Minimum impact walking

Walk as if you are kissing the Earth with your feet
Thich Nhat Hanh *Peace is every step*

The popularity of the 'Great Outdoors' as an escape route from the chaos of modern living has experienced something of a boom over the last decade or so. It is therefore important to be aware of the pressures that each of us as visitors to the countryside exert upon the land. The South Downs are particularly vulnerable, situated as they are in the most populous corner of the British Isles. Thousands of people explore the network of trails that criss-cross these historic chalk hills.

Minimum impact walking is all about a common-sense approach to exploring the countryside, being mindful and respectful of the wildlife and those who live and work on the land. Those who appreciate the countryside will already be aware of the importance of safeguarding it. Simple measures such as not dropping litter, keeping dogs on leads to avoid scaring sheep and leaving gates as you find them will already be second nature to anyone who regularly visits the countryside. However, there are several other measures that are not quite so well known and are worth repeating here.

ECONOMIC IMPACT

Rural businesses and communities in Britain have been hit hard in recent years by a seemingly endless series of crises. In addition, they have to compete with the omnipresence of chain supermarkets that are now so common in towns across Britain. Faced with such competition local businesses struggle to survive. Visitors to the countryside can help these local businesses by 'buying locally'. It benefits the local economy as well as the consumer.

Buy local

It's a fact of life that money spent at local level – perhaps in a market, or at the greengrocer, or in an independent pub – has a far greater impact for good on that community than the equivalent spent in a branch of a national chain store or restaurant. It's perhaps a step too far to advocate that walkers should boycott the larger supermarkets, which after all do provide local employment, but it's worth remembering that businesses in rural communities rely heavily on visitors for their very existence. If we want to keep these shops and post offices, we need to use them. The more money that circulates locally and is spent on local labour and materials, the greater the impact on the local economy and the more power the community has to effect the changes it wants to see.

Encourage local cultural traditions and skills
No two parts of the countryside look the same. Buildings, food, skills and language evolve out of the landscape and are moulded over hundreds of years to suit the locality. Discovering these cultural differences is part of the pleasure of walking in new places. Visitors' enthusiasm for local traditions and skills brings awareness and pride, nurturing a sense of place; an increasingly important role in a world where economic globalisation continues to undermine the very things that provide security and a feeling of belonging.

ENVIRONMENTAL IMPACT

By choosing a walking holiday you are already minimising your impact on the environment. Your interaction with the countryside and its inhabitants, whether they be plant, animal or human, can bring benefits to all. The following are some ideas on how you can go a few steps further in helping to minimise your impact on the natural environment while walking the South Downs Way.

Use public transport whenever possible
Both Sussex and Hampshire have a good public transport system (see pp44-7). There are plenty of bus and train links to get the walker to the Downs in the first place, making driving there unnecessary, and also various bus services linking the Way with nearby towns and villages as well as offering convenient start and finish points for day walks.

Never leave litter
Leaving litter shows a total disrespect for the natural world and others coming after you. As well as being unsightly, litter kills wildlife, pollutes the environment and can be dangerous to farm animals. Please take your rubbish with you so you can dispose of it in a bin in the next village. It would be very helpful if you could pick up litter left by other people, too.
● **Is it OK if it's biodegradable?** No. Apple cores, banana skins, orange peel and the like are an eyesore, encourage flies, ants and wasps and ruin a picnic spot for others. They also promote a higher population of scavengers such as carrion crows and magpies, an explosion of which can have a detrimental effect on rarer bird species. Those who use the excuse that orange peel is natural and biodegradable are simply fishing for an excuse to clear their conscience. Biodegradable? Yes, but surprisingly slowly. Natural? The South Downs have never been known for their orange groves.
● **The lasting impact of litter** A piece of orange peel left on the ground takes six months to decompose; silver foil 18 months; a plastic bag 10 years; clothes 15 years; and an aluminium can 85 years.

Erosion

● **Stay on the main trail** The effect of your footsteps may seem minuscule but when they are multiplied by several thousand walkers each year they become rather more significant. Avoid taking shortcuts, widening the trail or taking more than one path; your boots will be followed by many others. This is particularly pertinent on the South Downs where there is such a huge volume of visitors.

● **Consider walking out of season** Unfortunately, most people prefer to walk in the spring and summer which is exactly the time of year when the vegetation is trying to grow. Walking on the South Downs in the autumn and winter can be just as enjoyable as in the high season and eases the burden on the land during the busy summer months. The quieter season also gives the walker a greater chance of a peaceful walk away from the crowds and there are fewer people competing for accommodation.

Respect all wildlife, plants and trees

If you come across wildlife keep your distance and don't watch for too long. Your presence can cause considerable stress, particularly if the adults are with young or in winter when the weather is harsh and food is scarce. Young animals are rarely abandoned. If you come across young birds keep away so that their mother can return. Never pick flowers – leave them for others to enjoy too – and try to avoid breaking branches off or damaging trees in any way.

The code of the outdoor loo

As more and more people discover the joys of the outdoors, issues like toilet business rapidly gain importance. How many of us have shaken our heads at the sight of toilet paper strewn beside the path or, even worse, someone's dump left in full view? In some parts of the world where visitor pressure is higher than in Britain walkers and climbers are required to pack out their excrement. This could soon be necessary here. Human excrement is not only offensive to our senses but, more importantly, can infect water sources.

● **Where to go** Wherever possible **use a toilet**. Public toilets are marked on the trail maps in this guide and you will also find facilities in pubs, cafés and camp-sites along the Way. If you do have to go outdoors choose a site at least **30 metres away from running water** and 200 metres from any high-use areas such as hostels and beaches, or from any sites of historic or archaeological inter-est. Carry a small trowel and dig a small hole about 15cm (6") deep in which to bury your excrement. It decomposes quicker when in contact with the top layer of soil or leaf mould. Use a stick to stir loose soil into your deposit as well, as this speeds up decomposition even more. Do not squash it under rocks as this slows down the composting process. If you have to use rocks to cover it make sure they are not in contact with your faeces.

● **Toilet paper and tampons** Toilet paper takes a long time to decompose whether buried or not. It is easily dug up by animals and may then blow into water sources or onto the path. The best method for dealing with it is to **pack it out**. Put the used paper inside a paper bag which you then place inside a biodegradable bag. Then simply empty the contents of the paper bag at the next toilet you come across and throw the bag away. You should also pack out **tampons** and **sanitary**

towels in a similar way; they take years to decompose and may be dug up and scattered about by animals.

Wild camping

There is very little opportunity for wild camping along the length of the Downs. Most of the land is private farmland and much of this is arable cropland. If the urge to camp away from an organised site is too much to resist always ask the landowner first. If the opportunity for wild camping is there, take it. Camping in such an independent way is an altogether more fulfilling experience than camping on a designated site.

Living in the outdoors without any facilities allows the walker to briefly live in a simple and sustainable way in which everyday activities from cooking and eating to personal hygiene suddenly take on greater importance. Remember that by camping off the beaten track you accept added responsibilities. By taking on board the following suggestions for minimising your impact the whole experience of wild camping will be a far more satisfying one.

● **Be discreet** Camp alone or in small groups and spend only one night in each place. Pitch your tent late in the day and move off as early the next day as you can.
● **Never light a fire** The deep burn caused by camp fires, no matter how small, seriously damages the turf and can take years to recover. Cook on a camp stove instead.
● **Don't use soap or detergent** There is no need to use soap; even biodegradable soaps and detergents pollute streams. You won't be away from a shower for more than a couple of days. Wash up without detergent; use a plastic or metal scourer, or failing that some bracken, grass or grit.
● **Leave no trace** Enjoy the skill of moving on without leaving any sign of having been there. Before heading off check your campsite and pick up any litter (even if not left by you), so leaving the place in a better state than you found it.

ACCESS

The south-east corner of England is the most populated area of the British Isles and is criss-crossed by some of the busiest roads in the country. Thankfully, there are also countless public footpaths and rights of way for the large local population and visitors alike. But what happens if you want to explore some of the local woodland or tramp across a meadow? Most of the land on the South Downs is agricultural land and, unless you are on a right of way, it's off limits. However, the 'Right to Roam' legislation (see p65) opened up some previously restricted land to walkers.

Rights of way

As a designated National Trail (see box p57) the South Downs Way is a public right of way – this is either a footpath, a bridleway or a byway; the South Downs Way is made up of all three. Rights of way are theoretically established because the owner has dedicated them to public use. However, very few rights of way are formally dedicated in this way. If the public has been using a path without interference for 20 years or more the law assumes the owner has intended to dedicate

MINIMUM IMPACT & OUTDOOR SAFETY

❏ THE COUNTRYSIDE CODE

The Countryside Code, originally described in the 1950s as the Country Code, was revised and relaunched in 2004, in part because of the changes brought about by the CRoW Act (see opposite); it was updated again in 2012, 2014 and also 2016. The Code seems like common sense but sadly some people still appear to have no understanding of how to treat the countryside they walk in. An adapted version of the 2016 Code, launched under the logo 'Respect. Protect. Enjoy.', is given below:

Respect other people

● **Consider the local community and other people enjoying the outdoors** Be sensitive to the needs and wishes of those who live and work there. If, for example, farm animals are being moved or gathered keep out of the way and follow the farmer's directions. Being courteous and friendly to those you meet will ensure a healthy future for all based on partnership and co-operation.

● **Leave gates and property as you find them and follow paths unless wider access is available** A farmer normally closes gates to keep farm animals in, but may sometimes leave them open so the animals can reach food and water. Leave gates as you find them or follow instructions on signs. When in a group, make sure the last person knows how to leave the gate. Follow paths unless wider access is available, such as on open country or registered common land (known as 'open access land'). Leave machinery and farm animals alone – if you think an animal is in distress try to alert the farmer instead. Use gates, stiles or gaps in field boundaries if you can – climbing over walls, hedges and fences can damage them and increase the risk of farm animals escaping. If you have to climb over a gate because you can't open it always do so at the hinged end. Also be careful not to disturb ruins and historic sites.

Stick to the official path across arable/pasture land. Minimise erosion by not cutting corners or widening the path.

Protect the natural environment

● **Leave no trace of your visit and take your litter home** Take special care not to damage, destroy or remove features such as rocks, plants and trees. Take your litter with you (see p61); litter and leftover food doesn't just spoil the beauty of the countryside, it can be dangerous to wildlife and farm animals.

Fires can be as devastating to wildlife and habitats as they are to people and property – so be careful with naked flames and cigarettes at any time of the year.

● **Keep dogs under effective control** This means that you should keep your dog on a lead or keep it in sight at all times, be aware of what it's doing and be confident it will return to you promptly on command.

Across farmland dogs should always be kept on a short lead. During lambing time they should not be taken with you at all. Always clean up after your dog and get rid of the mess responsibly – 'bag it and bin it'. (See also box opposite and pp188-90).

Enjoy the outdoors

● **Plan ahead and be prepared** You're responsible for your own safety: be prepared for natural hazards, changes in weather and other events. Wild animals, farm animals and horses can behave unpredictably if you get too close, especially if they're with their young – so give them plenty of space.

● **Follow advice and local signs** In some areas there may be temporary diversions in place. Take notice of these and other local trail advice. Walking on the South Downs Way is pretty much hazard-free but you're responsible for your own safety so follow the simple guidelines outlined on pp66-8.

it as a right of way. If a path has been unused for 20 years it does not cease to exist; the guiding principle is 'once a highway, always a highway'.

On a public right of way you have the right to 'pass and repass along the way' which includes stopping to rest or admire the view or to consume refreshments. You can also take with you a 'natural accompaniment' which includes a dog, but obviously could also be a horse, on bridleways and byways. All 'natural accompaniments' must be kept under close control.

Farmers and land managers must ensure that paths are not blocked by crops or other vegetation, or otherwise obstructed, and the route is identifiable and the surface is restored soon after cultivation. If crops are growing over the path you have every right to walk or ride through them, following the line of the right of way as closely as possible. If you find a path blocked or impassable you should report it to the appropriate highway authority as they are responsible for maintaining public rights of way. Along the Way the highway authorities are Hampshire County Council, West Sussex County Council and East Sussex County Council (see box p58). The councils are also the surveying authority with responsibility for maintaining the official definitive map of public rights of way.

Right to roam

For many years groups such as the **Ramblers** (see box p40) and the **British Mountaineering Council** (🖳 thebmc.co.uk) campaigned for new and wider access legislation. This finally bore fruit in the form of the Countryside & Rights of Way Act of November 2000, colloquially known as the CRoW Act or 'Right to Roam'. It came into full effect on 31 October 2005 and gave access for 'recreation on foot' to mountain, moor, heath, down and registered common land in England and Wales. In essence it allows walkers the freedom to roam responsibly away from footpaths, without being accused of trespass, on about four million acres of open, uncultivated land. The areas of access land open to walkers are shown on OS Explorer maps. 'Right to Roam' does not mean free access to wander over farmland, woodland or private gardens, and much of the true chalk grassland of the South Downs has long since been ploughed up. Along with this, most of that which remains is already annexed as national and local nature reserves where access is relatively unrestricted anyway, so the results of the CRoW Act on the South Downs Way might not be quite as liberating as expected.

For those who wish to get off the beaten track and away from the crowds there are plenty of lesser-known rights of way. Follow any of these and you are likely to spend the whole day alone, which is not an easy thing to do in this part of England. However, if you want to leave the path entirely and beat your own trail through the woods and fields always check with local landowners.

❏ **Lambing**
Most of the Way passes through private farmland, some of which is pasture for sheep. Lambing takes place from mid March to mid May when dogs should not be taken along the path. Even a dog secured on a lead is liable to disturb a pregnant ewe. If you should see a lamb or ewe that appears to be in distress contact the nearest farmer.

Those who do exercise their 'right to roam' should remember that this added freedom comes with the responsibility to respect the immediate environment. This is particularly pertinent on the South Downs where most of the land is worked by farmers and is the home to a variety of wildlife. Always keep this in mind and try to avoid disturbing domestic and wild animals.

Outdoor safety and health

AVOIDANCE OF HAZARDS

Walking does not come much more hazard-free than on the South Downs. However, these low southern hills should be given as much respect as their loftier counterparts. Good preparation is just as important here as it is on the northern mountains. The following common-sense advice should ensure that those out for a day trip as well as those embarking on the whole route enjoy a safe walk. Always make sure you have **suitable clothes** to keep you warm and dry, whatever the conditions, as well as a spare change of inner clothes.

Take more **food** than you expect to eat. High-energy snacks such as chocolate, fruit, biscuits and nuts are useful for those last few gruelling miles each day. With the Downs being made of permeable chalk there is a distinct lack of running water so make sure you have at least a one-litre **water bottle** or **pouch** that can be refilled when the opportunity arises. You need to drink plenty of water when walking; 3-4 litres per day depending on the weather. There are a few drinking water taps placed conveniently along the path; these are marked on the maps in Part 4. If you start to feel tired, lethargic or get a headache it may be that you are not drinking enough. Thirst is not always a good indicator of when to drink; stop and have a drink every hour or two, even if you're not feeling thirsty. A good indicator of whether you are drinking enough is the colour of your urine – the lighter the better. If you are not needing to urinate much and your urine is dark yellow you may need to increase your fluid intake.

Every rucksack should have inside it a torch, whistle, simple first-aid kit (see p38) and compass, though you may not need to use the latter as the trail is easy to follow. A whistle is also unlikely to be used due to the close proximity of people and villages. The **emergency signal** is six blasts on the whistle or six flashes with a torch.

It is a good idea to be aware of where you are throughout the day. **Check your location** on the map regularly. Getting lost on the Downs is unlikely to be a major cause for concern but it can turn a pleasant day's walk into a stressful trudge back in the dark, praying that the pub chef has not gone home. If you do get lost it is unlikely to be long before someone passes by who does know their Downs from their Bottoms (the name given to the interior valleys of the Downs).

If you are walking alone you must appreciate and be prepared for the increased risk. It is always a good idea to leave word with somebody about where you are going; you can always ring ahead to book accommodation and let them know you are walking alone and what time you expect to arrive. Don't forget to contact whoever you have left word with to let them know you've arrived safely. Carrying a mobile phone can be useful though you cannot rely on a strong signal, or your phone's battery life.

Be aware that, because much of the South Downs Way is on a chalk ridge high above the surrounding countryside, there may be a steep climb down to, and back up from the adjacent towns and villages.

To ensure you have a safe trip it is well worth following this advice:

- Keep to the path – avoid steep sections of the escarpment and old quarries
- Be aware of the increased possibility of slipping over in wet or icy weather, especially where the chalk is exposed
- Whether you choose to wear hiking boots, trainers or even hiking sandals, be sure that your footwear has good grip and is well worn-in before you start
- Be extra vigilant with children
- Take extra care when leading dogs through areas of grazing animals
- In an emergency dial ☎ 999.

FOOTCARE

Caring for your feet is vital; you're not going to get far if they are out of action. Wash and dry them properly at the end of the day, change your socks every day and if it is warm enough take your boots and socks off when you stop for lunch to allow your feet to dry out. It is important to 'break in' new boots or shoes before embarking on a long walk. Make sure they are comfortable and try to avoid getting them wet on the inside. If you feel any 'hot spots' stop immediately and apply a few strips of zinc oxide tape and leave them on until the area is pain free or the tape starts to come off. If you have left it too late and a blister has developed you should surround it with 'moleskin' or any other blister treatment to protect it from abrasion. Popping it can lead to infection. If the skin is broken keep the area clean with antiseptic and cover with a non-adhesive dressing material held in place with tape.

SUNBURN, HYPOTHERMIA, HYPERTHERMIA & HEATSTROKE

Sunburn can happen, even in England and even on overcast days. The only surefire way to avoid it is to stay wrapped up but that's not always an option. What you must do, therefore, is to always wear a hat, preferably a wide-brimmed one, and to smother yourself in sunscreen (with a minimum factor of 15, although higher is much better) and apply it regularly throughout the day. Don't forget your lips, nose, the back of your neck and even under your chin to protect you against rays reflected from the ground.

Hypothermia, also known as exposure, occurs when the body can't generate enough heat to maintain its normal temperature, usually as a result of being wet, cold, unprotected from the wind, tired and hungry. The risk of hypothermia while walking on the Downs is extremely small. However, it is worth being aware of the dangers. Hypothermia is easily avoided by wearing

MINIMUM IMPACT & OUTDOOR SAFETY

suitable clothing, carrying and eating enough food and drink, being aware of the weather conditions and checking the morale of your companions.

Early signs to watch for are feeling cold and tired with involuntary shivering. Find some shelter as soon as possible and warm the victim up with a hot drink and some chocolate or other high-energy food. If possible give them another warm layer of clothing and allow them to rest until feeling better.

If allowed to worsen, strange behaviour, slurring of speech and poor co-ordination will become apparent and the victim can quickly progress into unconsciousness, followed by coma and death. In the unlikely event of a severe case of hypothermia, quickly get the victim out of wind and rain, improvising a shelter if necessary. Rapid restoration of bodily warmth is essential and best achieved by bare-skin contact: someone should get into the same sleeping bag as the patient, both having stripped to their underwear with any spare clothing under or over them to build up heat. Send urgently for help.

Hyperthermia occurs when the body generates too much heat, eg heat exhaustion and heatstroke. Not an ailment that you would normally associate with the south of England, heatstroke is a serious problem nonetheless. Symptoms of **heat exhaustion** include thirst, fatigue, giddiness, a rapid pulse, raised body temperature, low urine output and, if not treated, delirium and finally a coma. The best cure is to drink plenty of water. **Heatstroke** is another matter altogether, and even more serious. A high body temperature and an absence of sweating are early indications, followed by symptoms similar to hypothermia (see p67) such as a lack of co-ordination and convulsions. Coma and death will follow if treatment is not given instantly. Sponge the victim down, wrap them in wet towels, fan them, and get help immediately.

WEATHER FORECASTS

The South Downs is one of the driest parts of what is a notoriously wet island. However, the weather can still change from blazing sunshine to a stormy wet gale in the space of a day. The wind, in particular, can be surprisingly severe along the top of the Downs. Couple this with rain and a nice walk can turn into a damp battle against the elements. For detailed local weather outlooks online log on to ▯ bbc.co.uk/weather, or ▯ metoffice.gov.uk.

DEALING WITH AN ACCIDENT

● Use basic first aid to treat the injury to the best of your ability.

● Try to attract the attention of anybody else who may be in the area. The emergency signal is six blasts on a whistle, or six flashes with a torch.

● If possible leave someone with the casualty while others go to get help. If there are only two people, you have a dilemma. If you decide to get help leave all spare clothing and food with the casualty.

● Telephone ☎ 999 and ask for the ambulance service (or coastguard if relevant). They will assist in both offshore and onshore incidents. Be sure you know exactly where you are before you call. Report the exact position of the casualty and their condition.

Using this guide

This route guide has been divided according to logical start and stop points. However, these are not intended to be strict daily stages since people walk at different speeds and have different interests. The maps can be used to plan how far to walk each day but note that these are walking times only (see box below).

The **route summaries** describe the trail between significant places and are written as if walking the path from west to east. To enable you to plan your own itinerary **practical information** is presented clearly on the trail maps. This includes walking times for both directions, places to stay, camp and eat, as well as shops where you can buy supplies. Further service **details** are given in the text under the entry for each place.

For **map profiles** see the colour pages at the end of the book. For an overview of this information see itineraries on pp32-3 and the village and town facilities table on pp30-1.

See pp184-5 for the cumulative **distance chart**.

TRAIL MAPS

Scale and walking times   [see map key, p190]
The trail maps are to a scale of 1:20,000 (1cm = 200m; 3¹/₈ inches = one mile). Walking times are given along the side of each map and the arrow shows the direction to which the time refers. Black triangles indicate the points between which the times have been taken. **See note below on walking times**. The time-bars are a tool and are not there to judge your walking ability. There are so many variables that affect walking speed, from the weather conditions to how many beers you drank the previous evening. After the first hour or two of walking you will see how your speed relates to the timings on the maps.

GPS waypoints
The numbered GPS waypoints refer to the list on p183 & pp186-8.

❏ **Important note – walking times**
Unless otherwise specified, **all times in this book refer only to the time spent walking**. You will need to add 20-30% to allow for rests, photography, checking the map, drinking water etc. When planning the day's hike count on 5-7 hours' actual walking.

Up or down?

The trail is shown as a dashed line. An arrow across the trail indicates the gradient; two arrows show that it's steep. Note that the *arrow points uphill*, the opposite of what OS maps use on steep roads. A good way to remember our style is: '**front-pointing** on crampons **up** a steep slope' and 'open arms – Julie Andrews-style – **spreading out** to unfold the view **down** below'. If, for example, you are walking from A (at 80m) to B (at 200m) and the trail between the two is short and steep it would be shown thus: A— — — >> — — – B. Reversed arrow heads indicate downward gradient.

Accommodation

Apart from in large towns where some selection of places has been necessary, almost every place to stay that is within easy reach of the trail is marked. Details of each place are given in the accompanying text.

The number of **rooms** of each type is stated, ie **S** = single bed, **T** = twin beds, **D** = double bed, **Tr** = triple room (for three people) and **Qd** = quad (for four). Note that most of the triple/quad rooms have a double bed and one/two single beds (or bunk beds); thus for a group of three or four, two people may have to share the double bed but it also means the room can be used as a double or twin. See also pp19-20.

Rates quoted for a double or twin in B&B-style accommodation are **per person (pp) based on two people sharing a room** for a one-night stay; rates are usually discounted for longer stays and also if three or more people are sharing a room. Where a **single room (sgl)** is available the rate for that is quoted if different from the rate per person. The rate for **single occupancy (sgl occ)** of a double/twin room may be higher. Unless specified, rates are for bed and breakfast. At some places the only option is a **room rate**; this will be the same whether one or two people (or more if permissible) use the room.

The accommodation will either have **en suite** (bath or shower) facilities in the room or **private,** or **shared, facilities** (in either case this is a separate room, with a bath and/or shower, often just outside the bedroom); in some places the facilities may be private if only one room is booked.

The text also mentions whether the premises have: **wi-fi (WI-FI)**; if a bath (●) is available in/for at least one room, for those who prefer a relaxed soak at the end of the day; if **packed lunches** (Ⓛ) can be prepared subject to prior arrangement (though this has not been checked for cities or large towns where there are lots of options); and if **dogs** (🐾) are welcome in at least one room, or at campsites, subject to prior arrangement; see pp188-90.

If arranged in advance some B&B proprietors are happy to collect walkers from the nearest point on the trail and deliver them back again next morning; they may also be happy to transfer your **luggage** to your next accommodation place. Some may charge; check the details at the time of booking.

Other features

Features are marked on the map when pertinent to navigation. In order to avoid cluttering the maps and making them unusable not all features have been marked each time they occur.

WINCHESTER   MAP 1, pp74-5

Winchester is a city steeped in history. The area was settled as long ago as 450BC when the nearby **St Catherine's Hill** was inhabited by a Celtic tribe. After the Roman occupation came the Dark Ages of AD400-600 during which time it is believed that **King Arthur** reigned from here. Many romantics today believe the city to be the site of legendary Camelot.

Things brightened up after the Dark Ages when in 871 **King Alfred the Great** (849-899) made the city the capital of Saxon England. He has probably had the greatest influence on the city so it is not surprising that a **bronze statue** of him, constructed in 1901, stands on Broadway. **St Swithun** (see box below) is also inextricably linked with Winchester.

In 1066 **William the Conqueror** arrived in Hastings and made his way to Winchester where he duly took charge and ordered the building of the castle. Soon after, in 1079, work began on the cathedral.

Winchester has had a long and sometimes turbulent history but it is well worth spending an afternoon or the whole day exploring the compact city's many sights.

What to see and do

Winchester Cathedral (☎ 01962-857200, 🖳 winchester-cathedral.org.uk; Mon-Sat 9.30am-5pm, Sun 12.30-3pm; £8) stands elegantly in parkland in the city centre. The spectacular nave is said to be the longest Gothic cathedral nave in the world. The best time to visit the cathedral is during the Sunday morning service when the choir can be heard. The cathedral has witnessed many an historic event: **Henry III** was baptised

here in 1207 and it was also the scene of the marriage of **Mary Tudor** to **Philip of Spain** in 1554. In more recent history it became the final resting place in 1817 of **Jane Austen** (see box p72); her grave and memorial are in the north aisle of the cathedral. Tours included in the ticket price are the Cathedral Tour (hourly between 10am and 3pm), which includes a look at the 12th-century Winchester Bible and the Crypt Tour (Mon-Sat 10.30am, 12.30pm & 2.30pm). The Tower Tour (Jun-Sep Mon, Wed & Fri 2.15pm, Sat 11.30am & 2.15pm, Jan-May & Oct-Nov Wed 2.15pm & Sat 11.30am) costs £6.50. There's also a large *café* (Cathedral Refectory, see p76).

Even though the cathedral is the centrepiece of the city there are other equally fascinating places such as the extensive ruins of **Wolvesey Castle** (Apr-Sep daily 10am-5pm; free), the former palace (residence) for the bishops of Winchester, which in 1554 hosted Queen Mary's and Philip II of Spain's wedding breakfast, before being destroyed less than a century later by Roundheads in the English Civil War. At 8 College St, not far from Wolvesey Castle, is the house where **Jane Austen** died. However, this is a private residence so don't peer through the windows.

Nearby is one of Winchester's hidden gems: **St Swithun-upon-Kingsgate Church**, a tiny Church of England church, built on top of King's Gate, one of Winchester's two surviving city gates (the other being Westgate). Built during the Middle Ages, the church is unusual in that it actually formed part of the fabric of the old city walls.

ROUTE GUIDE AND MAPS

❏ The Legend of St Swithun

St Swithun, once Bishop of Winchester, died in AD862. Before his death he asked to be buried outside the old Minster and was duly interred in accordance with his wishes. St Swithun, however, had not counted upon the wishes of Bishop Aethelwold who on 15 July 971 decided to extend the Minster. The expansion plans required the temporary opening of St Swithun's grave before he was carefully re-interred within the new Minster's walls. On the day of the re-interment it began to rain and did not stop for forty days. To this day the legend says that if it rains on St Swithun's Day it will rain for the next forty days. Some would say this is not unusual for England in July.

❏ **Jane Austen**
Jane Austen, born near Basingstoke in Hampshire in 1775, is one of the most important English novelists, having written such classics as *Pride and Prejudice*,
Persuasion and *Northanger Abbey*. In 1816 she began writing *Sanditon* but in the
same year she contracted Addison's disease and the novel was never completed. As
her condition worsened she moved to a house in Winchester where she spent the last
few weeks of her life, dying at the age of 41 on 18 July 1817.

Also near the cathedral is the **City of
Winchester Museum** (☎ 01962-863064,
🖥 hampshireculturaltrust.org.uk/winches
ter-city-museum; Apr-Oct Mon-Sat 10am-
5pm, Sun noon-5pm, Nov-Mar Tue-Sat
10am-4pm, Sun noon-4pm; free). The
museum traces the history of the city from
the Romans to the Victorians and most
things in between.

Next to **Westgate**, one of the two surviving city gates, is the **Great Hall** (☎
01962-846476, 🖥 hants.gov.uk/greathall;
daily 10am-5pm; free but donations of £3
are welcome; tours are available on
request), Castle Ave, the only surviving part
of Winchester Castle. Here, on the west
wall, hangs, so legend has it, *the* table
around which King Arthur and his Knights
of the Round Table sat. Carbon dating has
quashed that particular story, however, and
the table is actually a few hundred years too
young to have been used by Arthur, having
been constructed around the end of the 13th
century; but it's still a mightily impressive
disc of oak, weighing over a ton and elabo-
rately painted during the time of Henry VIII
with a beautiful Tudor rose. The Great Hall
is also famous for the trial of **Sir Walter
Raleigh** for treason in 1603.

In the heart of the city is **City Mill** (☎
01962-870057, 🖥 nationaltrust.org.uk/win
chester-city-mill; daily Feb half-term to end
Nov 10am-5pm, early to late Dec and Jan to
Feb half-term 10am-4pm, other times Fri-
Mon 11am-4pm; admission £4, NT and
Wildlife Trust members free), sitting astride
the River Itchen, and thought to be the country's oldest working water mill. Although
there has been a mill on this site for centuries the present building dates from 1743.
Call ahead for times if you're interested in
the free-to-watch demonstrations of flour

milling. City Mill is the official **'Gateway'
to the South Downs National Park** and it
doubles as an information centre for the
park; it is now the official start of the walk
(see p77).

It is possible to visit **Winchester
College** (☎ 01962-621209, 🖥 winchester
college.org/guided-tours; one-hour tours
Mon, Wed, Fri & Sat 10.15am, 11.30am,
2.15pm & 3.30pm, Tue & Thur 10.15am &
11.30am, Sun 2.15pm & 3.30pm but the
days/hours may vary out of season; tour £8,
cash only) which was founded in 1382 by
William of Wykeham, then Bishop of
Winchester; it is said to be the oldest contin-
uously running school in the country.
Originally it was home to 70 pupils but it
now has over 700. Amongst the buildings
included in the tour are the 14th-century
chapel, the College Hall, the 17th-century
schoolroom and the medieval cloister.

Services
The very helpful **tourist information centre**
(TIC; ☎ 01962-840500, 🖥 visitwinchester
.co.uk; May-Sep Mon-Sat 10am-5pm, Sun
& bank holiday Mon 11am-4pm, Oct-Apr
Mon-Sat 10am-5pm, WI-FI) is on the ground
floor of the Guildhall on High St. You can
also book accommodation here (£4 booking
fee plus a 10% deposit), and rent bikes (half-
day/full-day £10/15, 10am-4.30pm). For
**information on South Downs National
Park** see City Mill, left column.

On the pedestrianised High St there are
countless **banks** and **ATMs** while the main
post office (Mon-Sat 8.30am-6pm, Sun
10.30am-4.30pm) is housed inside WH
Smith at the top of the High St.

There are several **supermarkets**,
including the biggest, Sainsbury's, adjoining **Brooks Shopping Centre** on Middle

Brook St, and a handy Co-op (daily 7am-11pm) near the railway station. Last-minute hiking equipment (including blister kits) can be found in Mountain Warehouse **outdoor gear shop** (Mon-Sat 9am-5.30pm, Sun 10.30am-4.30pm), on the High St.

Lloyds **Pharmacy** (Mon, Wed-Fri 8.45am-5.30pm, Tue & Sat 9am-5pm) is near the TIC at 155 High St. There's also a Boots and a Superdrug on the High St.

There's free **internet access** at the TIC and also inside the Discovery Centre (Mon-Fri 9am-7pm, Sat 9am-5pm, Sun 11am-3pm), a small, modern **library** with a *café*, on Jewry St.

Public transport
Both SouthWest Trains and Cross Country Trains operate **train** services to Winchester (see box p43). The **railway station** is about five minutes' walk from the city centre on Station Rd.

Several National Express **coach** services (Nos 032, 203, 310 & 539; see box p44) call at the **bus station** opposite the TIC. For Southampton you should take Bluestar's No 1 **bus** while for Petersfield and the villages in between take Stagecoach's No 67. Stagecoach's No 64 (from Alton) also calls here. For further details see pp44-7.

Where to stay
Being a popular tourist destination, Winchester is blessed with plenty of guesthouses and hotels. However, the demand on accommodation throughout the year is such that **booking well in advance** is strongly recommended to avoid a night on the park bench by the cathedral.

The nearest **campsite** is the well-equipped *Morn Hill Caravan Club Campsite* (☎ 01962-869877; camping May-end Sep; limited WI-FI; 🐾 if on a lead), 2¼ miles east of town. They charge around £6 per tent, depending on the season, plus around £6 per adult. Stagecoach's bus No 64 (see p47) goes from the bus station to Winchester Science Centre, which is very close to the campsite, so it is possible to use it as a place to stay, but note they only have six tent pitches. The campsite is

also two miles north-east of Chilcomb (Map 2) and 1½ miles north of the Cheesefoot Head car park (Map 3).

Five minutes' walk from the railway station is the welcoming *3 Worthy Lane B&B* (☎ 01962-864339, 🖥 3worthylane.weebly.com; 1D en suite, 1D shared bathroom; ☛; WI-FI; Mar-Dec), with two smart rooms, one of which is huge, a pretty back garden and a friendly cat. B&B costs £45pp (£80 sgl occ). Also not far from the station, and offering the chance to stay in a traditional old inn is *The Westgate* (☎ 01962-820222, 🖥 westgatewinchester.com; 10D en suite; ☛; WI-FI; 🐾 pub area only) at 2 Romsey Rd. B&B costs £42.50-62.50pp (sgl occ full room rate). Two rooms have fold out beds for up to two more adults/children.

Cathedral Cottage (☎ 01962-878975, 🖥 cathedralcottagebandb.co.uk; 1D en suite; WI-FI), at 19 Colebrook St, is just a stone's throw from the cathedral with a cosy room (from £47.50pp, sgl occ full room rate) overlooking a pretty cottage garden, in which you can have your English or continental breakfast served. Another room (1D separate facilities; from £37.50pp, £65 sgl occ) is also sometimes available. Nearby at 10 Colebrook Place is the delightful *Wolvesey View* (☎ 01962-852082 or ☎ 07984-612614, 🖥 wintonian.co.uk; 1S/1D/1Tr, shared bathroom; ☛; WI-FI) where welcoming host John offers B&B from £44pp (sgl £50-58, sgl occ from £68). The house used to belong to Sir Alec Guinness.

In a beautiful Queen Anne house at the top of St John's St is *St John's Croft* (☎ 01962-859976, 🖥 st-johns-croft.co.uk; 2D or T/1Qd, shared bathroom; ☛; WI-FI) with B& 'Aga-cooked'-B from £50pp (sgl occ £50-100). There are comfortable good-sized rooms with views over Winchester.

A short distance up Magdalen Hill at Nos 5-9 is *Magdalen House* (☎ 01962-869634, 🖥 magdalen-house.co.uk; 1D/1T/1Tr, private shower facilities; WI-FI) charging £40-42.50pp (sgl occ from £65). The breakfast room gives a good view over Winchester while you eat the generous 'light' breakfast (included) or the full fry up

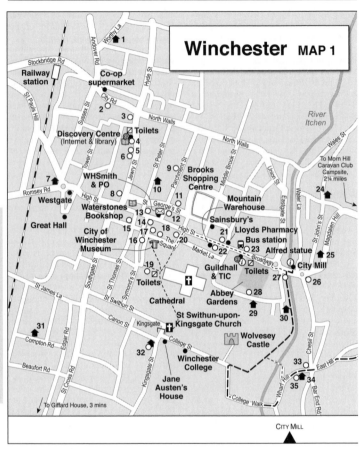

Winchester MAP 1

(an extra £5pp). Note; the double and twin are connecting rooms so they are only both let to guests who know each other.

Winchester Royal (☎ 01962-858751 or ☎ 0330-102 7242, 🖥 winchesterroyal hotel.com; 43D/28D or T/3 suites, all en suite; 🛏; WI-FI) is on St Peter St. This 16th-century townhouse was once a bishop's residence then a convent but now offers luxurious hotel accommodation with four-poster beds in two of the rooms. Rates vary but expect to pay £50-100pp (sgl occ full room rate), often less if booking more than

a week in advance: check their website for special offers.

Further from the bustling centre are several affordable guesthouses in a Victorian part of town: *5 Compton Road* (☎ 01962-869199, 🖥 winchesterbedandbreak fast.net; 2D or T/1T, shared bathroom; 🛏; WI-FI; ⓛ; 🐾) with B&B from £35pp (sgl occ from £45). They have drying facilities and serve a continental-style breakfast but are willing to cook eggs (though not meat) if requested in advance. The comfortable and popular *Giffard House*

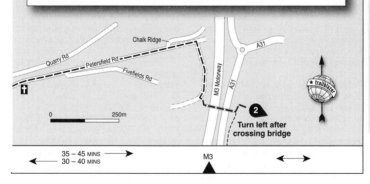

Where to stay
1 3 Worthy Lane B&B
7 The Westgate
10 Winchester Royal
24 St John's Croft
25 Magdalen House
29 Cathedral Cottage
30 Wolvesey View
31 5 Compton Rd
32 The Wykeham Arms
34 The Black Hole

Where to eat and drink
2 Gurkha's Inn
3 Porterhouse Steakhouse
4 Discovery Centre Café
5 Brasserie Blanc
6 Loch Fyne
8 Ruby Reds Burger Shack
9 Piecaramba!

Where to eat and drink *(cont'd)*
11 Caught – Fish & Chips
12 Forte Kitchen
13 Ask (Italian)
14 West Cornwall Pasty Co
15 Café Winchester
16 The Old Vine
17 Café Monde
18 The Eclipse Inn
19 Cathedral Refectory
20 Flat Whites
21 Chococo
22 Rick Stein Fish and Shellfish
23 Gandhi Restaurant
26 Chesil Rectory
27 Bishop on the Bridge
28 River Cottage Canteen
32 The Wykeham Arms
33 The Black Rat
35 Black Boy

Chalk Ridge
Quarry Rd
Petersfield Rd
Fivefields Rd
A31
M3 Motorway
A31
trailblazer
2 Turn left after crossing bridge

0   250m

35 – 45 MINS →
← 30 – 40 MINS

M3

ROUTE GUIDE AND MAPS

(off Map 1; ☎ 01962-852628, 🖳 giffard hotel.co.uk; 4S/1T/1D or T/7D, all en suite; 🖵; WI-FI) with B&B for £54.50-73pp (sgl from £83, sgl occ £97-134) is a guest house south of town at 50 Christchurch Rd.

At 75 Kingsgate St is *The Wykeham Arms* (☎ 01962-853834, 🖳 wykehamarms winchester.co.uk; 2S/10D/2T, all en suite; 🖵; WI-FI; 🐾), a cosy inn with quality rooms priced from £57.50 to £101pp (sgl/sgl occ £93-99); breakfast is not included in the rate. It's named after William of Wykeham who founded

Winchester College (see p72). Sounding as unattractive as its associated restaurant (The Black Rat; see Where to Eat), *The Black Hole* (☎ 01962-807010, 🖳 theblack holebb.co.uk; 10D, all en suite; 🖵; WI-FI; 🐾) is in fact a quality, if somewhat quirky guesthouse with a small roof terrace over-looking the city. They charge £42.50-55pp (sgl occ full room rate).

Where to eat and drink
Cafés The city centre is dotted with cafés. One of the most popular, and a great spot

for breakfast, is *Café Monde* (Mon-Sat 8am-6pm, Sun 9am-5pm), a stone's throw from the cathedral and with a clutch of tables spilling out onto the pavement outside. At the other end of a nearby alleyway is *Café Winchester* (Mon-Fri 7.30am-6pm, Sat 8am-6pm, Sun 9am-6pm) which does pastries, cakes and light lunches. The large, modern *Cathedral Refectory* (daily 9.30am-5pm) is another dependable option and also has plenty of outdoor seating for sunny afternoons. For something more quirky, try *Chococo* (🖥 chococo.co.uk; Mon-Fri 9.30am-5.30pm, Sat 9am-5.30pm, Sun 11am-5pm) which, as the name suggests, specialises in all things chocolate, including hot-chocolate drinks. They also serve tea, coffee, cakes and soups. Serving arguably the best coffee of all, though, is *Flat Whites* (daily 9am-5pm), a coffee and snack van with a seemingly permanent position just off the High St. They do decent cakes here too, and there are tables and chairs scattered beside the van so you don't have to take away. For healthy breakfasts and brasserie-type lunches, *Forte Kitchen* (Mon-Fri 8am-4pm, Sat 9am-5pm, Sun 9am-4pm) is an up-scale café at 78 Parchment St that's very popular.

Pubs There are numerous pubs to choose from. One of the most attractive and historic is *The Eclipse Inn* (☎ 01962-865676, 🖥 eclipseinnwinchester.co.uk; food Mon-Sat noon-2.30pm, Sun noon-3pm; WI-FI; 🐾) at 25 The Square. It's a tiny whitewashed, timber-framed house which once served as a 16th-century rectory and is rumoured to be haunted. The food is good-value here. Another good traditional pub is *Black Boy* (☎ 01962-861754, 🖥 theblack boypub.com; food Tue 7-9pm, Wed-Fri noon-2pm & 7-9pm, Sat noon-2.30pm & 7-9pm, Sun noon-2.30pm; WI-FI; 🐾 on lead) at 1 Wharf Hill, but note the irregular food-serving times.

Opposite the cathedral, on Minster St, *The Old Vine* (☎ 01962-854616, 🖥 oldvine winchester.com; food Mon-Fri noon-2.30pm & 6.30-9.30pm, Sat noon-3pm & 6.30-9.30pm, Sun noon-3pm & 6.30-9pm; WI-FI; 🐾 bar only), is another refurbished old pub that offers a traditional ploughman's

lunch and handmade pork pies as well as more substantial pub fare. Staff members can be brusque, though.

The Wykeham Arms (see Where to stay; Mon-Sat noon-3pm, Sun noon-3.30pm; daily 6-9.30pm), south of the cathedral, is much friendlier, serves top-class fare (main dishes around £16) and feels more like a country pub.

Less cosy, but with a great location, *Bishop on the Bridge* (🖥 bishoponthe bridge.co.uk; food Mon-Sat noon-9pm, Sun noon-8pm) is worth visiting for its sun terrace overlooking the River Itchen.

Restaurants & takeaways One of the most enjoyable places to eat is the café-cum-diner *Piecaramba!* (🖥 piecaramba.co .uk; Mon-Sat 11am-9pm, Sun 11am-5pm), 11 Parchment St, a pie-and-mash specialist with a soft spot for comic books. Superhero stories are plastered across the walls, while complimentary comic books are scattered around for diners to peruse. The menu, meanwhile, is dominated by pies (including beef, chicken, lamb and veggie varieties), which go for just £5.50, or £8.50 as part of a pie-and-mash meal. Great value. Great fun.

There are numerous places to eat on nearby Jewry St too. *Ruby Reds Burger Shack* (🖥 rubyredsburgershack.co.uk; Mon-Thur noon-9pm, Fri noon-10pm, Sat 9am-10pm, Sun 10am-9pm), at 5 Jewry St, does burgers from £6.50, burritos from £7.50, and pancake breakfasts as well as cocktails, beers and shakes.

Further up, at No 24, is *Porterhouse Steakhouse* (☎ 01962-810532, 🖥 www.por terhouserestaurant.co.uk; Sun-Thur noon-10.30pm, Fri & Sat noon-11pm) with high-quality steaks (£11.95-28.95). Along the road is a branch of the seafood chain *Loch Fyne* (☎ 01962-872930, 🖥 www.lochfyne seafoodandgrill.co.uk; Mon-Fri noon-10pm, Sat-Sun 9am-10pm) with courtyard seating.

For something more upscale, there's a branch of the famous French chef Raymond Blanc's *Brasserie Blanc* (☎ 01962-810870, 🖥 brasserieblanc.com; Mon-Fri noon-10pm, Sat 9am-10.30pm, Sun 9am-9pm), also on Jewry St. A two-course set lunch costs £11.95 (Mon-Sat); £15.45 for three courses.

Down on the High St, and similarly upscale, *Rick Stein Fish and Shellfish* (☎ 01962-353535, 🖥 rickstein.com; Mon-Fri noon-3pm & 6-10pm, Sat noon-10pm, Sun noon-9pm) is one of three TV-chef restaurants to open here and was Stein's first restaurant outside Cornwall. Mains cost £16 to £42; the set lunches (£19.95-24.95) are a better deal. The other is *River Cottage Canteen* (☎ 01962-457747, 🖥 rivercottage .net; Mon-Fri 11am-10.30pm, Sat 10am-10.30pm, Sun 10am-6pm), part of Hugh Fearnley-Whittingstall's River Cottage chain. Two- and three-course set menus cost £15.95 and £19.95. It's located in the pleasant Abbey Mill Gardens and there are one or two tables on a veranda overlooking the park.

The Black Rat (☎ 01962-844465, 🖥 theblackrat.co.uk; daily 7-9.15pm, plus noon-2.15pm at weekends), 88 Chesil St, is one of two fancy restaurants at either end of Chesil St. It was awarded a Michelin star in 2017; it was first awarded one in 2011). Expect to spend around £40-50pp for a really memorable evening meal. The other, at 1 Chesil St, is *Chesil Rectory* (☎ 01962-851555, 🖥 chesilrectory.co.uk; Mon-Thur noon-2.20pm & 6-9.30pm, Fri-Sat noon-2.20pm & 6-10pm, Sun noon-3pm & 6-9pm), voted one of Britain's most romantic restaurants by *The Times* newspaper in 2013, and housed in one of Winchester's best-preserved medieval buildings, which dates from around 1425, and was once owned by Henry VIII. Lunchtime and early evening set menus cost £17.95 for two courses or £21.95 for three.

For something more down to earth, grab some pizza or pasta at the Italian food chain, *Ask* (☎ 01962-849464, 🖥 www.ask italian.co.uk; Sun-Thur 11am-10pm, Fri & Sat 11am-11pm), 101 High St, or go for a curry at *Gandhi Restaurant* (☎ 01962-863940, 🖥 gandhirestaurant.com; daily noon-2.30pm & 5.30-11.30pm) at 163 High St. For subcontinental fare with a Himalayan twist there's *Gurkha's Inn* (☎ 01962-842843, 🖥 gurkhasinnwinchester. com; daily noon-2.30pm & 5.30-11pm), a popular Nepalese restaurant and takeaway at 17 City Rd. Alternatively, *Caught – Fish & Chips* (Mon-Sat 11.30am-9pm) is a good chippy on St George's St, while *West Cornwall Pasty Co* (Mon-Fri 8.30am-5.30pm, Sat 8.30am-6pm, Sun 9am-5.30pm), on the High St, is your best bet for a pasty on the go.

The route guide

WINCHESTER TO EXTON   MAPS 1-7

These **12 miles (19.5km, 4¼-5¾hrs)** begin at the City Mill (there is a large wooden plaque here marking the start of the Way) in the centre of Winchester and follow the River Itchen south before crossing it to leave the city and enter the rolling East Hampshire countryside.

Until May 2017 the route began at the cathedral in the centre of Winchester and went from the cathedral grounds, along the main shopping street, past the statue of King Alfred then down beside the River Itchen. You may prefer to start the route this way.

On crossing the bridge spanning the noisy motorway (M3) spare a thought for the remains of **Twyford Down**. This once beautiful hill a few miles to the south was, despite vociferous demonstrations, ruthlessly sliced in two as part of a highly controversial road improvement scheme in the early 1990s.

Once away from the noise of the road the path crosses a field before arriving at **Chilcomb** (see below). The church aside, there's little in the way of shops or services to keep you in Chilcomb so once you have admired the thatched cottages head on up the lane for the gradual but steady ascent to **Cheesefoot Head** (Map 3) where there are great views to the north over the Itchen Valley.

CHILCOMB   MAP 2

Chilcomb is the first of several beautiful Hampshire villages passed through on the way to Sussex. In fact Chilcomb is one of the older settlements, with a **church** (off the path to the south) that pre-dates Winchester Cathedral.

Campers will find tent pitches at *Morn Hill Caravan Club Campsite* (see p73), two miles north-east of here; turn left where the path hits the lane just before Chilcomb then follow the lane up to the busy A31. Turn right and follow this road as far as the big roundabout a mile further east. Keep to the left, over the roundabout,

then go straight over a second, almost adjacent roundabout, and you'll see the campsite in front of you.

There's also a charming **B&B** called *Complyns* (☎ 01962-861600 or ☎ 07890-447982, 🖥 complyns.co.uk; 1S/1D/1T, shared bathroom; 🛏; wi-fi; Ⓛ) in a 17th-century former farmhouse, which charges from £32.50pp (sgl/sgl occ from £40). They have a boiler house where you can dry clothes. In the garden there is also a cosy **shepherd's hut** (£25pp, sgl occ £30) with a double bed.

If you're going to **Cheriton** (35-45 mins; see below), take the path in the corner of the field (see Map 4, p81) rather than following the busy A272.

CHERITON   MAP 4a

On hot sunny days the locals can be seen paddling in the clear waters of the tiny River Itchen, which bubbles out of the chalk about a mile south of Cheriton and runs straight through the village passing beautiful thatched houses and the village green. The village is about 35-45 minutes from the Way so unfortunately, unless you are planning on staying the night here, you are likely to miss Cheriton's quaint charms. Those who do visit should bear in mind that it was not always such a peaceful and charming spot. In 1644, during the English Civil War, the Battle of Cheriton took place just to the east of the village, off Lamborough Lane. The clash between the Parliamentarians and the Royalists resulted in the deaths of 2000 men with the Parliamentarians coming out on top. To this day it is claimed that 'Lamborough Lane ran with the blood of the slain'.

In the centre of the village is the very useful *Cheriton Post Office & Stores* (☎ 01962-771251; Mon-Sat 7am-6pm, Sun 7.30am-1pm), a combined shop, newsagent, off-licence and **post office**. *(cont'd on p82)*

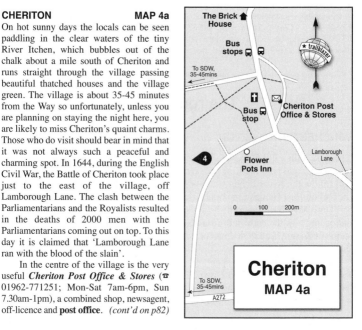

The Brick House

Bus stops 🚌 🚌

★ trailblazer

To SDW, 35-45mins

🛈   ✉ Cheriton Post
Bus 🚌 Office & Stores
stop

4   ○ Flower Pots Inn

Lamborough Lane

0   100   200m

To SDW, 35-45mins

A272

Cheriton
MAP 4a

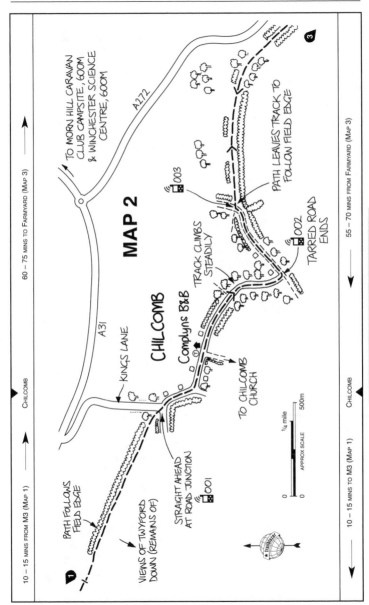

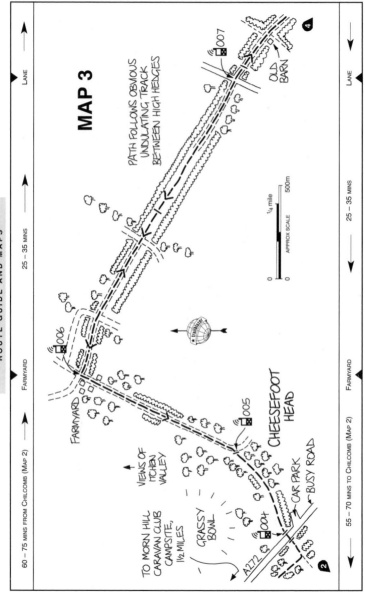

MAP 3

PATH FOLLOWS OBVIOUS UNDULATING TRACK BETWEEN HIGH HEDGES

007

OLD BARN

LANE

25 – 35 MINS

25 – 35 MINS

LANE

006

FARMYARD

FARMYARD

VIEWS OF ITCHEN VALLEY

005

CHEESEFOOT HEAD

CAR PARK

BUSY ROAD

TO MORN HILL CARAVAN CLUB CAMPSITE, 1½ MILES

GRASSY BOWL

004

A272

60 – 75 MINS FROM CHILCOMB (MAP 2)

55 – 70 MINS TO CHILCOMB (MAP 2)

¼ mile

500m

APPROX SCALE

ROUTE GUIDE AND MAPS

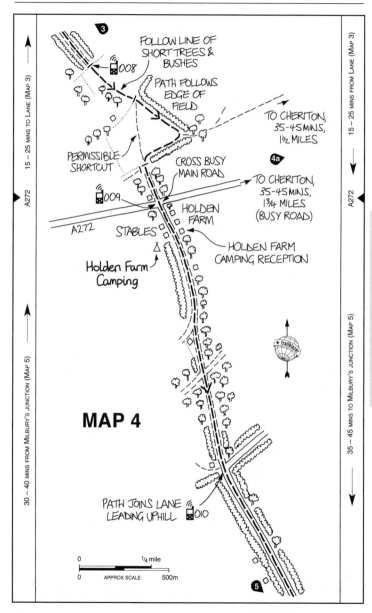

3

FOLLOW LINE OF
SHORT TREES &
BUSHES

📱 008

PATH FOLLOWS
EDGE OF
FIELD

TO CHERITON,
35-45 MINS,
1½ MILES

PERMISSIBLE
SHORTCUT

CROSS BUSY
MAIN ROAD

4a

TO CHERITON,
35-45 MINS,
1¾ MILES
(BUSY ROAD)

📱 009

HOLDEN
FARM

A272

STABLES

HOLDEN FARM
CAMPING RECEPTION

Holden Farm
Camping

MAP 4

★ trailblazer

PATH JOINS LANE
LEADING UPHILL 📱 010

0   ¼ mile

0   APPROX SCALE   500m

5

15 – 25 MINS TO LANE (MAP 3)   A272   15 – 25 MINS FROM LANE (MAP 3)

30 – 40 MINS FROM MILBURY'S JUNCTION (MAP 5)   A272   35 – 45 MINS TO MILBURY'S JUNCTION (MAP 5)

ROUTE GUIDE AND MAPS

(**Cheriton** *cont'd from p78)* However, the post office opens only on Monday (1.30-4.30pm) and Thursday (9am-noon). Stagecoach's No 67 **bus** service (Winchester–Petersfield; see pp44-7) stops in the centre of the village, next to the church.

The charming ***Flower Pots Inn*** (☎ 01962-771318, 💻 flowerpotscheriton.co.uk; food daily noon-1.15pm, Mon-Sat 7-8.30pm; 🐕) is a great spot for a meal and a pint. It has its own **brewery**; their Flowerpots Bitter is definitely worth a taste. Note the pub is closed 2.30-6pm (Sun 3-7pm).

For **B&B,** there's ***The Brick House*** (☎ 01962-771334, 💻 brickhousecheriton.co.uk; 1D en suite/1D private shower; WI-FI; Ⓛ), just past the village centre. They charge £45-47.50pp (sgl occ £80-85).

Immediately after the turning to Cheriton, and right on the Way, you'll find ***Holden Farm Camping*** (Map 4; ☎ 07599-553740, 💻 holdenfarm.co.uk; 🐕; Easter to end Sep) with around 20 tent pitches (£12pp) in a large field opposite the farmhouse. There are showers, toilets and washing-up facilities, as well as fire pits for each pitch. They prefer to know people are coming but will always make space for SDW walkers; the charge can be paid in cash on arrival.

The route continues from here along leafy country lanes and tracks through a typically English landscape of patchwork fields, hedgerows and pockets of woodland. Along this section is ***The Milbury's*** (Map 5; ☎ 01962-771248, 💻 themilburyspub.synthasite.com; food Tue-Sat noon-2pm & 6-9pm, Sun-Mon noon-2pm; WI-FI; 🐕 on lead), a pub full of character, and an ideal lunch stop. A filled baguette and chips costs from £5.95; most mains are around £10. They also do **B&B** (2D/1T all en suite; 🛁; Ⓛ) for £37.50pp (sgl occ from £40). It's worth dropping in just for a drink (though the pub is closed 3-6pm in winter) and to admire the 250-year-old **indoor treadmill** and 300ft-deep (92m) well lit all the way to the bottom. They also have a traditional skittles alley.

If you're staying at ***Dean Farmhouse*** (off Map 5; ☎ 01962-771286, 💻 warrdeanfarm.co.uk; 1D private facilities, 1D/1T both en suite; 🛁; WI-FI; Ⓛ) take the next road north to Kilmeston. B&B, with a substantial continental breakfast, costs from £40pp (sgl occ full room rate)

The highlight of this stage appears rather unexpectedly at the top of **Beacon Hill** (Map 6, p84), a National Nature Reserve and the first real taste of steep downland scenery. The view over the Meon Valley to Old Winchester Hill is a fine reward for the day's effort. Beacon Hill is one of a number of hills in southern England where beacons or bonfires were lit to warn of invasions, most notably in the 16th century because of the Spanish Armada and more recently in June 2012 as part of the celebrations for the Queen's Diamond Jubilee.

There have been plans to change the course of the South Downs Way across the Meon Valley for many years. For now the trail still goes through the pretty village of **Exton** (see p84) – and all the better for it – though there is an alternative route for cyclists (clearly signposted) which skirts around the south of the village.

Symbols used in text (see also p70) 🐕 Dogs allowed subject to prior arrangement
🛁 Bathtub in at least one room Ⓛ packed lunch available if requested in advance

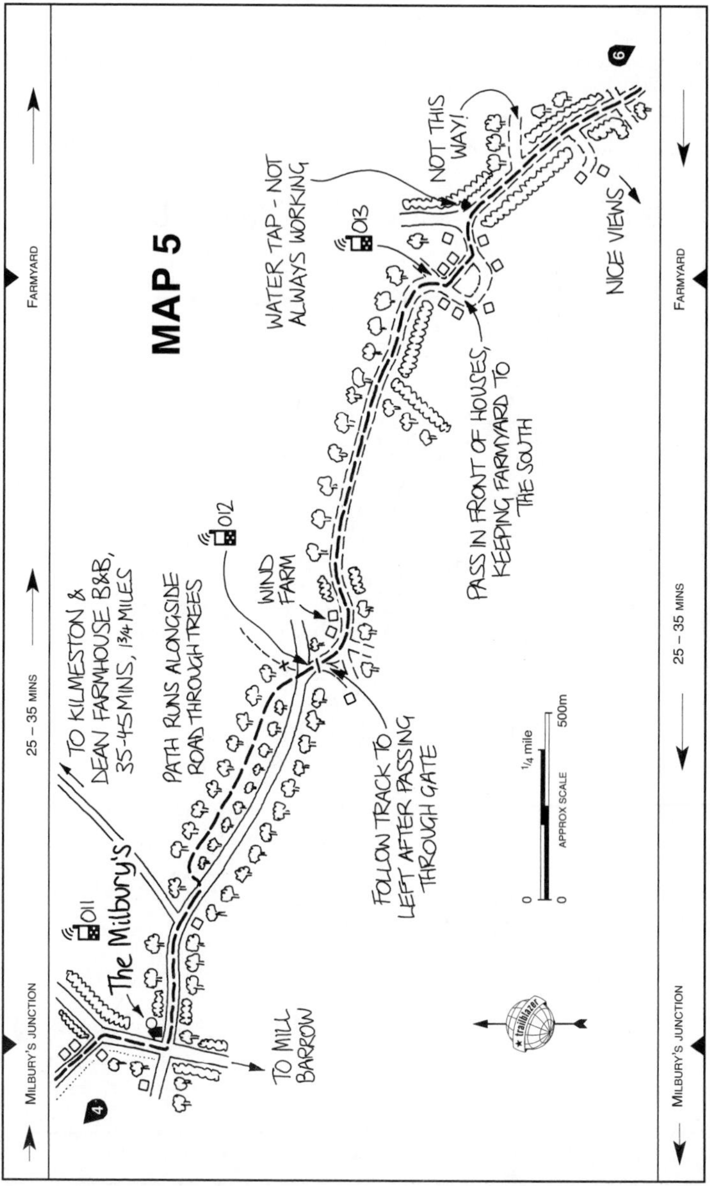

MAP 5

FARMYARD

← 25 – 35 MINS →

TO KILMESTON & DEAN FARMHOUSE B&B, 35-45 MINS, 1¾ MILES

PATH RUNS ALONGSIDE ROAD THROUGH TREES

WIND FARM

☎ 012

WATER TAP - NOT ALWAYS WORKING

☎ 03

NOT THIS WAY!

NICE VIEWS

PASS IN FRONT OF HOUSES, KEEPING FARMYARD TO THE SOUTH

☎ 011

The Milbury's

TO MILL BARROW

FOLLOW TRACK TO LEFT AFTER PASSING THROUGH GATE

¼ mile

500m

APPROX SCALE

0

0

MILBURY'S JUNCTION

← 25 – 35 MINS →

FARMYARD

MILBURY'S JUNCTION

ROUTE GUIDE AND MAPS

EXTON

The Meon valley is known for its natural beauty and also for the Meon villages, all of which claim to be the prettiest in the area. Exton is the smallest of them, if you discount the adjoining hamlets of Meonstoke and Corhampton, and dates

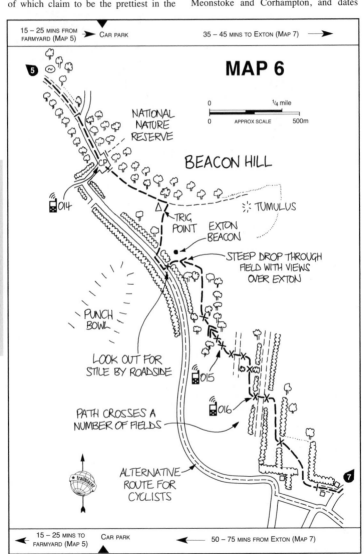

MAP 7

15 – 25 MINS FROM FARMYARD (MAP 5) ▶ CAR PARK

35 – 45 MINS TO EXTON (MAP 7) ⟶

MAP 6

5

NATIONAL NATURE RESERVE

0   ¼ mile
0   APPROX SCALE   500m

BEACON HILL

☐014

TUMULUS

TRIG POINT

EXTON BEACON

STEEP DROP THROUGH FIELD WITH VIEWS OVER EXTON

PUNCH BOWL

LOOK OUT FOR STILE BY ROADSIDE

☐015

☐016

PATH CROSSES A NUMBER OF FIELDS

★ trailblaze

ALTERNATIVE ROUTE FOR CYCLISTS

7

15 – 25 MINS TO FARMYARD (MAP 5) ◀ CAR PARK

50 – 75 MINS FROM EXTON (MAP 7) ◀

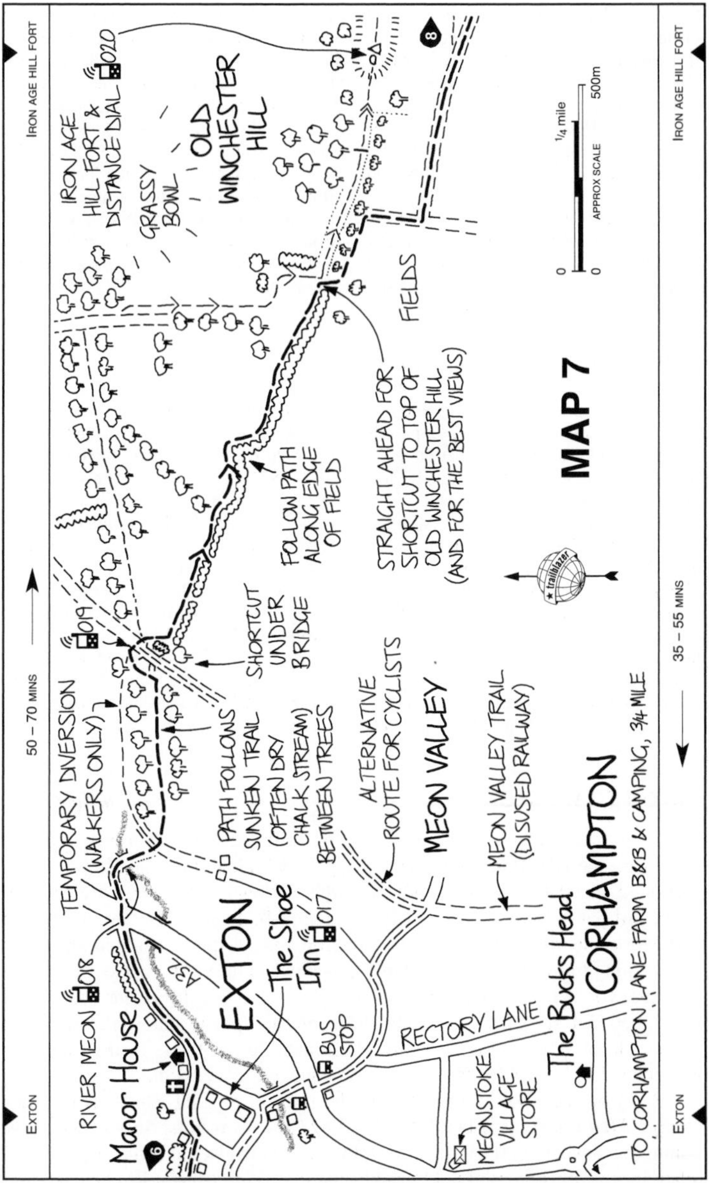

MAP 7

IRON AGE HILL FORT

IRON AGE HILL FORT & DISTANCE DIAL 020

OLD WINCHESTER HILL

GRASSY BOWL

FIELDS

FOLLOW PATH ALONG EDGE OF FIELD

STRAIGHT AHEAD FOR SHORTCUT TO TOP OF OLD WINCHESTER HILL (AND FOR THE BEST VIEWS)

8

50 – 70 MINS

TEMPORARY DIVERSION (WALKERS ONLY)

019

SHORTCUT UNDER BRIDGE

PATH FOLLOWS SUNKEN TRAIL (OFTEN DRY CHALK STREAM) BETWEEN TREES

ALTERNATIVE ROUTE FOR CYCLISTS

MEON VALLEY

MEON VALLEY TRAIL (DISUSED RAILWAY)

35 – 55 MINS

RIVER MEON 018

Manor House

6

EXTON

The Shoe Inn 017

A32

BUS STOP

RECTORY LANE

The Bucks Head CORHAMPTON

MEONSTOKE VILLAGE STORE

TO CORHAMPTON LANE FARM B&B & CAMPING, ¾ MILE

0   ¼ mile
0   500m
APPROX SCALE

ROUTE GUIDE AND MAPS

EXTON

IRON AGE HILL FORT

back to at least AD940 when it was first mentioned in official documents. It also merited an entry in the Domesday Book of 1086, described as a hamlet of one church and two mills.

Manor House (☎ 01489-877529, 🖥 extonbedandbreakfast.com; 1D en suite, 1D private bathroom; ▼; WI-FI but not in rooms) offers B&B for £62.50-70pp (sgl occ £105-120). Minimum two-night stay at weekends. *The Shoe Inn* (☎ 01489-877526, 🖥 theshoeexton.co.uk; food Mon-Fri noon-2.15pm & 6-9pm, Sat/Sun noon-3pm & 6-8.30/9pm; 🐾) is a friendly

village pub with real ales and good food though it's closed 3-6pm during the week. It offers baguettes (£6.50), Ploughman's (£7.50), pastries and soups at lunchtime, while the evening menu includes slow-cooked belly of pork (£14.95) and haddock in beer batter (small/large £8.95/12.95); they always have a vegan option too. Booking is advised in the evenings, particularly at weekends. The pub's name derives from the building next door which used to be the village cobbler's. There's a nice beer garden across the road.

CORHAMPTON   MAP 7, p85
A short distance south of Exton, Corhampton is useful for its shop and two good places to stay, one of them a pub. If you do stay down here note that there's a shortcut back to the South Downs Way following the disused railway track.

Meonstoke Village Store (Mon-Sat 6am-7pm, Sun 7am-4pm) incorporates the **post office** (Mon-Fri 9am-5.30pm, Sat 9am-12.30pm) and is 500m south of Exton. There's a good range of local produce here.

The Bucks Head (☎ 01489-877313, 🖥 thebuckshead.co.uk; food Mon-Fri noon-2.30pm & 6-8.30pm, Sat noon-3pm & 6-8.30pm, Sun noon-4pm; WI-FI; 🐾) is another welcoming pub and they also offer **B&B** (2T/3D, all en suite; ▼; WI-FI; Ⓛ) from

£45pp (sgl occ £70). Note the pub closes between 3pm and 5.30pm on weekdays.

About a mile down Corhampton Lane (off Map 7) is *Corhampton Lane Farm* (☎ 01489-878755, 🖥 corhamptonlanefarm.co .uk; 2Tr both with private facilities; ▼; WI-FI; Ⓛ; 🐾) with **B&B** for £40pp (sgl occ £50). Luggage transfer, pick up/drop off at Exton, and lifts to and from the village/pub by arrangement. Often recommended: 'best B&B on the whole trip' said one reader! **Campers** (£5 per pitch; 🐾) can use the toilet, kitchen and wash basin in the barn, and can even sleep in the barn in bad weather. Breakfast (£10) is available for campers if requested in advance.

EXTON TO BURITON   MAPS 7-12

This fine stretch of the Way covering **12½ miles (20km, 4½-6hrs)** takes the walker beside **Old Winchester Hill** (Map 7), a typical downland hill of chalk grassland and steep ancient woodland and a National Nature Reserve. The top of the hill boasts one of the finest **Iron Age hill-fort** sites in the south. The old earthworks clearly mark the outline of the fort and a display board has an artist's impression of how it once would have looked when the earthy banks were lined with the wooden stakes that formed the walls of the fort. It is clear why it was positioned here since the views in all directions are spectacular, stretching as far as the Isle of Wight on a clear day. Presumably the soldiers of the time also appreciated the views for the strategic advantage it gave them.

Right on the SDW, shortly before the turn-off to **East Meon**, is the welcoming *Meon Springs* (Map 8; ☎ 01730-823134, 🖥 meonsprings.com), a fly-fishing base where you can pick up refreshments (rolls, baguettes, pasties and other snacks, plus hot and cold drinks, and even cold beers!). It opens at 8am

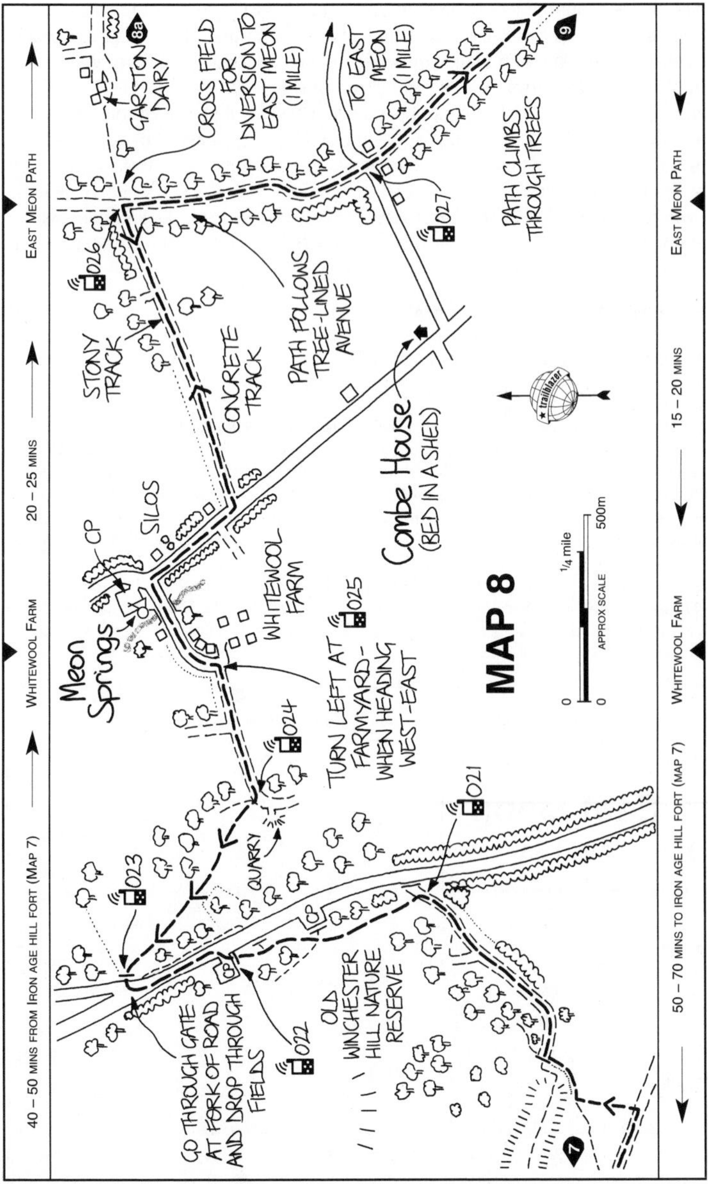

MAP 8

40 – 50 MINS FROM IRON AGE HILL FORT (MAP 7)

WHITEWOOL FARM

20 – 25 MINS

EAST MEON PATH

GARSTON DAIRY 8a

CROSS FIELD FOR DIVERSION TO EAST MEON (1 MILE)

TO EAST MEON (1 MILE)

9

PATH CLIMBS THROUGH TREES

026

STONY TRACK

027

CONCRETE TRACK

PATH FOLLOWS TREE-LINED AVENUE

Meon Springs

CP

SILOS

WHITEWOOL FARM

Combe House (BED IN A SHED)

025

TURN LEFT AT FARMYARD WHEN HEADING WEST-EAST

024

QUARRY

¼ mile

500m

APPROX SCALE

023

021

022

OLD WINCHESTER HILL NATURE RESERVE

GO THROUGH GATE AT FORK OF ROAD AND DROP THROUGH FIELDS

7

ROUTE GUIDE AND MAPS

WHITEWOOL FARM

15 – 20 MINS

EAST MEON PATH

50 – 70 MINS TO IRON AGE HILL FORT (MAP 7)

and closes when the last fishermen go home (normally just before sunset), and there's an honesty box for payment if no one's around. They also rent bikes here, can help you with bike spares/repairs, and are happy to fill up your water bottles. You can **camp** (£10pp; 🐾) here too if you have a tent. There's a toilet and washing facilities but no showers. Campers can just turn up but occasionally they are fully booked so it's worth checking the calendar on their website or phoning ahead. They have yurts and shepherd's huts too, but these can only be booked for multi-day stays. Just over half a mile to the south of here is *Combe House, Bed in a Shed* (Map 8; ☎ 01730-823541, 🖥 southdownsbnb .com; 1D or T en suite; WI-FI; ⓛ) with B&B in a self-contained annex from £50pp (sgl occ from £55).

EAST MEON   MAP 8a

East Meon is only a half-hour detour from the official path and is well worth the effort for a lunch stop or overnight stay. There are records of a settlement here as far back as AD400 and the whole area was once a royal estate belonging to King Alfred. If in the village, take a look at the 900-year-old **church** at the foot of the hill where you can also admire the 14th-century **courthouse**, once part of a monastery.

The **post office** (Mon-Fri 9am-5pm, Sat 9am-noon) and **East Meon Stores** (Mon-Fri 7am-6pm, Sat 7am-5pm, Sun 8am-1pm) are on the High St. The Stores are surprisingly well stocked. Note, they accept cash only. Stagecoach's No 67 **bus** service (Winchester–Petersfield) stops here; see pp44-7.

Where to stay and eat

In the centre of the village, *Ye Olde George Inn* (☎ 01730-823481, 🖥 yeoldegeorgeinn .net; WI-FI; 🐾) does upmarket pub **food** (Mon-Sat noon-2.30pm & 6.30-9.30pm, Sun noon-3pm & 6.30-8pm: book ahead at weekends); mains cost £15-25. They also offer **B&B** (3D/2D or T, all en suite; 🛏; WI-FI; ⓛ; 🐾) for £45-55pp (sgl occ from £65). Note, the pub is closed 3-6pm, Monday to Saturday but open all day on Sunday.

ROUTE GUIDE AND MAPS

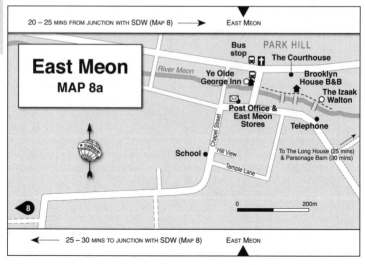

20 – 25 MINS FROM JUNCTION WITH SDW (MAP 8) ⟶   EAST MEON

East Meon
MAP 8a

PARK HILL

Bus stop

The Courthouse

River Meon

Ye Olde George Inn

Brooklyn House B&B

The Izaak Walton

Post Office & East Meon Stores

Telephone

Chapel Street

School ●

Hill View

To The Long House (25 mins) & Parsonage Barn (30 mins)

Temple Lane

8

0   200m

⟵ 25 – 30 MINS TO JUNCTION WITH SDW (MAP 8)   EAST MEON

Beside the trickling River Meon, **Brooklyn House B&B** (☎ 01730-823075, 💻 brooklynhousebnb.co.uk; 1D private facilities/1D en suite; 🛏; WI-FI; Ⓛ; 🐾) charges £40-45pp (sgl occ £70-80). They will collect you from Butser Hill or Coombe Cross if arranged in advance.

The Long House (off Map 8a & Map 9; ☎ 01730-823239, 💻 thelonghouseeast meon.co.uk; 2D en suite/1D or T adjacent private bathroom; 🛏; intermittent WI-FI; 🐾; Ⓛ) lies just round the corner from the end of Frogmore Lane, about a mile from the village on the Ramsdean road. B&B in this friendly place with possibly the world's most powerful shower costs from £45pp (sgl occ £55). About 300m south of here

Parsonage Barn (Map 9; ☎ 01730-823090, 💻 parsonagebarn.co.uk; 2D both en suite; 🛏; WI-FI; Ⓛ; 🐾 but not in the room) is a 17th-century converted barn with two luxurious doubles that go for £52.50-60pp (sgl occ full room rate). The proprietor is a walker and loves to have walkers.

The Izaak Walton (☎ 01730-823252, 💻 izaakwalton.biz; food Tue-Thur & Sat noon-2pm & 7-9pm, Fri noon-9pm, Sun noon-7.30pm, roast till 4pm; WI-FI; 🐾) is a freehouse pub named after a famous local angler, and offers a cheaper pub-grub option (mains £7-10) to Ye Olde George Inn. It's closed every Monday, though, apart from bank holiday Mondays, and the pub closes 2.30-6pm Tuesday to Thursday.

After the turn off to East Meon there is a tough pull up the slope for about two miles to the fabulous **Sustainability Centre** (Map 9, p90) and *Wetherdown Lodge* (☎ 01730-823549, 💻 sustainability-centre.org; 2T/10Tr/1 five-bed room, shared facilities; 🛏; intermittent WI-FI), a hostel which is part of the centre. As you'd expect from the name, everything is environmentally friendly and they use renewable energy. The five-bed room has a double bed with a bunk bed over it and a set of bunk beds. The rate in the hostel rooms is £35 for one person in a room and then £22 for each extra person; this includes a continental breakfast. Booking in general is recommended as the hostel is sometimes booked for sole occupancy use; online booking is available through their website. **Campers** (£12pp; 🐾 on lead) will appreciate the fact that they allow camp fires in designated areas (£6 for firewood & kindling). They also have three **yurts** each sleeping 2-4 people (Apr-Oct only, booking essential and two-night minimum stay for weekends; bedding provided for up to two people; £77.50 for two people including one batch of firewood for the heater). The (solar) shower block is open April to October; running water and compost toilets are available all year. The hostel has self-catering facilities but there is also the on-site *Beech Café* (☎ 01730-823755; Tue-Sun & Bank Hol Mondays 10am-3.30pm; WI-FI; Ⓛ; 🐾 on lead) which can provide packed lunches if booked in advance.

If you're staying here and need an evening meal, the closest pub that does food is the excellent *Bat & Ball* (☎ 023-9263 2692, 💻 batandballclanfield.co .uk; food Mon-Sat noon-2.30pm & 6-9pm, Sun noon-8pm, winter to 2.30/3pm; WI-FI; 🐾 bar only), about half an hour's walk away, just before the village of Hambledon.

It is around here that the true line of the Downs begins, stretching east as a high-level ridge, interrupted only by a few river valleys, all the way to Beachy Head near Eastbourne.

The Way continues along the broad ridge with fine views over the Meon valley to the north culminating in the highest point of the South Downs at

ROUTE GUIDE AND MAPS

Butser Hill (270m). **Butser Hill** (see Map 10) is another National Nature Reserve, earning its status for its fine chalk grassland. It is home to over 30 species of butterfly including the tiny, difficult-to-spot but exquisite chalkhill blue (see p49). It was also the original starting point for the South Downs Way before it was decided to extend the path all the way to Winchester.

Before you reach the car park at the top of the hill, a signpost directs you north, towards *Upper Parsonage Farm* (off Map 10; ☎ 01730-823490, 🖳 upperparsonagefarm.co.uk; 1D en suite; WI-FI; Ⓛ; 🐴), about half a mile from

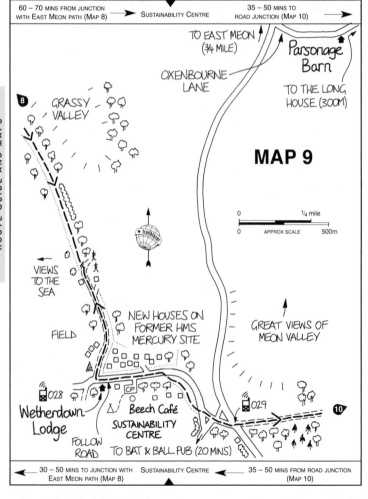

ROUTE GUIDE AND MAPS

60 – 70 MINS FROM JUNCTION WITH EAST MEON PATH (MAP 8) → SUSTAINABILITY CENTRE · 35 – 50 MINS TO ROAD JUNCTION (MAP 10) →

8
GRASSY VALLEY

TO EAST MEON (¾ MILE)

OXENBOURNE LANE

Parsonage Barn

TO THE LONG HOUSE (300M)

MAP 9

0 ¼ mile
0 APPROX SCALE 500m

★ trailblazer

VIEWS TO THE SEA

FIELD

NEW HOUSES ON FORMER HMS MERCURY SITE

GREAT VIEWS OF MEON VALLEY

📶028

Wetherdown Lodge

FOLLOW ROAD

CP

Beech Café
SUSTAINABILITY CENTRE
TO BAT & BALL PUB (20 MINS)

📶029

10

← 30 – 50 MINS TO JUNCTION WITH EAST MEON PATH (MAP 8) · SUSTAINABILITY CENTRE ← 35 – 50 MINS FROM ROAD JUNCTION (MAP 10)

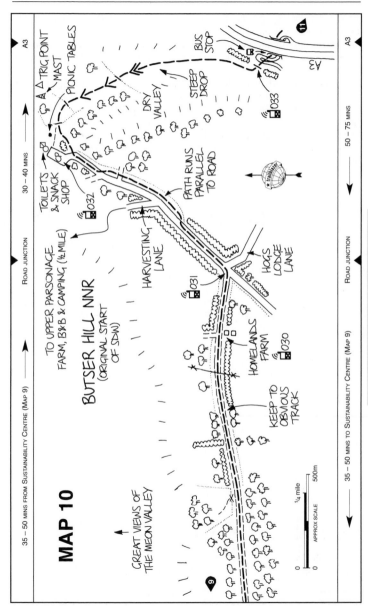

the Way, on Harvesting Lane. This 1400-acre farm has **B&B** accommodation in either a large double room (£47.50-52.50pp, sgl occ full room rate), or in a cosy **shepherd's hut** in the garden (1D; rates on request). You can also **camp** (£10pp) in the garden; there is room for around six tents. Toilets and showers are available for both.

From the car park, which has toilets and a snack shop, the Way slopes down towards the less-than-attractive A3 dual carriageway that slices through the lower flanks. Once past the din of racing traffic the path climbs steadily back to the top of the downland escarpment above Buriton, passing through **Queen Elizabeth Country Park** (Map 11; see box opposite), a magnificent natural mixed woodland that covers the rolling Downs for miles around, just as it has

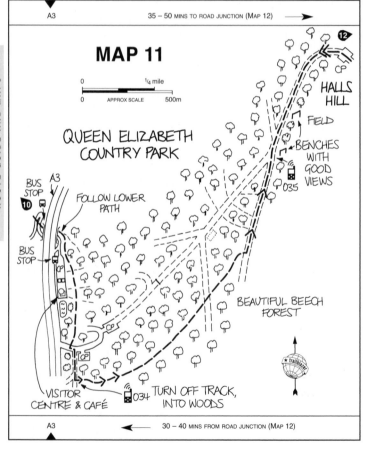

A3   35 – 50 MINS TO ROAD JUNCTION (MAP 12) ⟶

MAP 11

0   ¼ mile
0   APPROX SCALE   500m

QUEEN ELIZABETH COUNTRY PARK

BUS STOP **10**

A3

FOLLOW LOWER PATH

BUS STOP

12

CP

HALLS HILL

FIELD

BENCHES WITH GOOD VIEWS

035

BEAUTIFUL BEECH FOREST

VISITOR CENTRE & CAFÉ

034 TURN OFF TRACK, INTO WOODS

trailblazer

A3   ⟵   30 – 40 MINS FROM ROAD JUNCTION (MAP 12)

done through the centuries. If the accommodation in **Buriton** is booked up you could head into **Petersfield**, where there are several more places.

❏ **Queen Elizabeth Country Park** [Map 11]
The South Downs Way cuts right through the heart of this vast protected area which includes the chalk downland of Butser Hill. To the east of the hill the park is dominated by one of the largest expanses of unbroken woodland cover in the South-East, comprising both ancient broadleaved wood and beech and conifer plantations.

The park (open all the time) is popular with daytrippers and picnickers largely thanks to its proximity to the main A3 road. The **Visitor Centre** (☎ 023-9259 5040, 🖥 hants .gov.uk/qecp; Mar-Oct daily 10am-5.30pm, Nov-mid Dec & early Jan-Feb daily 10am-4.30pm) can provide maps and guides to the park. The centre houses a **shop** and *café* offering cakes and snacks. The **toilets** are open from 8.30am.

Stagecoach's No 37 **bus** (see p47; Havant–Petersfield) stops on the A3. The northbound stop lies just beyond the slip road under the A3 (the slip road needs to be used with care). Access to the park from the stop on the south side is no problem. Either way this is a **request stop** so make sure you let the driver know you want to stop here and also if you are waiting at the bus stop make sure you can be seen.

BURITON   MAP 12, p95
Buriton is yet another pretty village commanding an enviable position at the foot of the wooded downland escarpment.

The **Church of St Mary** by the duck pond is of particular interest as the interior dates back to the 12th century.

Wheel Drive's No 94 **bus** operates between here and Petersfield (see pp44-7).

Where to stay and eat
A good accommodation choice if you can face the 1½-mile walk up the lane is *Nursted Farm* (☎ 01730-264278, 🖥 nurst edfarm.co.uk; 1Tr/1T both en suite; ▼; WI-FI; Ⓛ). It is a magnificent old farmhouse with B&B from £40pp (sgl occ from £60). There's also a self-contained, self-catering annex (min two nights; rates on request), which sleeps two (or four if two are happy to use the sofa bed). There is plenty of wildlife to spot in the garden and the owner

has lived here all his life so knows a thing or two about the area.

The Five Bells (☎ 01730-263584, 🖥 fivebells-buriton.co.uk; food Mon-Sat noon-2pm & 7-9pm, Sun noon-4pm; WI-FI; 🐾 bar only) is a great pub with friendly staff and excellent food (most mains cost around £9). They have some **self-catering accommodation** (two chalets; 1D) which can be booked for single-night stays if it is available; contact them for details. Nearby *The Village Inn* (☎ 01730-233440, 🖥 vil lageinnburiton.co.uk; WI-FI; 🐾) is a more upscale pub, with excellent **food** (daily noon-2.30pm & 6-9pm), although portions can be on the small side. It also has beautifully appointed rooms (14D all en suite; ▼; WI-FI; Ⓛ; 🐾). **B&B** costs £47.50-82.50pp (sgl occ full room rate). Passers-by can pop in during the morning for breakfast (8-10am) or for a coffee and cake.

PETERSFIELD   MAP 12a, p97
This market town still retains pockets of charm, despite attempts to turn it into something bland and modern with supermarkets and a small shopping arcade.

Petersfield Museum (☎ 01730-262601, 🖥 petersfieldmuseum.co.uk; Mar-Dec Tue-Sat 10am-4pm; £3), housed in the

1858 former police station, has old newspaper cuttings, photos, antique maps of the local area and Flora Twort Gallery, which exhibits the Petersfield-inspired watercolours and pastels of the late Flora Twort.

An oasis of calm amongst the bustle is afforded by **Petersfield Physic Garden** (🖥

petersfieldphysicgarden.org.uk; daily 9am-6pm, winter to 4pm; free), reached via an alley off the High St. It features many of the characteristics and plant varieties of a 17th-century town garden with herbs, topiary and an orchard and plenty of benches to relax on with your takeaway lunch.

Walkers on a day off might fancy a dip in Petersfield's **heated open-air swimming pool** (☎ 01730-265143, 🖳 petersfieldpool .org; Apr-Sep 6.15am-8.30pm; £5) on Tor Way.

Services

The **Tourist Information Centre** (☎ 01730-268829, 🖳 www.visit-hampshire .co.uk, click on Explore; Mon-Sat 9am-5pm) is in the **library** (days/times but open to 7pm Wed & Fri); the library has free wi-fi and free **internet** access. Staff can help book accommodation (£2.50 phone booking fee; 10% booking fee on first night) and also provide information on public transport services in the area. Alternatively look at 🖳 visitpetersfield.com.

On the High St there are various **banks** with ATMs, as well as a Boots **pharmacy** (Mon-Sat 8.30am-5.30pm, Sun 10.30am-4.30pm) and an M&S Foodstore (Mon-Fri 8am-8pm, Sat 8am-7pm, Sun 10.30am-4.30pm), while just off it is a large Waitrose **supermarket** (Mon-Sat 7.30am-8pm, Sun 11am-4pm). There's a large Tesco south of the town centre.

The **post office** (Mon, Wed, Thur & Fri 9am-5.30pm, Tue 9.30am-5.30pm, Sat 9am-12.30pm) is on the edge of The Square. There are two good bookshops: **Waterstones** and **One Tree Books** (Mon-Sat 9am-5pm), which also has a nice *café* (Madeleine's, see Where to eat).

Public transport

Petersfield is a stop on SouthWest Trains' London Waterloo to Portsmouth **train** service (see box p43). National Express's No 31 **coach** service (see box p44) from London calls here.

Buses (see pp44-7) leave from the town centre. The most useful services are: Emsworth & District's No 54 (to Chichester) and their Nos 91 & 92 (to Midhurst; Mon-Sat); Stagecoach's No 67 (to Winchester), No 37 (to Havant), and No 38 (to Alton); and Wheel Drive's No 94 (to Buriton).

For a **taxi** or luggage transfer contact: **14U cars** (☎ 01730-300738, ☎ 07795-101895, 🖳 14ucarspetersfield.com).

Where to stay

Campers will have to trudge 1¼ miles out of town to reach the very basic *Ridge Farm Campsite* (☎ 07850-873055; 🐾), where a field and a single portaloo toilet await those who wish to pitch their tent (£10 for a tent and up to two adults). The turn-off for the campsite is about 200 metres past *The Cricketers Inn* (☎ 01730-261035, 🖳 cricketersinnsteep.co.uk; WI-FI; 🐾), which does **food** (Wed-Sun noon-3pm & daily 6-9pm), but serves pizzas only on Monday and Tuesday evening. **B&B** (1T/7D/1Tr, all en suite; ©; 🐾) costs £42.50-46.50pp (sgl occ full room rate). To get to the campsite, walk north-west along Station Rd, turn right at the roundabout up Bell Hill, and keep walking straight, over the A3 dual carriageway, and past The Cricketers Inn before taking the next left turn down a country track.

Back in Petersfield itself, and tucked away behind a high hedge at 4 Heath Rd, is the pretty little 16th-century *Border Cottage* (☎ 01730-263179, 🖳 bordercot tage.co.uk; 1D en suite; WI-FI; ©) which offers B&B from £32.50pp (sgl occ £50) with a continental breakfast served in your room; a room-only rate (£25pp, sgl occ £40) is available and they can suggest places for you to go to if you would prefer a cooked breakfast. At the end of Sheep St, *1 The Spain* (☎ 01730-263261, 🖳 1the spain.com; 1D/1T both en suite, 1D private bathroom; ☞; ©; 🐾) is a well-kept 18th-century townhouse with B&B from £42.50pp (sgl occ from £55).

Just west of the railway station, *Rushes Road B&B* (off Map 12a; ☎ 01730-261638, 🖳 rushes-road.co.uk; 1D or T private bathroom; ☞; WI-FI; ©), at No 80, is run by a friendly tour guide. B&B costs from £35pp (sgl occ £50). From Swan St, walk under the railway bridge, turn left onto Rushes Rd then take the next right.

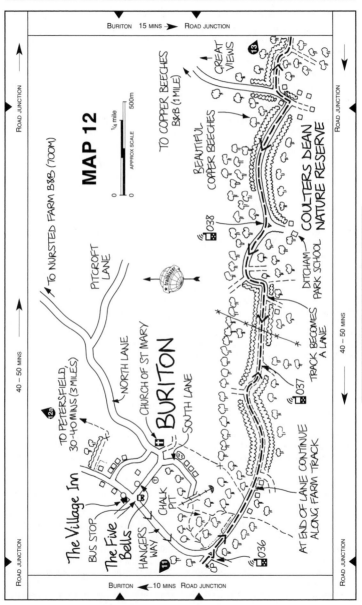

Closest to the Way at No 64A The Causeway, *Causeway Guest House* (☎ 01730-262924, ☎ 07899-682945, 🖥 petersfieldbedandbreakfast.co.uk; 2S/1D/1Tr, shared bathroom; 🛁; WI-FI; Ⓛ) offers B&B from £35pp (sgl/sgl occ £40-60). They also have a microwave for guests to use.

Under new management, *The Good Intent* (☎ 01730-263838, 🖥 goodintentpetersfield.co.uk; 1D/1Tr both en suite, 1D private bathroom; 🛁; WI-FI; 🐕) is a pub with three B&B rooms. They charge £30-45pp (sgl occ £60-70). It is a short walk out of town, on College St, A classier choice, and also under new management, *The Old Drum* (☎ 01730-300208, 🖥 theolddrum .com; 1S/3D/1Qd, all en suite; WI-FI; 🐕) is a beautiful old pub with friendly staff, good food, a selection of real ales and very smart rooms. B&B costs £57.50-62.50pp (sgl occ £95-115). The quad has its own kitchen and goes for £135-155 even if fewer than four stay there. A notch or two above that, *JSW* (☎ 01730-262030, 🖥 jswrestaurant.com; 4D, all en suite; 🛁; WI-FI; Wed-Sat only) is an upmarket restaurant (see Where to Eat) offering top-quality B&B accommodation. Rooms come only as a package with breakfast and dinner – the latter is a 6-/8-course tasting menu; prices range from £107.50-to £177.50pp (sgl occ rates start at £160).

Where to eat and drink
Petersfield is replete with eating places, some of which are excellent, particularly the town's numerous independent cafés.

Cafés One of a number of cafés in contention for best-in-town status, the modern, family-friendly *Fork Handles Kitchen* (☎ 01730-266250, 🖥 forkhandleskitchen.co .uk; Mon-Wed 8.30am-5pm, Thur-Fri 8.30am-11pm, Sat 9am-11pm, Sun 9am-4pm; WI-FI; 🐕) not only comes with great food and friendly service, but also has the added advantage of having plenty of space – perfect for walkers with big rucksacks. More snug, but rightly popular, *Natural Apothecary* (☎ 01730-858183, 🖥 thenaturalapothecary.co.uk; Mon-Sat 8.30am-5pm; WI-FI; 🐕 bar area) is a health-conscious café with rustic décor, wholesome food and

great tea, coffee and cakes. Another fine choice, on the corner of Bakery Lane, is the bright and cheery *Julie's Tearooms* (Mon-Sat 9am-4pm), a traditional-style English tearoom that's good for cream teas, cherry bakewell and the like, although they also do jacket potatoes, and made-to-order paninis and baguettes.

Close to the railway station, *Madeleine's Delicatessen* (Mon-Sat 8.45am-5pm) is another great place for filled sandwiches and baguettes; you can eat in here too. Their spin-off café, *Madeleine's Kitchen* (Mon-Sat 9am-4.30pm), is housed on the opposite side of the road, inside One Tree Books (see Services). Beside St Peter's Church, *Cloisters Café* (daily 8am-4.30pm, food served until 3pm) is tiny but has extra seating outdoors, overlooking The Square. There's a good choice of breakfasts here.

On the other side of The Square, *Heidi's Swiss Patisserie* (☎ 01730-231889; shop Mon-Sat 8.30am-5pm, coffee lounge to 4pm; WI-FI) is a good-value bakery with some seating, and another good place for made-to-order sandwiches.

Vegetarians and vegans need look no further than *Earth* (daily 9am-8pm), Petersfield's only fully vegan café.

Pubs New management has revitalised *The Old Drum* (see Where to Stay; food Mon noon-3pm, Tue-Sat noon-3pm & 6-9pm, Sun noon-4pm; WI-FI; 🐕), an 18th-century pub with good food and fine ales, and which was once a favourite hangout of author HG Wells. Round the corner, *The Square Brewery* (☎ 01730-264291, 🖥 squarebrewery.co.uk; food Mon-Fri 11am-3pm, Wed & Thur also 6-9pm, Sat 10am-4pm, Sun 10am-5pm; WI-FI; 🐕) is a welcoming locals-favourite Fuller's-owned pub. It no longer brews its own beer, but it does have live music some evenings. Also on The Square, *The George* (☎ 01730-233343, 🖥 www.thegeorgepetersfield.co .uk; food Mon-Fri 9-11am, noon-3pm & 6-9pm, Sat 9-11.30am, noon-4pm & 6-9pm, Sun 9-11.30am & noon-3pm; WI-FI; 🐕) is an upmarket pub and restaurant, which feels more like a city bar than a market-town pub,

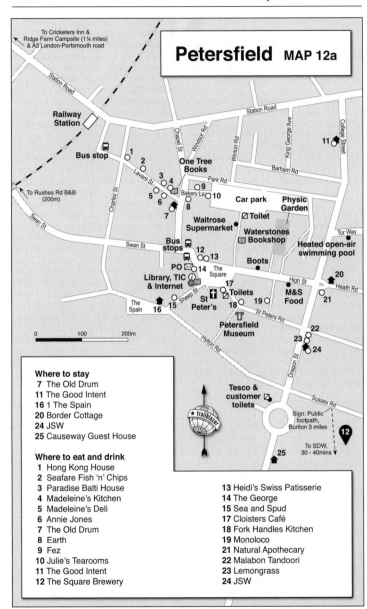

Petersfield MAP 12a

To Cricketers Inn &
Ridge Farm Campsite (1¼ miles)
& A3 London-Portsmouth road

Station Road

Railway
Station

Bus stop

To Rushes Rd B&B
(200m)

Station Road

Chapel St

Windsor Rd

Winton Rd

King George Ave

College Street

Lavant St

One Tree
Books

Park Rd

Barham Rd

Charles St

Bakery La

Car park

Physic
Garden

Toilet

Waitrose
Supermarket

Waterstones
Bookshop

Heated open-air
swimming pool

Tor Way

Swan St

Swan St

Bus
stops

Boots

High St

Heath Rd

Library, TIC
& Internet

PO

The
Square

M&S
Food

The
Spain

Sheep St

St
Peter's

Toilets

St Peters Rd

Petersfield
Museum

Hylton Rd

Dragon St

Tesco &
customer
toilets

Sussex Rd

Sign: Public
footpath,
Buriton 3 miles

To SDW,
30 - 40mins

0   100   200m

★ trailblazer

ROUTE GUIDE AND MAPS

1 Hong Kong House
2 Seafare Fish 'n' Chips
3 Paradise Balti House
4 Madeleine's Kitchen
5 Madeleine's Deli
6 Annie Jones
7 The Old Drum
8 Earth
9 Fez
10 Julie's Tearooms
11 The Good Intent
12 The Square Brewery

13 Heidi's Swiss Patisserie
14 The George
15 Sea and Spud
17 Cloisters Café
18 Fork Handles Kitchen
19 Monoloco
21 Natural Apothecary
22 Malabon Tandoori
23 Lemongrass
24 JSW

Where to stay
7 The Old Drum
11 The Good Intent
16 1 The Spain
20 Border Cottage
24 JSW
25 Causeway Guest House

Where to eat and drink

but is popular nonetheless. Note, you can get breakfast here too.

The Good Intent (see Where to stay; food Mon-Sat noon-3pm & 5-9pm, Sun noon-8pm; WI-FI; 🐾) serves standard pub grub such as sausages and mash (£9.95).

Restaurants & takeaways One of the coolest places to eat is tucked away down the narrow alleyway known as Bakery Lane: *Fez* (☎ 01730-231266, 🖵 fezpetersfield.com; daily 10am-10pm, food served from 11.30am) is a Turkish restaurant, meze bar and café rolled into one and is a great place for lunch, an evening meal, or even just a coffee (they have tables in the alleyway). A three-course lunch/dinner costs £11.95/17.95. Nearby, on Lavant St, *Annie Jones* (☎ 01730-262728, 🖵 anniejones.co.uk) is a **restaurant** (Thur-Sat noon-1.30pm & 7-9.30pm, Sun noon-2.30pm), **tapas bar** (Tue-Thur noon-2pm & 6-9.30pm, Fri-Sat noon-2pm & 6-10pm, Sun noon-3pm) and **café** (Tue-Fri 10am-4pm, Sat 9am-4pm, Sun 10am-3.30pm) with terribly complicated opening hours, but good food and a pleasant atmosphere. In a lane off the High St, *Monoloco* (☎ 01730-266119, 🖵 monolo.co; Mon 9am-4pm, Tue-Sat 9am-4pm & 6-10pm) began as a popular **café** and now also opens five evenings a week as a steakhouse: you cook your own steak at the table on hot lava stones.

South-east of the centre, at 16-18 Dragon St, *Lemongrass* (☎ 01730-267077, 🖵 lmpetersfield.co.uk; daily noon-2.30pm & 5.30-10.45pm) is a good quality, but inexpensive Thai restaurant with dishes such as green curry for £8.50. Next door *Malabon Tandoori* (☎ 01730-268352, 🖵 malabonrestaurant.co.uk; daily noon-2.30pm & 5-11.30pm) serves Indian & Bangladeshi meals to eat-in or takeaway. For a smarter Indian-food option, try *The Paradise Balti House* (☎ 01730-265162, 🖵 paradise-restaurant.com; Sun-Thur noon-2.30pm & 5.30-11.30pm, Fri 5.30pm-midnight, Sat noon-2.30pm & 5.30pm-midnight) at 23 Lavant St. The best Chinese takeaway, meanwhile, is *Hong Kong House* (☎ 01730-265256; Tue-Sun 5-10pm), also on Lavant St.

For fish & chips, try *Seafare* (☎ 01730-265702; Mon 5-10pm, Tue-Thur 11.30am-2pm & 5-10pm, Fri-Sat 11.30am-2pm & 4.30-10pm) on Lavant St, or the more stylish *Sea and Spud* (☎ 01730-262188, 🖵 seaandspud.co.uk; Mon-Sat noon-9.30pm) on historic Sheep St.

Fine dining can be had four days a week at *JSW* (see Where to stay; Thur-Sat noon-1.30pm, Wed-Sat 7-8.30pm), a swish, Michelin-starred restaurant where a two-course lunch/dinner will cost £35/45. Saturdays are reservation only.

BURITON TO COCKING   MAPS 12-16

The route from Buriton follows tracks and lanes along the top of the South Downs escarpment for **10½ miles (17km, 3¾-4¾hrs)**. It is very wooded before reaching South Harting (Map 13) so although the views are limited there is plenty of beautiful shady woodland to enjoy. About 10 minutes south of the Way where it crosses the B2146 is **Uppark House** (see box below).

❏ Uppark House

Uppark House (off Map 13, see opposite; ☎ 01730-825857, 🖵 www.nationaltrust.org.uk/uppark; house daily Mar to late Oct 12.30-4.30pm; gardens and café year-round 10am-5pm) is a magnificent 17th-century country home perched high on a hill with extensive views across the Downs and beyond. The Georgian interior and gardens can be toured for £10.50; visiting the gardens only costs £7. Note, the café is only open to ticket holders. One of the most remarkable things about Uppark is the near-perfect restoration of the building after it was all but gutted by a rampant fire in 1989.

Emsworth & District's No 54 **bus service** calls here (see pp46-7).

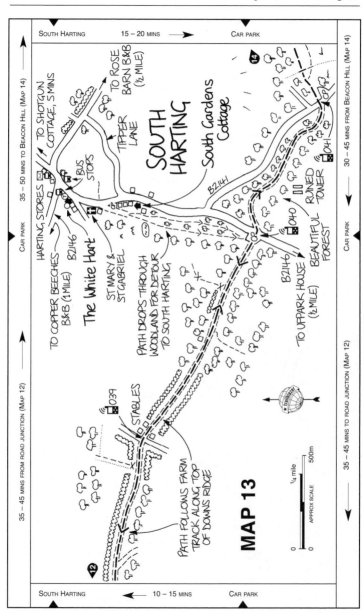

SOUTH HARTING   MAP 13, p99

From the top of Harting Down the village of South Harting with its distinctive church steeple is clearly visible and looks very inviting.

Note, the road down to the village from the Way doesn't have a footpath, so it's much safer, and more pleasant, to use the pathway running parallel to the road and immediately west of it. It's not a long walk but you do have to climb back up the hill through the woods on the return.

The **Church of St Mary & St Gabriel** is interesting and contains an impressive statue of the Archangel Gabriel, by sculptor Philip Jackson, suspended from the ceiling; see photo below. The **village stocks** are still by the path outside the church.

Services

Harting Stores (Mon-Fri 7am-6pm, Sat-Sun 8am-noon) is an excellent village shop, which sells a wide variety of provisions as well as hot pies and pasties, wine and beer. It also incorporates the local **post office** (Mon-Fri 9am-5.30pm, Sat 9am-noon).

© JANE THOMAS

Visit South Harting church to see Philip Jackson's statue of the Archangel Gabriel

Emsworth & District's No 54 (Petersfield–Chichester) **bus** service calls here as does their 91 (Midhurst–Petersfield); see pp44-7.

Where to stay

The most beautiful B&B in the village is the spectacular old timber-framed, thatched 16th-century *South Gardens Cottage* (☎ 01730-825040, 🖳 julia@randjholmes.plus .com; 1T en suite; �¤‚), with a garden that's ablaze with flowers in the summer. B&B costs from £45pp (sgl occ rates on request); they also have a single room but it is only let for a group of three. Their garden gate opens onto the footpath from the Way; it goes past the back of their house. They do not use the front door as it opens on to the road.

Up North Lane, *Shotgun Cottage* (☎ 01730-826878, 🖳 qejoy@hotmail.com; 1D or T en suite/1Tr private facilities; ➖; 🐾; WI-FI) charges from £40pp (sgl occ £40-50; three sharing from £110). To reach the cottage turn right into Pays Farm, which is on the right-hand side of the road.

The upmarket *White Hart* (☎ 01730-825124, 🖳 www.the-whitehart.co.uk; 4D /1T/1Qd, all en suite; ➖; WI-FI; 🐾) offers B&B for £39.50-100pp (sgl occ £70-190); room only rates are also available and the best rates are for advance booking only.

Half a mile south-east of the village, is *Rose Barn B&B* (off Map 13; ☎ 01730-825341, 🖳 spanglefish.com/eastharting bandb; 1D en suite; WI-FI; Ⓛ; 🐾) with accommodation in a self-contained room. B&B costs from £35pp (sgl occ from £40); breakfast is served in the main house.

Just over a mile west of South Harting along the Petersfield road (B2146) and directly accessible from the Way (see Map 12), is *Copper Beeches* (☎ 01730-826662, 🖳 copperbeeches.net; 1D/1Qd both en suite; ➖; WI-FI; Ⓛ; 🐾) with B&B from £40pp (sgl occ £60). The 'quad' has a double bed and bunk beds. During Goodwood events they accept bookings for a minimum of three nights.

Just outside **Elsted** and almost equidistant between South Harting and Midhurst (just over three miles from each) is *The*

Elsted Inn (☎ 01730-813662, 🖥 theelsted inn.com; 2T/2D all en suite; ☞; WI-FI in the bar; Ⓛ; 🐾), a well-run, popular pub. The friendly owners will collect walkers staying with them from the Way and take them back next morning subject to prior arrangement. B&B costs £42.50-47.50 (sgl occ full room rate). They serve food (Mon-Sat noon-2pm, Tue-Sat 7-9pm, Sun noon-3pm).

Where to eat and drink
The White Hart (see Where to stay; WI-FI; 🐾 bar only; food Mon-Fri noon-3pm & 6-9pm, Sat noon-3pm & 6-9.30pm, Sun noon-7pm) does excellent food and is open every day, although breakfasts (7.30/8-10am) need to be reserved in advance if you're not staying here.

After South Harting the trees begin to thin out as the Way passes over **Harting Down**. The views open up over the patchwork fields below and the path climbs even higher onto **Beacon Hill** (Map 14), one of two Beacon Hills on the Way. There then follows another wooded section, the **Monkton Estate** (Map 15), where it's worth listening out for peacocks, before the path continues through the pastureland of **Cocking Down** down to the main road leading to Cocking.

COCKING   MAP 16, p104

Cocking is pleasant enough but the busy main road that slices the village in two has rather taken the soul out of the place despite one or two pretty, old cottages. The consolation is that it is not too far from the Way. It is best reached by ignoring the obvious route down the busy main road and continuing, instead, to the farm buildings 10 minutes east of this road and following the farm track north down the hill to the village.

Behind Malthouse B&B you'll find a bronze plinth known as the **Cocking History Column**. Containing relief panels detailing the town's history, it was sculpted by local resident Philip Jackson (see p100) and unveiled in 2005.

Services
The very small **Cocking Stores** (🖥 cock ingstores.co.uk; Mon-Sat 7am-5pm, Sun 8am-1pm) also houses the **post office** (Mon-Fri 9am-5pm, Sat 9am-noon).

The **bus stop** is on the main road and Stagecoach's No 60 (see pp44-7; Chichester–Midhurst) service passes through regularly.

Where to stay, eat and drink
The most convenient place to stay, particularly for campers, is on a busy working farm right beside the Way. It's part of Manor Farm, where they rear cattle, pigs and various crops. There's **B&B** (in a simple room with a fabulous view) from £35pp (sgl occ from £45) at *Hilltop Cottages* (☎ 01730-814156; 1D or T, bathroom across the landing; ☞; WI-FI; Ⓛ) with hearty breakfasts often including their own sausages. A friendly German Shepherd dog also lives here. If the Bluebell Inn closes (see p104), they may also offer dinners. There's basic **camping** (Easter to end Oct; 🐾 on leads) for £5pp, although this will rise once their shower/toilet block has been installed, hopefully in

ROUTE GUIDE AND MAPS

❏ **Glorious Goodwood – not so glorious for walkers**
Goodwood (🖥 goodwood.com), near Singleton, has long been associated with country pursuits such as horse-racing and shooting but is also host to sports such as flying and motor-racing. The Festival of Speed, held every July, celebrates the history of motor sport and is one of many events held here around the year. Whilst these are probably not of interest to walkers of the South Downs Way, the relevance is that accommodation in the area is often booked up months in advance so it is probably worth checking the dates for events (see the Goodwood website) before you set off.
    Compass Travel's No 99 bus service calls here if prebooked (see pp46-7).

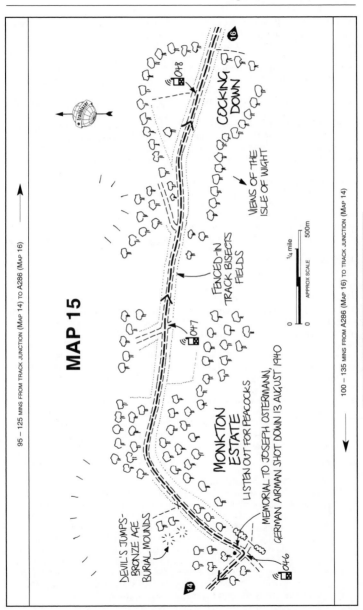

2018. Until then, all campers get is a field and a single portaloo toilet/shower. Breakfast available if ordered in advance. There's also a **farm shop** (Fri-Sun 11am-4pm) selling eggs and home-made sausages as well as sandwiches, drinks and ice-cream.

There's also a warm welcome for walkers at *Moonlight Cottage* (☎ 01730-813336, ☐ moonlightcottage.co.uk; 1D or T en suite, 1S/1T/1D share bathroom; ▼; WI-FI; Ⓛ; ⋈) with **B&B** for £40-47.50pp (sgl/sgl occ £60/70). If arranged in advance they are happy to provide a baggage-transfer service; contact them for details. They also have a **bunkhouse** (4 beds; £22pp inc bedding & towels, £30pp inc breakfast; ⋈; Mar-Oct) with access to washing facilities, toilets and basic self-catering facilities (kettle, fridge & microwave); booking is essential. Directly opposite and owned by the same people, the 16th-century *Malthouse* (see Moonlight Cottage for contact details; 1T/1Tr both en suite, 1Tr pri-

vate bathroom; ▼; WI-FI; Ⓛ) offers **B&B** for £47.50pp (sgl occ £75). Breakfast is eaten at Moonlight. **Camping** (£10pp, £18pp inc breakfast; shower/toilet facilities) is available in their garden.

On Bell Lane there's *Downsfold* (☎ 01730-814376, ☐ downsfold.co.uk; 1D/1T, share bathroom; ▼; WI-FI; Mar-Oct), with B&B from £40pp (sgl occ from £45).

B&B at *The Bluebell Inn* (☎ 01730-810200, ☐ thebluebellinnatcocking.co.uk; 3D en suite, 1D/1T share facilities; WI-FI; Ⓛ; ⋈ part of pub area only) costs £45-62.50pp (sgl occ £65-90). **Food** is served daily (Mon-Tue 6-8pm, Wed-Sun noon-2pm & 6-8pm) and they have a bar menu as well as an à la carte menu. However, as we go to press the pub is currently up for sale.

If everywhere is booked take Stagecoach's No 60 (see pp46-7) to Midhurst (see below), about 2-3 miles to the north, where there is a wider choice of accommodation.

MIDHURST   off MAP 16
Midhurst has some accommodation options, a good range of eating places, a Tesco Express, NatWest and Barclays banks with ATMs and other services should you find yourself here. Several **bus services** (see pp44-7) operate from here: to Worthing (Stagecoach's No 1), to Chichester (Stagecoach's No 60) and to Petersfield (Emsworth & District's Nos 91 & 92 and Stagecoach's 92).

The friendly *Pear Tree Cottage* (☎ 01730-817216, ☐ peartreecottagebandmid hurst.co.uk; 1T/2D plus 4ft sofa bed, all en

suite; WI-FI) is on Lamberts Lane. B&B costs from £45pp (£60-65pp during Goodwood events; sgl occ £60-130). The rooms are self-contained and have a fridge, microwave, toaster and kettle; the twin can sleep an additional child and the doubles up to four people. The owner leaves the ingredients for a continental breakfast in the room the night before. They don't do packed lunches because there is often enough food in the breakfast for guests to make one but also they are behind a Tesco Express (daily 6am-10pm). Failing this have a look at ☐ visit midhurst.com for additional suggestions.

❏ The two Cowdray Gold cups
The Cowdray Estate is probably best known for the Polo Club and the polo matches (both national and international) held there during the year; the main event is the Gold Cup which is held in July. The second 'Gold Cup' refers to the colour of the paint seen on the window frames and doors of cottages and buildings that are part of the estate, particularly around Midhurst. The 'cowardy custard' yellow, as some locals call it, was first used on the cottages by the 2nd Viscount Cowdray who was a Liberal MP (yellow being the colour particularly associated with the Liberal Party), thus it was a good way of promoting the Liberal Party. The paint was made specially for the Viscount and was originally called 'Cowdray Gold' but is now known as 'Gold Cup', though it is not exactly the same shade as the original colour.

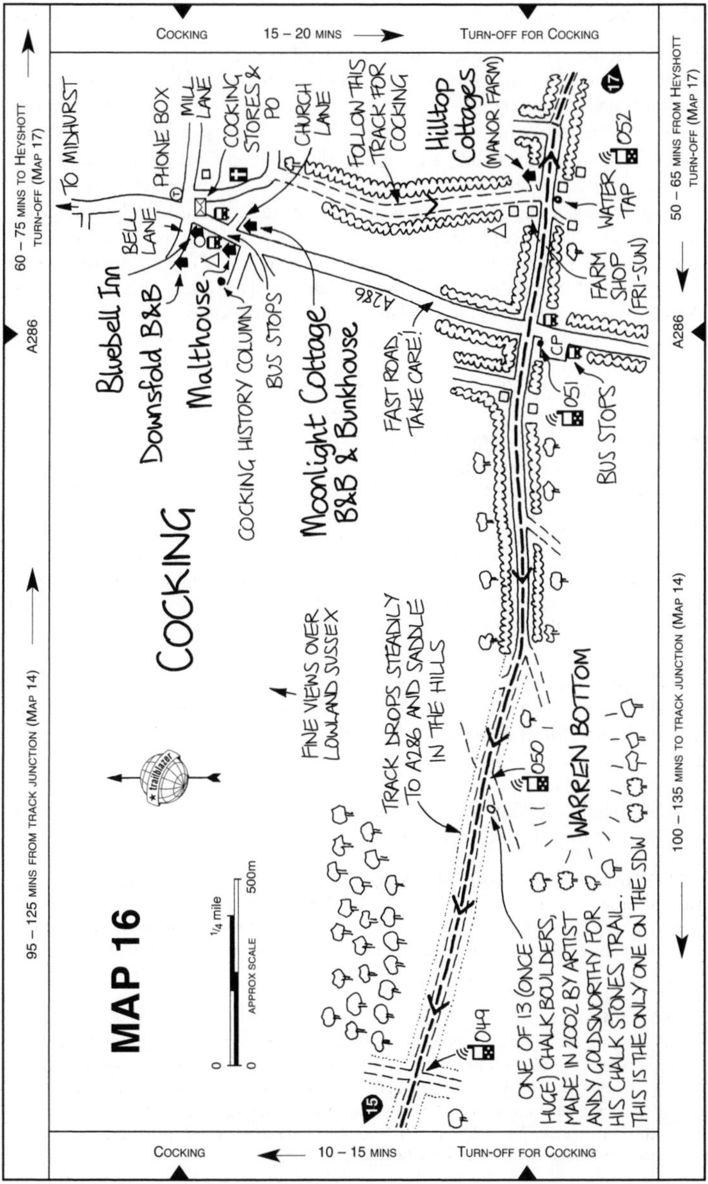

60 – 75 MINS TO HEYSHOTT TURN-OFF (MAP 17)

A286

50 – 65 MINS FROM HEYSHOTT TURN-OFF (MAP 17)

95 – 125 MINS FROM TRACK JUNCTION (MAP 14)

A286

100 – 135 MINS TO TRACK JUNCTION (MAP 14)

TO MIDHURST

PHONE BOX

MILL LANE

COCKING STORES & PO

CHURCH LANE

FOLLOW THIS TRACK FOR COCKING

HILLTOP COTTAGES (MANOR FARM)

WATER TAP

☐☐ 052

☐ 17

BELL LANE

Bluebell Inn

Downsfold B&B

Malthouse

COCKING HISTORY COLUMN

BUS STOPS

FARM SHOP (FRI–SUN)

Moonlight Cottage B&B & Bunkhouse

A286

FAST ROAD, TAKE CARE!

☐☐ 051

BUS STOPS

COCKING

FINE VIEWS OVER LOWLAND SUSSEX

TRACK DROPS STEADILY TO A286 AND SADDLE IN THE HILLS

☐☐ 050

WARREN BOTTOM

MAP 16

¼ mile
APPROX SCALE
500m
0
0

ONE OF 13 (ONCE HUGE) CHALK BOULDERS, MADE IN 2002 BY ARTIST ANDY GOLDSWORTHY FOR HIS CHALK STONES TRAIL. THIS IS THE ONLY ONE ON THE SDW

☐☐ 049

☐ 15

ROUTE GUIDE AND MAPS

COCKING TO AMBERLEY   MAPS 16-22

It is **11½ miles (18.5km, 3¾-5¼hrs)** from the Cocking turn off to the Amberley turn off. From the main road south of Cocking, the Way follows a chalk lane, climbing steadily through fields to rejoin the high escarpment. There is a **water tap** (see Map 16) by the farm buildings. Just after that you will notice that the window frames on the cottages here, including Hilltop Cottages (see p102), are painted yellow; this shows they are part of the Cowdray Estate (see box p104).

The track here used to be bordered on one side by dense woodland and on the other by a high hedge so the view was somewhat obscured in parts but the former South Downs Joint Committee and Graffham Down Trust created a wildlife corridor in order to link up two rich grassland sites – Heyshott Down (Map 17) and Graffham Down (Map 18). **Heyshott Down** is one of the nature reserves in this area which is managed by the Murray Downland Trust (see p59) – making it easier for a lot of the flora and fauna here to survive. The best view is probably from the trig point (Map 17), about 50m off the path.

HEYSHOTT   MAP 17a, p108

It's a steep and sometimes muddy descent from the Way, but Heyshott does have a nice pub and a B&B. *Leggs Cottage* (☎ 01730-814181; 1D or T en suite; ☞; WI-FI) charges from £45pp (sgl occ from £60).

The Unicorn Inn (☎ 01730-813486, ☐ unicorn-inn-heyshott.co.uk; food Tue-Sat noon-2pm & 6-9.30pm, Sun noon-2.30pm;

WI-FI; 🐾 bar area & garden) is a smart country pub with excellent food. Main dishes include beer-battered cod & chips (£13) as well as more unusual offerings like pheasant & chorizo pie (£13.50). The views across the hay meadows to the Downs escarpment are lovely. Note, the pub is closed on Sunday and Monday evenings.

The path then continues past a **Bronze Age burial ground** (Map 18) with tumuli clearly visible among the tussocks of grass. Shortly after is the turn south to *New House Farm Camping* (off Map 18; ☎ 01243-811685, ☐ nhfcamping .com; 🐾 on leads; £5 per pitch and £5pp) 1¼ miles from the Way and on the edge of East Dean. It's a basic place with portaloos and a cold water tap but no showers. The track continues on through a mixture of woodland and grassland, passing the turn-off for **Graffham**.

GRAFFHAM   MAP 18a, p110

There is little to see in Graffham but it has a lazy, peaceful air about it, being well away from any major roads, so makes for a

pleasant overnight stay or lunch stop. The very well-stocked **Graffham Village Shop** (☐ graffhamvillageshop.co.uk; Mon-Sat

---

❏ **Tumuli**
All along the crest of the Downs are numerous burial mounds known as tumuli. These are in the region of 4000 to 4500 years old. Some are overgrown or are not particularly distinct but many are surprisingly well preserved. A glance at an Ordnance Survey map of the area will indicate exactly where they are. Next time you stop for lunch on that nice grassy hump just remember you may be sitting on the grave of someone who has been dead for 4500 years.

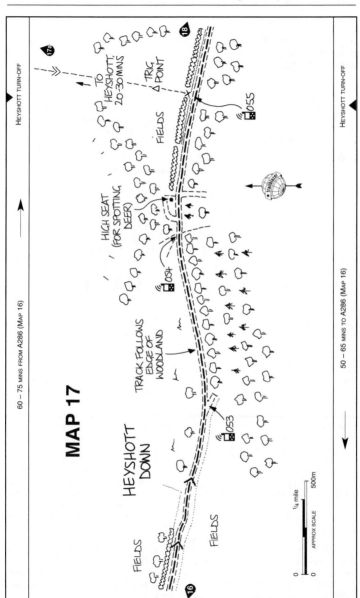

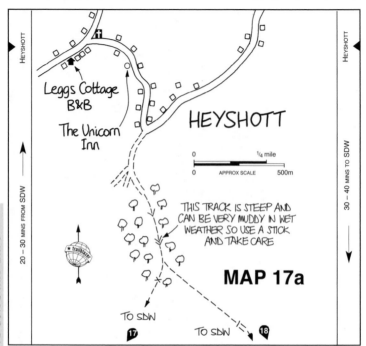

Leggs Cottage B&B

The Unicorn Inn

HEYSHOTT

0   ¼ mile
0   APPROX SCALE   500m

THIS TRACK IS STEEP AND CAN BE VERY MUDDY IN WET WEATHER SO USE A STICK AND TAKE CARE

★ trailblazer

MAP 17a

TO SDW

TO SDW

17

18

HEYSHOTT

HEYSHOTT

20 – 30 MINS FROM SDW

30 – 40 MINS TO SDW

ROUTE GUIDE AND MAPS

7am-7pm, Sun 7am-5pm) is more like a mini supermarket than a village store. It also sells hot drinks and baked goods and even has a small **café** area with a few seats and free wi-fi. There's a pop-up **post office** (Tue 9am-noon, Thur 12.30-4pm) in the village hall next door.

Compass Travel's No 99 **bus service** calls here if booked in advance (see pp46-7).

Campers can head up the road for about a mile to the well-run and welcoming *Graffham Camping & Caravanning Club Site* (☎ 01798-867476, 🖥 campingandcaravanningclub.co.uk; limited WI-FI; 🐾 on leads; end Mar to early Nov), set in a peaceful, forested location. The showers are decent and there are laundry facilities. Backpackers are charged £6-10pp depending on the season.

Brook Barn (☎ 01798-867356, 🖥 brookbarn-graffham.co.uk; 1D/1T shared bathroom but private if only one room booked; ➥; WI-FI; Ⓛ; 🐴), on Selham Rd, offers B&B for £35-45/45-55pp shared/private bathroom (sgl occ from £65). The rate includes a continental breakfast, a cooked one costs an extra £10pp (minimum two people). Z-beds can be put in the double for up to four additional people (£32pp). Dogs (and horses!) are welcome, too.

There's also B&B behind The White Horse pub, at *Willow Barns* (☎ 01798-867493, 🖥 willowbarns.co.uk; 3D/3D or T, all en suite; ➥; WI-FI; Ⓛ), where light, stylish rooms are set around a small courtyard. They generally charge from £75pp (sgl occ full room rate) but rates vary depending on the day of the week and if there are special events in the area. There is a minimum 2-night booking policy at weekends in summer. They don't accept children aged under 12.

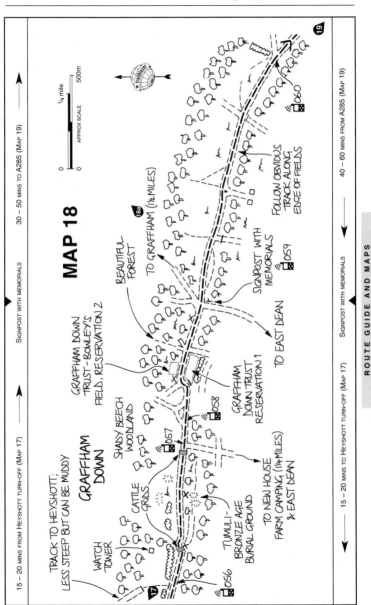

The White Horse (☎ 01798-867331, 🖳 whitehorsegraffham.com; **food** Tue-Fri noon-2pm, Sat & Sun to 2.30pm, Tue-Sat 6.30-9pm; WI-FI; 🐾 bar area only and on lead) itself is a friendly place with some interesting real ales (it's a free house), a quiet garden and spectacular views onto the hills. Note, the pub is closed on Mondays from January to March and also that the food hours may change so check before you go.

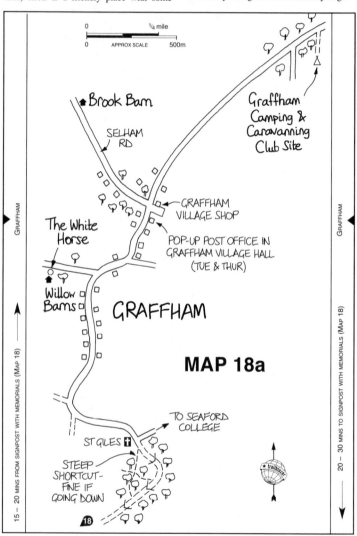

After the Graffham turn off the Way eventually drops down across pasture to the A285 main road (Map 19). Compass's No 99 **bus** service calls here if booked in advance; see pp44-7.

Climbing back up towards Bignor Hill the views open out spectacularly to the south. The rather outlandish-looking tent structure visible by the coast is the

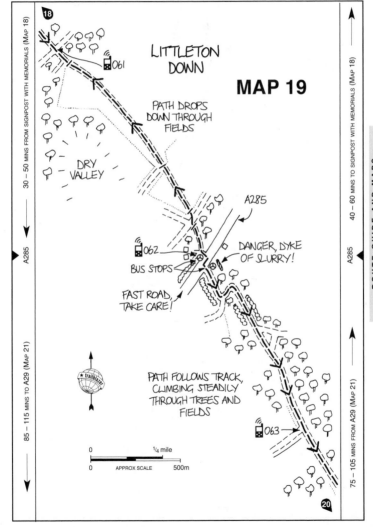

LITTLETON DOWN

MAP 19

PATH DROPS DOWN THROUGH FIELDS

DRY VALLEY

A285

DANGER, DYKE OF SLURRY!

062

BUS STOPS

FAST ROAD, TAKE CARE!

PATH FOLLOWS TRACK, CLIMBING STEADILY THROUGH TREES AND FIELDS

063

061

0   ¼ mile
0   APPROX SCALE   500m

30 – 50 MINS FROM SIGNPOST WITH MEMORIALS (MAP 18)

A285

85 – 115 MINS TO A29 (MAP 21)

40 – 60 MINS TO SIGNPOST WITH MEMORIALS (MAP 18)

A285

75 – 105 MINS FROM A29 (MAP 21)

ROUTE GUIDE AND MAPS

★ trailblazer

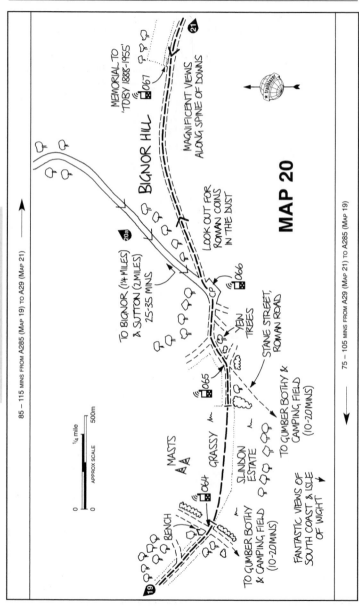

85 – 115 MINS FROM A285 (MAP 19) TO A29 (MAP 21) →

75 – 105 MINS FROM A29 (MAP 21) TO A285 (MAP 19) →

MEMORIAL TO "TOBY 1888-1955"

067

BIGNOR HILL

MAGNIFICENT VIEWS ALONG SPINE OF DOWNS

MAP 20

LOOK OUT FOR ROMAN COINS IN THE DUST

066

TO BIGNOR (1¼ MILES) & SUTTON (2 MILES) 25-35 MINS

20a

YEW TREES

STANE STREET, ROMAN ROAD

065

TO CUMBER BOTHY & CAMPING FIELD (10-20MINS)

¼ mile

500m

APPROX SCALE

MASTS

064

GRASSY

SLINDON ESTATE

BENCH

19

TO CUMBER BOTHY & CAMPING FIELD (10-20MINS)

FANTASTIC VIEWS OF SOUTH COAST & ISLE OF WIGHT

21

Butlins holiday complex at Bognor Regis. Of far greater interest is **Stane St** (Map 20), the Roman road built around AD50 to connect Noviomagus (Chichester) with Londinium (London).

Close to Bignor Hill, a mile south of the Way, is the excellent National Trust camping barn *Gumber Bothy* (see Map 20; ☎ 01243-814484, 🖳 gumberbothy @nationaltrust.org.uk; mid Mar to end Oct), a converted Sussex flint barn, which has simple accommodation (padded sleeping platforms without bedding) for £12pp. They also allow **camping** here for the same price. Facilities include showers, toilets, a basic kitchen with a gas cooker (but no fridge), a barbecue and a pay phone. Booking in advance is recommended. Note that there is no vehicle access here (although there are bike racks). Nor are there any power outlets or plug points.

The Way follows part of the old Roman road over **Bignor Hill**. Look out for the signpost in Latin in the car park (not actually of Roman origin!) and look out, too, for any Roman coins that may be buried among the flint and chalk. It's well worth going down to **Bignor** (see below) from here to see the mosaics at **Bignor Roman Villa**.

SUTTON & BIGNOR   MAP 20a, p114

The main reason for dropping off the hills to these twin villages to see the fabulous mosaics at **Bignor Roman Villa** (see below) but you can also stay comfortably here and eat well. There's a *teashop* at the villa. The **church** at Sutton dates from the 11th century; publisher John Murray (1909-95) is buried in the churchyard.

Very close to the Roman Villa is an excellent B&B, *Stane House* (☎ 01798-869454, 🖳 stanehouse.co.uk; 1D/1T en suite, 1D private facilities; 🍽; WI-FI; (L),

---

❑ **Bignor Roman Villa**   **Map 20a, p114**

Just off the old Roman road of Stane Street are the remains of Bignor Roman Villa (☎ 01798-869259, 🖳 bignorromanvilla.co .uk; daily Mar-Oct 10am-5pm, last entry 4pm; £6). It was discovered by a farmer, George Tupper, who was ploughing his field in 1811.

Believed to date from the 3rd century AD, Bignor Villa was one of the biggest in England and probably home to a wealthy farmer considering its enviable

© BRYN THOMAS

position on fertile land close to the main road between Chichester and London. Bignor is most famous for the superb floor mosaics, said to be some of the world's best-preserved examples. Many are in near perfect condition, including a 24-metre length of the 70-metre corridor. It is the longest mosaic on display in Britain.

There's a picnic area, and a *teashop* (10.30am-4pm) but it serves only tea, coffee and cakes; no sandwiches or hot meals.

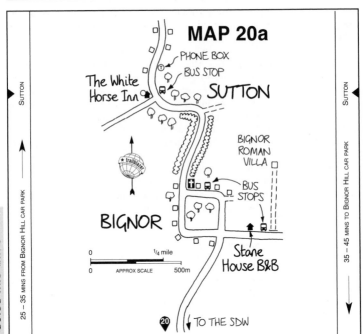

with rooms from £42.50pp (£65 sgl occ). A mile further on is *The White Horse Inn* (☎ 01798-869221, 🖳 whitehorse-sutton.co.uk; 5D, all en suite; 🍷; WI-FI; 🐕 in bar only), a magnificent isolated country pub with **B&B** from £42.50pp (sgl occ £75), though they sometimes have special offers on their website. They also have a large **restaurant** (food Tue-Sun noon-2.15pm & 6-9pm) and

the food is exquisite: all home-cooked and sourced locally, with the bread, sausages and ice-cream made on the premises. Note, the pub is closed between 3pm and 6pm and on Sunday and Monday evenings.

Compass's No 99 **bus service** calls at both Sutton and Bignor if pre-booked (see pp44-7).

Continuing along the Way, there are sensational views to the east along the length of the Downs, as well as two possible routes north to the village of Bury (see p116). Both follow pavement-less roads, although the country lane further west is more pleasant to walk along than the busier A29.

❑ **Important note – walking times**
All times in this book refer only to the time spent walking. You will need to add 20-30% to allow for rests, photography, checking the map, drinking water etc.

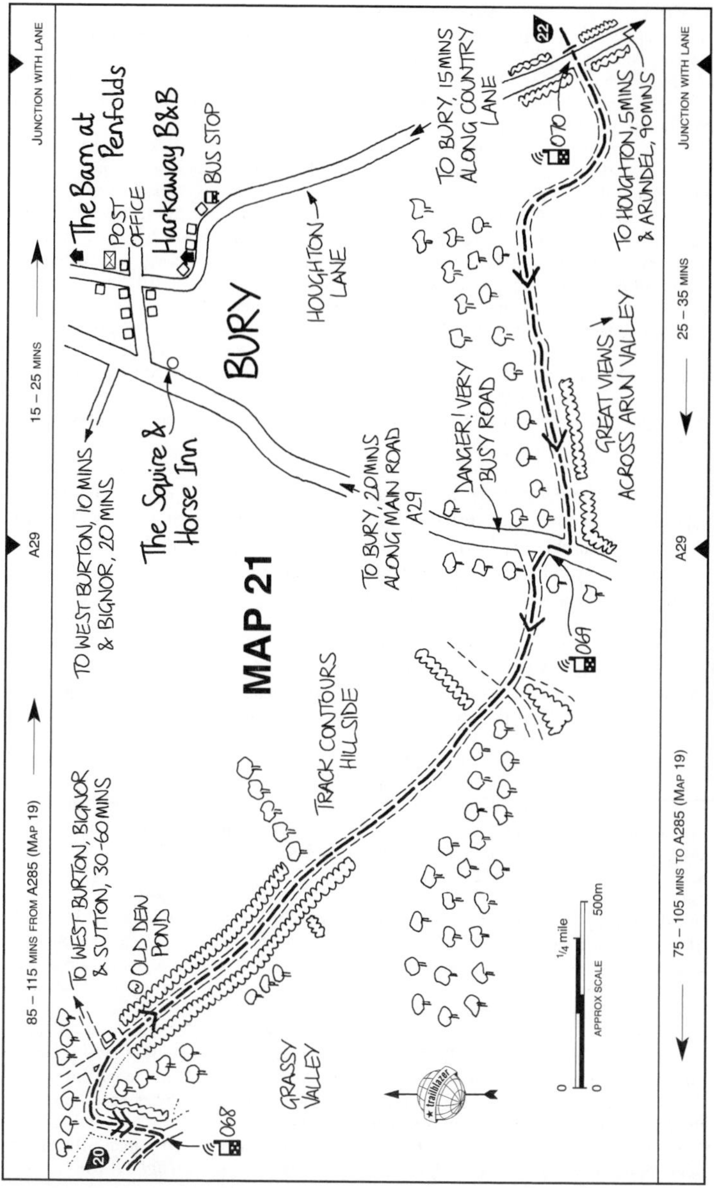

MAP 21

BURY

JUNCTION WITH LANE

A29

15 – 25 MINS

The Barn at Penfolds

POST OFFICE

Harkaway B&B

BUS STOP

HOUGHTON LANE

The Squire & Horse Inn

TO WEST BURTON, 10 MINS & BIGNOR, 20 MINS

TO BURY, 20 MINS ALONG MAIN ROAD A29

TO BURY, 15 MINS ALONG COUNTRY LANE

010

TO HOUGHTON, 5 MINS & ARUNDEL, 90 MINS

JUNCTION WITH LANE

A29

25 – 35 MINS

DANGER! VERY BUSY ROAD

GREAT VIEWS ACROSS ARUN VALLEY

06A

85 – 115 MINS FROM A285 (Map 19)

TO WEST BURTON, BIGNOR & SUTTON, 30 – 60 MINS

OLD DEW POND

TRACK CONTOURS HILLSIDE

GRASSY VALLEY

068

20

¼ mile

APPROX SCALE

500m

trailblazer

75 – 105 MINS TO A285 (Map 19)

22

ROUTE GUIDE AND MAPS

BURY MAP 21, p115

This unassuming village offers accommodation, food and a mobile **post office** (Mon & Thur 11.15am-12.15pm).

Compass's 69 **bus service** (Alfold to Worthing) calls here on Tuesdays and Thursdays (1/day) and their 71 service (Storrington to Chichester) on Wednesdays (1/day). For details see pp44-7

The Barn at Penfolds (☎ 01798-831496, 💻 thebarnatpenfolds.co.uk; 2D en suite; ♥; WI-FI; Ⓛ), on Houghton Lane, offers **B&B** for £35-42.50pp (sgl occ from £55); they require a minimum stay of two nights at some times of the year. They also have a cosy **shepherd's hut** (heated and insulated; 🐕) with its own shower and toilet and a deck area outside; it's £42.50pp per night (sgl occ from £55) including breakfast.

Harkaway (☎ 01798-831843, 💻 harkaway.freeuk.com; 1D en suite, 1S/1T share bathroom; WI-FI; Ⓛ), also on Houghton Lane, offers B&B for £32.50-35pp (sgl/sgl occ £35-50). Since there is no village shop here requests for a packed lunch must be made at least 24 hours in advance.

The Squire & Horse Inn (☎ 01798-831343, 💻 squireandhorsebury.co.uk; **food** Mon-Sat noon-3pm & 6-9pm, Sun noon-8.30pm; WI-FI; 🐕 bar area and garden), by the main road, is a freehouse with an award-winning chef and a busy restaurant. Main dishes include steak, Sussex ale and mushroom steamed pudding (£12.95), and chicken breast stuffed with goat's cheese & basil (£15.50). Note, the pub is closed from 3pm to 5.30pm every day except Sunday.

Follow the route down into the Arun valley for the villages of **Houghton Bridge** (see below) and **Amberley** (see p118). If you have time it is well worth visiting **Arundel** (see p118), five miles further south along the River Arun. You can reach it by following the riverside footpath but it's quicker to jump on the train. Trains run hourly throughout the day.

HOUGHTON BRIDGE MAP 22

The village of Houghton Bridge, itself just a short walk from the village of Amberley, can easily be reached from the SDW as the trail almost passes through it. The **railway station** (called Amberley Station) has trains to London Victoria and south to Arundel and beyond; see box p43. There are, however, no useful **bus** services other than school day services operated by Sussex Bus (💻 thesussexbus.com): their No 619 goes in the early morning to Amberley, Storrington, and Steyning and their No 719 does the return route in the mid afternoon. One of Compass's No 74 services continues to Houghton mid afternoon on school days; see pp44-7).

Right by the station you'll find the entrance to **Amberley Working Museum** (☎ 01798-831370, 💻 www.amberleymuseum.co.uk; mid Feb to end Oct Wed-Sun & Bank hols, daily during school holidays 10am-5pm, last entry 4pm; £11.50; call for details), situated in an old chalk pit. This extensive museum features a blacksmith's and foundry, as well as workshops producing traditional items such as brooms and walking sticks. There's a ***café*** here too. The quarry tunnel at Amberley was used as a film location in the James Bond film *A View To A Kill* in 1984.

Where to stay and eat

Foxleigh Barn (☎ 01798-839113, 💻 pete@foxleighbarn.co.uk; 🐕 on leads only and all mess must be cleared up; Easter to Oct), is conveniently located right on the SDW by the B2139. Their B&B is generally fully booked and they don't take walk-in guests but they do offer **camping** (£20 per night for a pitch for up to two people) in a camp field with use of a toilet and shower for campers only.

Alternatively you could **wild camp**, free of charge, at ***High Titten***, a local

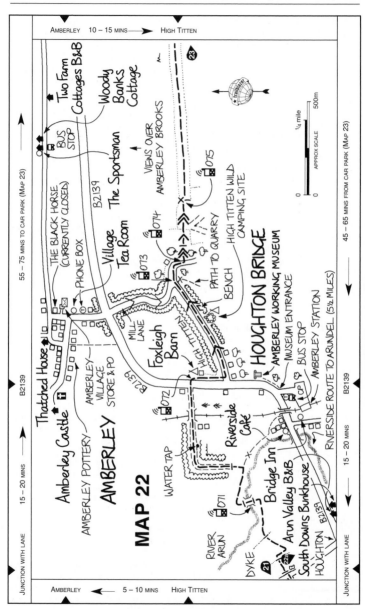

authority-owned walled garden with one open-sided **camping barn** with a raised sleeping platform, and another smaller barn, as well as room for around five tent pitches. There's a camp-fire area, but no water or toilets.

Just west of the river, the excellent *South Downs Bunkhouse* (☎ 01798-831100, ▣ southdownsbunkhouse.co.uk; 3 x 4-, 1 x 8-bed dorms, shared facilities; WI-FI; Ⓛ; ▶ in utility room) has bunk-bed dormitories and charges from £22pp if you bring your own sleeping bag, or you can rent a duvet, sheet and towel for an extra £4-5pp. Each bunk has its own power socket and USB charging port, and there's also a communal living room, self-catering and laundry facilities, and even a barbecue you can use in the courtyard outside. Continental breakfast (£5pp) is also available if requested in advance.

Next door, and run by the same people, *Arun Valley B&B* (☎ 01798-831100, ▣ arunvalleybandb.co.uk; 1D or T private bathroom, 1D or T/1Tr en suite; ●; WI-FI;

Ⓛ; ▶ but can't sleep in the bedrooms) has very comfortable rooms from £55pp (sgl occ from £70), including a full breakfast. One room is in the garden cottage.

You can get breakfasts and light lunches at *Riverside* (☎ 01798-831066, ▣ dine bytheriver.co.uk; summer daily 9am-5pm, hot food served till 3pm, in winter Tue-Fri10am-4pm, Sat & Sun 9am-4.30pm; WI-FI; ▶), a café, bar and restaurant that's especially popular when the weather is good as they have a riverside garden where they serve all-day breakfasts, pizzas, and cakes amongst other items.

Just across the road is the *Bridge Inn* (☎ 01798-831619, ▣ bridgeinnamberley .com; food Mon-Fri noon-2.30pm & 6-9pm, Sat noon-4pm & 6-9pm, Sun noon-4pm & 5.30-8pm; WI-FI; ▶ bar and garden only), a friendly, award-winning pub with real ales and very good food. The pub closes at 9pm on Sundays.

AMBERLEY   MAP 22, p117

Perched on a sandstone ridge below the chalk Downs with the wild marshland of **Amberley Brooks** stretching to the north, Amberley claims to be the prettiest village on the Downs and it would be hard to argue otherwise. The quiet lane leading to the church and castle is lined with thatched cottages; hollyhocks and foxgloves bloom in the small front gardens in the summer months. Unlike other downland villages where local flint is prominent in the architecture, many of Amberley's cottages were built using local sandstone, making the village distinctive. There are records referring to Amberley dating back to AD680.

The pretty **church** was built by Bishop Luffa between 1091 and 1125. Next to the church is the **castle** (now a hotel, see Where to stay) which used to be the bishop's residence until it was recognised as a castle upon completion of the walls in 1377. More information on the history of the village and the local area can be found at Amberley Working Museum (see p116). **Amberley**

Village Pottery (☎ 01798-831876, ▣ am berleypottery.co.uk; Thur-Tue 11am-3pm), housed in an 1867 former chapel on Church St, is open to visitors

The community-run **Amberley Village Store** (▣ amberleystores.co.uk; Mon-Sat 7am-5pm, Sun & bank hols 8am-5pm or 4pm in winter) stocks a good range of groceries and also houses the **post office** (Mon, Thur & Fri 9am-1pm, Tue 9am-noon).

Amberley **railway station** is about a mile away in Houghton Bridge; see p116 for details of Compass Travel's 74/74A bus services that call in Amberley and continue to the railway station on school days.

Where to stay and eat

Thatched House (☎ 01798-831329, ▣ www.thatchedhouseamberley.co.uk; 1D/1T with private bathroom; ●; WI-FI; Ⓛ) isn't actually thatched but is nonetheless an excellent place to stay. Even though they have two rooms they only let one at a time unless people know each other. B&B costs from £45pp (£60-65 sgl occ), though rates are higher during Goodwood events.

Away from the village, about a mile down the lane at **Crossgates** is *The Sportsman* (☎ 01798-831787, 🖥 www .greyhoundbrewery.co.uk/sportsman; 3D/ 2D or T, all en suite; ☛; WI-FI; 🐾), a very pleasant pub with sweeping sunset views across Amberley Brooks from both its beer garden and conservatory. As well as good **food** (Tue-Sat noon-2.30pm & 6.30-9pm, Sun noon-5pm) and some fine real ales, they also offer **B&B** from £42.50pp (sgl occ from £65). Next door to the pub is *Woody Banks Cottage* (☎ 01798-831295, 🖥 woodybanks.co.uk; 1T private shower room; WI-FI; Ⓛ) with B&B from £39.50pp (sgl occ rates on request); the room also has its own sitting room and another bedroom is available for family and friends.

About 90 metres further along is *Two Farm Cottages B&B* (☎ 01798-831266, 🖥 twofarmcottages.co.uk; 1D/1T private bathroom; ☛; WI-FI). Rooms go for £45pp (sgl occ £75). Although they have two

rooms, they only rent both out at the same time to groups or families, so you'll never be sharing facilities with guests you don't know.

If you fancy a splurge, there's every luxury at *Amberley Castle* (☎ 01798-831992, 🖥 amberleycastle.co.uk; 19D, all en suite; ☛; WI-FI). A room with a whirlpool bathroom costs around £137.50pp (sgl occ full room rate), though it is always worth enquiring about special offers. There's a grand **restaurant** (daily noon-2pm & 7-9pm; with a dress code) serving a 7-course tasting menu for £85pp or a three-course meal for £67.50pp in the evening. Afternoon tea (3-4pm) costs £30pp. Booking is recommended.

Amberley Village Tea Room (☎ 01798-839196; 🐾; Apr-Sep Thur-Tue 10am-5.30pm, Sat & Sun only in Feb-Mar & Oct-Nov) prides itself on sourcing locally produced food and their clotted cream teas are very popular. They also serve toasted teacakes, crumpets, tea breads and mouthwatering slices of homemade chocolate cake.

ARUNDEL MAP 22a, p121

The town of Arundel is about 1½ hours from the South Downs Way via the riverside path from Houghton Bridge or a 5-minute train ride from Amberley station (see box p43). Those who are walking the entire South Downs Way in one trip will find that a visit to this historic town makes an ideal rest day.

Arundel boasts a fine cathedral but it is the perfectly preserved castle with its grand turreted walls that really catches the eye. **Arundel Festival** (🖥 arundelfestival.co .uk) is held in the castle in August.

What to see and do

The **castle** (☎ 01903-882173, 🖥 arundel castle.org; Easter to early Nov Tue-Sun 10am-5pm, plus Mon during Aug and bank holidays) is the centrepiece of this historical town. Rising grandly from the trees it looms over the Arun Valley and is everything you imagine an English castle to be, complete with imposing walls, turrets and

winding stone staircases. Of Norman origin it is now home to the dukes of Norfolk but is open to the public most of the year. There are four levels of ticket ranging from Bronze (grounds and chapel only £11) to Gold Plus (castle rooms and bedrooms, castle keep, chapel and grounds £20).

Arundel's gothic-style **cathedral** (🖥 arundelcathedral.org) is somewhat upstaged by the immense castle down the road but is still a fine building in its own right. Founded by Henry, the 15th Duke of Norfolk, the cathedral is relatively new, dating back to 1873. A good time to visit is during the Corpus Christi festivities in early June when the main aisle of the cathedral is covered in a spectacular carpet of flowers.

Arundel Museum (☎ 01903-885866, 🖥 arundelmuseum.org; daily 10am-4pm; £3.50) is down by the river, opposite the entrance to the castle. The museum's exhibits focus on local history with an interesting display on the castle, the Catholic dukes of Norfolk and their association with the town. Also of particular interest is the 12th-century coffin with the finely decorated lid, the Roman sword dating from the 4th century and the old photographs portraying local life through the years.

Arundel Wetland Centre (☎ 01903-883355, 🖥 www.wwt.org.uk; daily late Mar-late Oct 9.30am-5.30pm, rest of year 9.30am-4.30pm; £11.18, save 10% if you book online, free for WWT members, see p59) is a natural wetland site bordered by ancient woodland and is a perfect diversion for anyone interested in birds. The hides provide opportunities for viewing a variety of warblers and waders as well as the odd buzzard circling above the oak trees.

Swimmers might fancy a dip in **Arundel Lido** (☎ 01903-884772, 🖥 arundel-lido.com; late Apr to mid Sep, term-time weekdays noon-7pm, weekends and school hols 10am-7pm; adult £7), a heated open-air pool with views of the castle.

Services
Although of limited use, there's a **tourist information point** (daily 10am-4pm), with leaflets and such, at the entrance to the museum; for online information visit 🖥 www.arundel.org.uk or 🖥 sussexbythesea.com. For public **internet** access, the **library** (Mon-Wed 1-5pm, Thur-Sat 9am-1pm) is at the western end of Tarrant St.

If you're looking for the ingredients of a good picnic, **Pallant of Arundel** (☎ 01903-882288; Mon-Sat 9am-6pm, to 5pm in Jan, Sun & Bank Hol Mons 10am-5pm) is the town's excellent **deli** and specialist grocery store. Food supplies can also be found at the small **shop**, McColl's, near the bridge at the bottom of the High St, while across the bridge is a Co-op **supermarket** (daily 7am-10pm).

The **post office** (Mon-Fri 9am-5.30pm, Sat to 12.30pm) lies just across the road from McColl's.

Some pharmaceutical items are available in the Co-op but the nearest **pharmacy** is now inconveniently located in the local NHS health surgery on Canada Rd (beyond the roundabout at the western end of Maltravers St). There's an **ATM** outside the museum.

Chocoholics will be pleased to know that Arundel is home to **Castle Chocolates** (☎ 01903-884419, 🖥 castlechocolates.com; daily 10am-6pm), 11 Tarrant St, who claim to produce what is 'probably the finest confectionery, chocolate and fudge in the South of England'. For fudge they have competition with **Roly's Fudge Pantry**, doing brisk trade at the bottom of the High St (No 25).

Public transport
Those coming to Arundel by **train** will find that the **railway station** is a 10-minute walk from the town centre; services (see box p43) are operated by Southern.

National Express's 315 **coach** service (see box p44) calls in Arundel. Compass Travel's No 85/85A (see pp46-7) is the only choice for travel by **bus** to Chichester; the bus stop is near the bridge.

For a **taxi** call Castle Cars (☎ 01903-884444, 🖥 castlecarsltd.co.uk).

Where to stay
Arundel is a popular tourist centre so you must book well in advance, unless you're camping, in which case just turning up will normally suffice. Over some weekends (eg during local events, see p14) there may be a two-night minimum stay for some places.

There's **camping** at *Maynards Caravan Park* (☎ 01903-882075; 🐾 on leads; Feb-Dec), 500m walk up the hill beyond the railway station. They have a shower and toilet block, nice flat grassy pitches, and charge £10 for a tent and up to two people.

On the road leading from the town centre to the railway station is *Arundel Park Hotel* (☎ 01903-882588, 🖥 arundelparkhotel.co.uk; 1S/10D/3T/1Tr, all en suite; 🛁; WI-FI; mid Jan to mid Dec); it has

---

Symbols used in text (see also p70)   🐾 Dogs allowed subject to prior arrangement
🛁 Bathtub in at least one room   Ⓛ packed lunch available if requested in advance

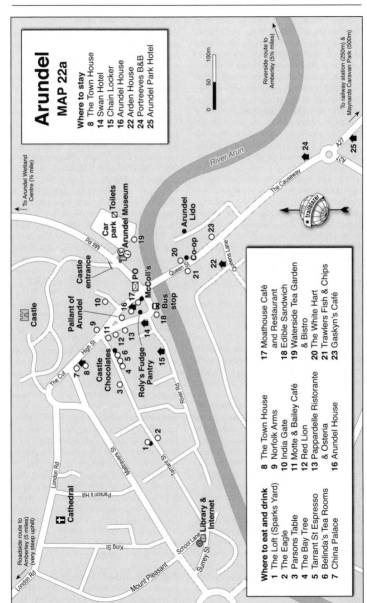

Arundel
MAP 22a

Where to stay
8 The Town House
14 Swan Hotel
15 Chain Locker
16 Arundel House
22 Portreeves B&B
24 Arden House
25 Arundel Park Hotel

To Arundel Wetland Centre (½ mile)

River Arun

Riverside route to Amberley (5¼ miles)

To railway station (250m) & Maynards Caravan Park (500m)

Car park ☑ Toilets
Arundel Museum

Mill Rd

Castle entrance

Castle

Pallant of Arundel

Castle Chocolates

Roly's Fudge Pantry

High St.

The Cut

PO
McColl's
Bus stop

Queen St.
Arundel Lido
Co-op
Queens Lane

The Causeway

A27

River Rd

London Rd
Parson's Hill
Cathedral
Maltravers St
Tarrant St
School Lane
Surrey St.
Library & Internet
King St
Mount Pleasant

Roadside route to Amberley (5 miles) (very steep uphill)

London Rd

0   50   100m

Where to eat and drink
1 The Loft (Sparks Yard)
2 The Eagle
3 Parsons Table
4 The Bay Tree
5 Tarrant St Espresso
6 Belinda's Tea Rooms
7 China Palace
8 The Town House
9 Norfolk Arms
10 India Gate
11 Motte & Bailey Café
12 Red Lion
13 Pappardelle Ristorante & Osteria
16 Arundel House
17 Moathouse Café and Restaurant
18 Edible Sandwich
19 Waterside Tea Garden & Bistro
20 The White Hart
21 Trawlers Fish & Chips
23 Gaskyn's Café

★ trailblazer

plenty of rooms and an unpretentious style. B&B costs £32.50-47.50pp (sgl/sgl occ from £55/65-95). Nearby is *Portreeves B&B* (☎ 01903-885392, 🖳 portreeves.co .uk; 2D or T, both en suite; ➡; WI-FI; 🐾). It's a well-run, friendly place offering B&B from £42.50pp (sgl occ from £65) in their apartments. However, the apartments are often let on a self-catering basis for a week or more, particularly in the summer months, so it is essential to book in advance. A sofa bed can be put in the apartments for additional people; contact them for details.

In the centre of Arundel in a former fisherman's cottage at 14 River Rd is *Chain Locker* (☎ 01903-882661, 🖳 chainlocker .org.uk; 1D private bathroom; ➡; WI-FI). Being a cottage it is a small place and the room and bathroom are on the ground floor. They don't do breakfast but it's wonderful value; from £45 (sgl occ £40).

Arundel House (☎ 01903-882136, 🖳 arundelhousewestsussex.com; 5D, all en suite; WI-FI), near the post office at 11 High St, is an intimate little boutique restaurant with rooms. It's in a good location and a gorgeous place to stay. B&B costs £35-75pp (sgl occ rates on request).

Nearby is the elegant *Swan Hotel* (☎ 01903-882314, 🖳 swanarundel.co.uk; 4T/ 7D/3Tr, all en suite; ➡; WI-FI; ⓛ; 🐾) with B&B from £45pp but it can cost around £75pp (sgl occ from £65).

The Town House (☎ 01903-883847, 🖳 thetownhouse.co.uk; 4D/2D or T, all en suite; ➡; WI-FI), opposite the castle at the top of the High St (No 65), is a very attractive place with immaculate and stylish rooms. Expect to pay £55-70pp (sgl occ from £75). It also has an excellent restaurant (see Where to eat and drink).

On Queen's Lane, a few minutes from the centre, is *Arden House* (☎ 01903-884184, 🖳 www.ardenhousearundel.com; 4D or T, all en suite/3D or T shared facilities; WI-FI; ⓛ). B&B costs £39.50-49.50pp (sgl occ £69-89) but during Goodwood and other major events the rate is £62.50-75pp (sgl occ £115-140); phone bookings are preferred. They also have a lockable garage for up to four bicycles.

Where to eat and drink
Arundel is bursting with excellent pubs, cafés and restaurants, most of which are centred on or around the High St.

Cafés Starting down by the river, *Waterside Tea Garden & Bistro* (daily 9.30am-6pm) is a no-frills café with good-value food (cream teas £4.50, chip butties £3.10) and simple terrace seating, over-looking the river; a wonderful spot on a sunny day. Also beside the river, on the other side of the bridge, *Edible Sandwich* (☎ 01903-885969; Mon-Fri 6.30am-4.30pm, Sat-Sun 8am-4.30pm; 🐾) doesn't have such good riverside seating, but it's friendly, opens early, and does good pas-tries, cakes and coffee. Nearby, at 9 High St, is the hugely popular *Moathouse Café and Restaurant* (☎ 01903-883297; Mon-Sat 8am-5.30pm, Sun 8.30am-5.30pm, closes earlier in winter; WI-FI; small 🐾), with an excellent range of breakfasts, toasties, filled baguettes and hot drinks.

Up towards the top of the High St, and also very popular, is the bright and modern *Motte & Bailey Café* (🖳 mnbcafe.co.uk; Mon-Sat 8.30am-5pm, Sun 9.30am-5pm, Thur-Sat also open 6.30-10.30pm), which as well as being arguably the best café in town also opens some evenings for tapas.

Sidling off down Tarrant St will bring you to two more fine cafés: *Belinda's Tea Rooms* (☎ 01903-882977; daily 9am-5pm; well-behaved 🐾), housed in a charming 16th-century building, has been serving teas and light lunches amongst the wooden beams for several decades now. But for the best coffee beans in town, head next door to the pocket-sized *Tarrant St Espresso* (☎ 01903-885350; Tue-Sat 8.30am-4pm, Sun 10am-2pm; WI-FI; 🐾); they also do filled rolls and salads. South of the river, mean-while, is the award-winning *Gaskyns Café* (🖳 gaskyns.co.uk; Wed-Sat 9am-4pm, Sun 10am-4pm), a licensed café which prides itself on being family friendly and serving locally sourced produce.

Pubs One of the best pubs in town is *The Eagle* (☎ 01903-882304; bar Mon-Fri 5-11pm, Sat & Sun 11am-11pm; WI-FI; 🐾), on Tarrant St. They serve an impressive array of beers (including Harvey's) and sometimes have live music at weekends. It's a popular place; locals spill out onto the pavement on warm summer evenings. They do bar snacks but no food.

On the High St, ***The Red Lion*** (☎ 01903-882214, 🖳 redlionarundel.com; food Sun-Fri noon-9pm, Sat 10am-9pm; WI-FI; 🐕 on a lead) is a large no-nonsense pub with a rear garden and serving cheap and filling dishes. There's a choice of real ales, and it opens for breakfast on Saturdays. Opposite, ***Norfolk Arms*** (☎ 01903-882101, 🖳 norfolkarmsarundel.com; WI-FI; 🐕 bar only), has a traditional restaurant (daily 6-9pm) serving English dishes as well as a pub-grub menu in its rather quiet bar (daily noon-6pm).

Restaurants & takeaways The very highly regarded ***Parsons Table*** (☎ 01903-883477, 🖳 theparsonstable.co.uk; Tue-Sat noon-2.30pm & 6-9.30pm) is a relative newcomer to the Arundel dining scene, but has taken it by storm. Run by husband-and-wife team Lee and Liz Parsons, it prides itself on dishes made from locally sourced seasonal ingredients, and the results are excellent. A set two-course lunch will set you back £18; evening mains start at around £17. Also of the highest quality, ***The Town House*** (see Where to stay; food Tue-Sat noon-2pm & 7-9.30pm) allows you to dine beneath a fabulous 16th-century Florentine carved ceiling. The food gets rave reviews; two courses at lunchtime/in the evening cost £17.50/25.50. Another smart place, albeit less showy, ***The Bay Tree*** (☎ 01903-883679, 🖳 thebaytreearundel.co.uk; Mon 9am-3pm, Tue-Fri 11.30am-3pm, Sat & Sun 9am-4.30pm, daily 6.30-9.30pm), at 21 Tarrant St, serves contemporary British food and is consistently recommended. You may need to book for dinner. Further along Tarrant St, in Sparks Yard, ***The Loft*** (☎ 01903-885588, 🖳 the loftarundel.com; Mon-Sat 9.30am-5.30pm, Sun 11am-5pm; WI-FI) is a quality, family-friendly, café-cum-restaurant offering beer, wine and healthy meals. Back on the High St, ***Arundel House*** (see Where to stay; Wed-Thur & Sun 11am-4pm, Fri & Sat 11am-8pm) is another excellent place to eat, where two- and three-course set meals cost £16.95 and £21.95 respectively.

Although there are better-known Italian-food chain restaurants in town, it's worth seeking out the Italian-run ***Pappardelle Ristorante & Osteria*** (🖳 pappardelle.co.uk). The informal **Osteria** (☎ 01903-882025; Mon-Sat 9am-11.30pm, Sun 10am-10.30pm) downstairs serves drinks and light meals with antipasto from £4.95 and open sandwiches (£7.95). The traditional **Ristorante** (bookings ☎ 01903-882025) is open Tuesday to Saturday (noon-2pm & 6-9.30pm). The pizzas are excellent.

For decent Indian food, head to ***India Gate*** (☎ 01903-884224; daily noon-2.30pm & 5.30-11.30pm), just off the High St at 3 Mill Lane. At 67 High St, ***China Palace*** (☎ 01903-883702; daily noon-2.15pm & 6pm-midnight) is a smarter than average Chinese restaurant. The best chippy in town is ***Trawlers Fish & Chips*** (Mon-Sat 11.45am-2pm & 5-9pm, Sun 4-8pm) on Queen St.

AMBERLEY TO STEYNING — MAPS 22-27a

The first half of this **10-mile (16km, 3½-5hrs)** stretch is an easy stroll along the high crest of the Downs with great views over the swamp-like **Amberley Wild Brooks** and the Low Weald. The quickest way to **Storrington** (Map 24) is along the path leading off the Way at GPS Waypoint 079. Alternatively take the road leading off from the Rackham Hill car park.

> **❑ Important note – walking times**
> All times in this book refer only to the time spent walking. You will need to add 20-30% to allow for rests, photography, checking the map, drinking water etc.

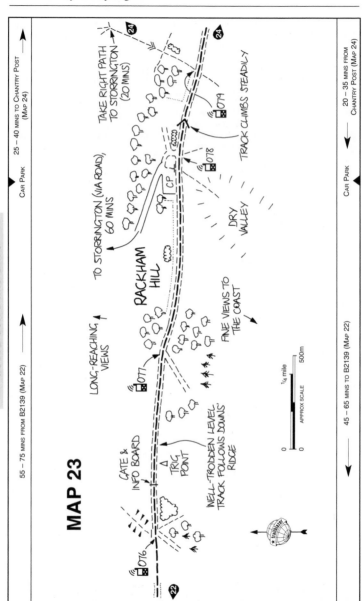

MAP 23

55 – 75 MINS FROM B2139 (MAP 22)

25 – 40 MINS TO CHANTRY POST (MAP 24)

CAR PARK

45 – 65 MINS TO B2139 (MAP 22)

20 – 35 MINS FROM CHANTRY POST (MAP 24)

CAR PARK

TAKE RIGHT PATH TO STORRINGTON (20 MINS)

TRACK CLIMBS STEADILY

019

078

CP

DRY VALLEY

TO STORRINGTON (VIA ROAD), 60 MINS

RACKHAM HILL

FINE VIEWS TO THE COAST

LONG-REACHING VIEWS

017

GATE & INFO BOARD

TRIG POINT

WELL-TRODDEN LEVEL TRACK FOLLOWS DOWNS' RIDGE

016

¼ mile

APPROX SCALE

500m

0

0

STORRINGTON   MAP 24, p126

In comparison to many of the other towns and villages along the Downs the busy little town of Storrington is functional rather than attractive. It is a convenient place for topping up on supplies, getting a bite to eat or for finding a bed for the night but apart from that there is little reason to make the detour.

There's a small **museum** (Wed & Sat 10am-4pm, Sun 10am-1pm; free) covering the local history of the area. Near the museum is a wonderfully ornate **Indian doorway**, set into the wall on Browns Lane.

Services

Storrington has everything you would expect in a small but prosperous town. The reception at the **library** (☎ 01903-839050; Mon-Fri 9.30am-5.30pm, Sat 10am-4pm) doubles up as the **tourist information point** and they also have **internet** access (free for library card holders; everyone else £1.50/hr; WI-FI is free for all).

Waitrose **supermarket** (Mon-Sat 8am-8pm, Sun 10am-4pm) is in a small shopping arcade just off the High St. At the other end of the High St is the **post office** (Mon-Fri 9am-5.30pm, Sat 9am-4pm). Just round the corner at 1 North St is Lloyds **pharmacy** and there's a branch of Boots (Mon-Sat 9am-5.30pm) on the High St. There are also three banks with **ATMs** on the High St.

If you need bike parts or repairs, head to **South Downs Bikes** (🖳 southdowns bikes.com; Mon-Fri 9am-6pm, Sat 9am-5pm, Sun 10am-4pm). For camping-stove fuel, try **Bunce's Home Hardware** (Mon-Sat 8.30am-5pm).

Stagecoach's No 1 (Midhurst–Worthing) **bus** service calls here as do Compass's bus No 100 (Burgess Hill–Pulborough) and their No 74/74A (to Horsham); see pp46-7.

Where to stay

There is a much wider choice of places to stay in Arundel (see p120) and Steyning (see p131). In fact the only accommodation

here is at the 400-year-old *White Horse* (☎ 01903-745760, 🖳 thewhitehorsestorring ton.com; 10D/3D or T, all en suite; WI-FI) which offers B&B from £42.50pp (sgl occ full room rate).

Where to eat and drink

There are several cafés and tearooms including the bright and cheery *Joanna's Boutique Tearoom* (🖳 joannasboutiquetea room.com; Mon-Sat 9am-5pm, Sun 10am-4pm), with cream teas and cakes, all-white décor, and a friendly welcome.

Also very popular, *Vintage Rose Tearoom* (☎ 01903-744100, 🖳 vintage rosetearoom.co.uk; Mon-Fri 9am-5pm, Sat 9am-4.30pm, Sun 10am-3pm; WI-FI) is housed in a Grade II-listed building, and serves teas and coffees – on interestingly mismatched china – as well as light lunches.

For cheaper fare, including tea, coffee, pastries and all-day breakfasts, there's *Truffles Bakery* (☎ 01903-742459; Mon-Sat 8am-5pm; WI-FI), near Waitrose. The Waitrose, meanwhile, has a branch of *Costa Coffee* (Mon-Sat 7am-6.30pm, Sun 8am-5pm) attached to it.

Pubs include *The Anchor Inn* (☎ 01903-742665, 🖳 anchorinnstorrington.co .uk; food Mon-Sat noon-6pm, Sun noon-4pm; WI-FI; 🐾 on a lead), at the eastern end of town, and the marginally more attractive *The Moon* (☎ 01903-744773, 🖳 themoon pub.co.uk; food Mon-Fri noon-2.30pm & 6-9.30pm, Sat noon-3pm & 6-9.30pm, Sun carvery noon-2.30pm, full menu inc burgers & pizzas 2.30-8.30pm; WI-FI; 🐾); they also have a have a takeaway menu when the kitchen is open.

For something a bit fancier, *13 Church Street* (☎ 01903-746964, 🖳 thirteenchurch street.co.uk; Tue-Sat noon-3pm & 6-10.30pm) serves high-quality, freshly prepared Thai specialities. Mains cost between £17 and £20.

Storrington also has a popular Indian restaurant: *Cottage Tandoori* (☎ 01903-743605; daily noon-2.30pm & 6-11pm).

ROUTE GUIDE AND MAPS

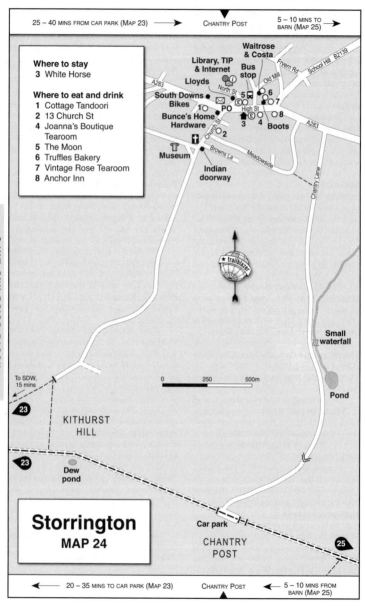

Where to stay
3 White Horse

Where to eat and drink
1 Cottage Tandoori
2 13 Church St
4 Joanna's Boutique Tearoom
5 The Moon
6 Truffles Bakery
7 Vintage Rose Tearoom
8 Anchor Inn

Waitrose & Costa

Library, TIP & Internet

Bus stop

Lloyds

South Downs Bikes

Bunce's Home Hardware

North St

A283

Fryem Rd

School Hill B2139

Old Mill

High St

PO

Boots

A283

Church St

Browns La

Meadowside

Chantry Lane

Museum

Indian doorway

★ trailblazer

Small waterfall

Pond

To SDW, 15 mins

23

23

KITHURST HILL

Dew pond

0   250   500m

Storrington
MAP 24

Car park

CHANTRY POST

25

ROUTE GUIDE AND MAPS

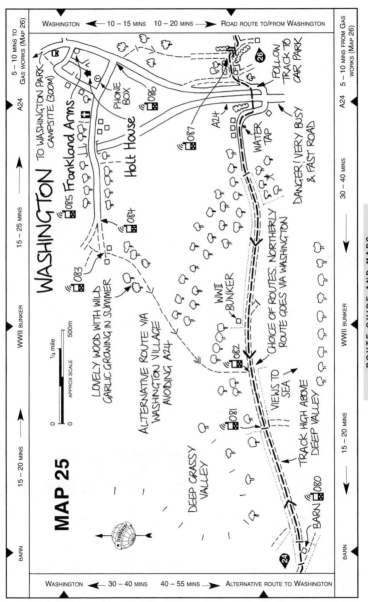

MAP 25

15 – 20 MINS

15 – 25 MINS

5 – 10 MINS TO GAS WORKS (MAP 26)

A24

WASHINGTON ← 10 – 15 MINS   10 – 20 MINS → ROAD ROUTE TO/FROM WASHINGTON

WASHINGTON

TO WASHINGTON PARK CAMPSITE (300M)

⌘085 Frankland Arms

PHONE BOX

⌘086

Holt House

⌘087

A24

WATER TAP

DANGER! VERY BUSY & FAST ROAD

FOLLOW TRACK TO CAR PARK

26

⌘084

⌘083

LOVELY WOOD WITH WILD GARLIC GROWING IN SUMMER

ALTERNATIVE ROUTE VIA WASHINGTON VILLAGE AVOIDING A24

WWII BUNKER

⌘082

CHOICE OF ROUTES. NORTHERLY ROUTE GOES VIA WASHINGTON

VIEWS TO SEA

⌘081

TRACK HIGH ABOVE DEEP VALLEY

DEEP GRASSY VALLEY

BARN ⌘080

24

¼ mile

APPROX SCALE

0   500m

trailblazer

A24 5 – 10 MINS FROM GAS WORKS (MAP 26)

30 – 40 MINS

15 – 20 MINS

ROUTE GUIDE AND MAPS

BARN   WWII BUNKER   WWII BUNKER   BARN

WASHINGTON ← 30 – 40 MINS   40 – 55 MINS → ALTERNATIVE ROUTE TO WASHINGTON

WASHINGTON MAP 25, p127

Despite the proximity of the busy A24 dual carriageway this village is a peaceful place with most of the traffic noise being absorbed by the trees. There is an alternative South Downs Way path which leads the walker directly into the village.

Stagecoach's **bus** No 1 stops here en route between Midhurst and Worthing. Compass's No 100 (Burgess Hill–Pulborough) also calls here as does Metrobus's No 23 (Crawley–Worthing) service. See pp44-7.

For **camping**, walk a few hundred metres north of the village, on London Rd, to the very welcoming *Washington Park* (☎ 01903-892869, 🖳 washcamp.com; WI-FI £5

for 48hrs; 🐾 on lead; open all year) which charges £8 per tent for backpackers plus £5pp. Showers are free and they also have laundry facilities (coin operated). There's **B&B** for £37.50-41pp (sgl occ £40-45) at friendly *Holt House* (☎ 01903-893542, or ☎ 07796-936444, 🖳 annesimmonds_holt house@yahoo.co.uk; 1D en suite, 1D/1T shared bathroom; 🛁; WI-FI; Ⓛ; 🐾) at the end of the road that runs off The Holt. You can get pub **food**, including late breakfasts, at *Frankland Arms* (☎ 01903-892220, 🖳 franklandarms.co.uk; WI-FI; 🐾 on lead; food Mon-Fri 10.30am-2.30pm & 6-9pm, Sat 10.30am-3pm & 6-9.30pm, Sun 11am-4pm). Thursday evening is curry night.

The A24 dual carriageway (Map 25) is something of a blot on the landscape but it is soon forgotten once the steep climb up **Chanctonbury Hill** (Map 26) begins. At the top there are the somewhat storm-ravaged remains of **Chanctonbury Ring** (see box below), a beautiful circle of beech trees that was shaken into a ragged mess during the famous storm of October 1987.

Steyning (see p130), about one mile north of the path, is well worth the minor detour and not just to replenish supplies and energy. A couple of possible pathways lead down to the village; the best is the one to your left, just after you pass the trig point and just before you reach the small memorial to a local farmer (Map 27). The descent is a leisurely one with fine views over Steyning Bowl and down to the coastal towns of Worthing and Lancing.

❏ Chanctonbury Ring   Map 26

This exposed hilltop is one of the great viewpoints of the South Downs but more significantly it is the site of an Iron Age hill-fort believed to date back to the 6th century BC. Today it is equally famous for the copse of beech trees that were planted on the site of the fort by Charles Goring in 1760 and which grew to become one of the

most famous landmarks in Sussex. Sadly, the copse was badly damaged by the storm of October 1987 and despite a replanting programme the skyline has not yet recovered its distinctive crown of trees.

Chanctonbury Ring is also known for its folklore, tales of witchcraft, fairies and other mysterious goings-on. Perhaps the most famous story goes that while Satan was digging the nearby Devil's Dyke valley, spadefuls of earth landed here creating the hill you see today. The ring is also said to be haunted. It may be a beauty spot by day but it takes a brave person to spend the night there.

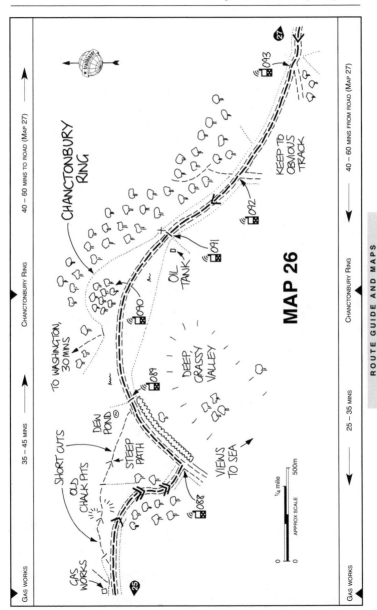

MAP 26

ROUTE GUIDE AND MAPS

To Steyning, 30mins

094

Dew Ponds

Fields

Views towards Worthing, Lancing & Brighton

Trig Point

Fields

095

Memorial to Farmer

MAP 27

Cross the road and follow the parallel path

0   1/4 mile
0   APPROX SCALE   500m

To Steyning (1/2 mile)

White House Caravan & Campsite

Best path to Steyning

27a

Newham Lane

Steyning Bowl

Grassy Valley

Path follows edge of field

28

40 – 60 MINS FROM CHANCTONBURY RING (MAP 26)

ROAD

45 – 60 MINS TO TURN FOR BOTOLPHS (MAP 28)

ROUTE GUIDE AND MAPS

40 – 60 MINS TO CHANCTONBURY RING (MAP 26)

ROAD

55 – 70 MINS FROM TURN FOR BOTOLPHS (MAP 28)

STEYNING   MAP 27a, p133

This small town has retained all the charm of a downland village and it is worth taking an afternoon off to wander around and maybe visit one or two of the sights. There are some beautiful old buildings, particularly along Church St where the **Grammar School (Brotherhood Hall)**, dating from 1614, really catches the eye with its black

timber framing. Next to the library is the small **Steyning Museum** (☎ 01903-813333, 🖳 steyningmuseum.org.uk; Tue, Wed & Fri 10.30am-12.30pm & 2.30-4.30pm, Sat 10.30am-4.30pm, Sun 2.30-4.30pm, closes at 4pm Oct-Mar, open Bank Hol Mons) with displays on local history. Entrance is free.

Services
There is an **information point** in the **library** (☎ 01903-270330; Mon-Fri 10am-5pm, Sat 10am-2pm); there is also **internet access** (free for library card holders and for 5 mins if don't have a card then £1.50/hr; free WI-FI) there.

The High St has plenty of **banks** and **ATMs** and there's a **post office** (Mon-Fri 9am-5.30pm, Sat 9am-12.30pm) too. The main **supermarket**, Co-op (daily 6am-10pm, Sun 9am-6pm) is also on the High St. Further down is a **pharmacy** and, virtually opposite, there is also a good **bookshop** (Mon-Sat 9.30am-5.30pm) that sells maps. For camping-stove fuel, there's a branch of **Bunce's Home Hardware** (Mon-Sat 8.30am-5pm).

Bus services (see pp44-7) calling here are Brighton & Hove Buses' No 2 to Brighton and Compass's No 100 (en route between Burgess Hill and Pulborough; see box p43 for details of rail services from Pulborough).

Where to stay
Campers should head to Newham Lane, where they'll find *White House Caravan and Campsite* (☎ 01903-813737; ✹; end Mar-Oct) which charges £10 for a pitch and up to two people. Note that there is no shower block and only one toilet here, although a new shower block (with more toilets) is in the pipeline. The walk into town takes about eight minutes.

Walker-friendly *Uppingham B&B* (☎ 01903-812099, ☐ uppingham-steyning .co.uk; 1S/1T with shared facilities, 1D private bathroom; ☛; WI-FI; Ⓛ; ✹) is in Kings Barn Villas, on the east side of Steyning. B&B costs from £35pp (sgl/sgl occ from £40).

Springwells House B&B (☎ 01903-812446, ☐ springwells.co.uk; 3D/3D or T, one room sleeping up to 5, all en suite; ☛; WI-FI; Ⓛ; ✹), 9 High St, offers B&B in an en suite room for £39.50-75pp (sgl occ £69-140). Two of the rooms have four-poster beds and a Z-bed can be put in most rooms (£20 per bed inc breakfast). One of the other delights of this lovely place is the heated swimming pool in the old walled garden.

Though the bar can sometimes be noisy, *Chequer Inn* (☎ 01903-814437, ☐ chequerinnsteyning.co.uk; 1D/1T/1Qd, all en suite; limited WI-FI), at 41 High St, offers comfortable B&B from £50pp (sgl occ £60). Note that they cannot offer breakfast before 7.30am but if requested in advance they will provide a takeaway breakfast.

Where to eat and drink
Cafés & restaurants Baked goods, breakfasts, tea and coffee can be had at the bakery *Truffles* (☎ 01903-816140; Mon-Sat 7.30am-5.30pm, Sun 8am-5pm; the café open 30 mins later than the shop, and during the week closes an hour earlier; WI-FI). For lunch packs there are takeaway buns, cakes and savouries at *Model Bakery* (☎ 01903-813785; Mon-Fri 8am-5pm, Sat 8am-1pm), on Church St, with a second, **takeaway-only** branch (☎ 01903-813126; Mon-Wed & Fri 8am-2pm, Thur to 1.30pm, Sat 7.30am-3pm) at the northern end of the High St.

A classier place is *The Steyning Tea Rooms* (☎ 01903-810103; daily 10am-6pm, winter hours variable; ✹), which does very good breakfasts – including traditional bacon sandwiches or scrambled eggs with smoked salmon – as well as light lunches and cream teas. Also popular is *Rhubarb Café* (☎ 01903-812644, ☐ rhubarbcafebistro.co.uk; Tue-Thur 9am-5pm, Fri-Sat 9am-6pm, Sun 10am-4pm), with extra seating in a 'secret' back garden. They also open in the evenings as a **bistro** (6-9pm) from Thursday to Saturday.

For something more intriguing, turn off the High St down Cobblestone Walk, a part-covered alleyway where, amongst a curious collection of boutique shops and gift stalls, you'll find the ever-so charming *Cobblestone Tea House* (☎ 01903-366171; daily 9am-5pm; WI-FI; ✹), housed in a 16th-century timber-framed cottage.

Arguably the best place to eat in Steyning is *The Sussex Produce Company* (☎ 01903-815045, ☐ thesussexproduce company.co.uk; Mon-Sat 8am-8pm & Sun 9am-5pm), an award-winning **deli** and local produce shop which has an excellent *café* (Mon-Sat 8.30am-4.30pm, Sun 9am-4.30pm, Fri & Sat 6-9pm; WI-FI) serving steak from Sussex Longhorn cattle and fish from the local port of Newhaven among all the other locally sourced ingredients. There's Harveys's beer, Fairtrade coffee and some fabulously healthy picnic fillers.

Nearby is **Baloos Bistro** (☎ 01903-814319, 🖳 baloos.co.uk; Tue-Sat 11am-2.30pm & 5.30-9pm, Sun 11am-4pm) with fine wine, juicy steaks and great Sunday roasts. They also do freshly filled sandwiches and bagels at lunchtimes.

Pubs *The White Horse* (☎ 01903-814084, 🖳 www.whitehorsesteyning.co.uk; food Mon-Sat noon-9.30pm, Sun noon-9pm; limited WI-FI; 🐾 on a lead), is a rather characterless gastro-pub at the crossroads on the High St, but the food is decent value, especially some of the lunchtime deals.

Chequer Inn (see Where to stay; limited WI-FI; 🐾 in parts of the pub only; food Mon-Sat 10am-2pm & 6.30-9pm, Sun 10am-2.30pm) is a more traditional pub with local ales, good food, and an antique three-quarter-sized snooker table that's still in use. They sometimes have live music on weekend evenings.

At the bottom end of the High St there is another traditional pub, *The Star Inn* (☎ 01903-813078; food Mon-Sat noon-3pm & 6-9pm, Sun noon-6pm; WI-FI; 🐾) serving dishes such as steak and ale pie.

For a straightforward pint of real ale, head to *The Norfolk Arms* (☎ 01903-812215; daily noon-2pm & 6-11pm; 🐾) at 18 Church St; a real old-style freehouse pub where you can enjoy your drink without the annoying distraction of food.

Acting almost as suburbs of Steyning, the twin villages of Bramber & Upper Beeding (see below) lie either side of the River Adur. They're easily accessed from Steyning, but can also be walked to directly from the Way (see Maps 28 & 29).

BRAMBER & UPPER BEEDING
MAP 27a

The main attraction is **Bramber Castle** (free, dawn to dusk). It was built by William de Broase in 1073 on a prominent knoll behind the village. In truth there is not much left of it, save for a few old ramparts and some collapsed sections of wall but the old moat, despite now having no water and having been taken over by trees, is still clearly visible. The only surviving part of the castle that's still in use is the **Church of St Nicholas** which was built around the same time. **St Mary's House** (☎ 01903-816205, 🖳 stmarysbramber.co.uk; May-Sep Thur, Sun & bank holidays plus Wed in Aug, 2-6pm; £10, garden only £6) is a magnificent place which claims to be the finest example of a 15th-century timber-framed house in Sussex. The perfectly manicured front garden, with its topiary and fish ponds, only adds to the charm. Despite the house being a private residence the owners do allow visitors in to admire the antiques, an Elizabethan *trompe l'oeil* painted room, four-poster beds, a 'mysterious, ivy-clad monks' walk' and octagonal

dining-room. It is a popular location for TV dramas, most notably *Dr Who*.

Services

On the main street in Upper Beeding there is a **newsagent** (Mon-Fri 5.30am-5pm, Sat 5.30am-1pm, Sun 5.30am-noon) as well as a **pharmacy** (Mon-Fri 9am-1pm & 2-5.30pm, Sat 9am-12.30pm). There's a small Budgens **shop** (Mon-Sat 6am-11pm, Sun 7am-11pm) that sells hot drinks and snacks, in a petrol station on the way out of town.

Brighton & Hove Buses' No 2 **bus** service (Steyning to Rottingdean) passes through both Bramber and Upper Beeding. Compass Bus No 100 also calls at both on its way between Pulborough and Burgess Hill; see pp44-7.

Where to stay

In **Upper Beeding** you'll find *Downs View B&B* (☎ 01903-816125, 🖳 upperbeeding .com; 1D/5D or T/1Qd, all en suite; 🛏; WI-FI; ⓛ), which featured on the Channel 5 TV series *To B&B the Best*. It gets great reviews from visitors and is a friendly place

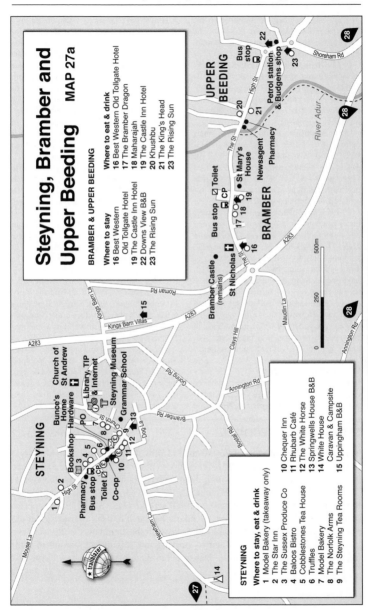

Steyning, Bramber and Upper Beeding MAP 27a

BRAMBER & UPPER BEEDING

Where to stay
16 Best Western
  Old Tollgate Hotel
19 The Castle Inn Hotel
22 Downs View B&B
23 The Rising Sun

Where to eat & drink
16 Best Western Old Tollgate Hotel
17 The Bramber Dragon
18 Maharajah
19 The Castle Inn Hotel
20 Khushbu
21 The King's Head
23 The Rising Sun

STEYNING

Where to stay, eat & drink
1 Model Bakery (takeaway only)
2 The Star Inn
3 The Sussex Produce Co
4 Baloos Bistro
5 Cobblestones Tea House
6 Truffles
7 Model Bakery
8 The Norfolk Arms
9 The Steyning Tea Rooms
10 Chequer Inn
11 Rhubarb Café
12 The White Horse
13 Springwells House B&B
14 White House
  Caravan & Campsite
15 Uppingham B&B

to stay. B&B in their comfortable rooms costs from £45pp (sgl occ £65-90). The breakfasts include homemade bread, muffins and jams.

The Rising Sun (☎ 01903-814424, 🖳 therisingsunupperbeeding.co.uk; 2D or T/1T all en suite, 3S shared bathroom; ➥; WI-FI; ⓛ), is a friendly pub with small, clean rooms with B&B for £40pp (sgl £40, sgl occ rates on request).

In **Bramber**, there are two smart options: *The Castle Inn Hotel* (☎ 01903-812102, 🖳 castleinnhotel.co.uk; 12D or T/4Tr, one room sleeping up to 5, all en suite; ➥; WI-FI; ⓛ; 🐾) is an old-worlde pub with B&B in a variety of rooms for around £40-55pp (sgl occ £50-72.50).

If you have cleaned the mud from your boots you could splash out on a four-posted bed room at the *Best Western Old Tollgate Hotel* (☎ 01903-879494, 🖳 oldtollgatehotel.com; 28D, two with four posters/6D or T/4T, all en suite; ➥; WI-FI; ⓛ) which incorporates a smart restaurant (see Where to eat) and lots of pristine rooms and charges from around £40pp (sgl occ full room rate). However, their rates vary by the day and are generally better if you book in advance, also at times they have some special offers, so it is worth checking online.

Where to eat and drink

In **Bramber** there is a surprising number of food outlets for such a small village. One of the best places is *The Castle Inn Hotel* (see

Where to stay; food daily 7-9am, noon-3pm & 6-9pm; WI-FI; 🐾), which is also open for breakfast for non-residents. They also serve real ale; see box p22. Eating at *Best Western Old Tollgate Hotel* (see Where to stay; food Mon-Fri 6.30-9.30am, noon-2pm & 6-9.30pm, Sat 7-10am, noon-3pm & 6-9.30pm, Sun 7-10am & noon-9.30pm; WI-FI) is a classy experience with a three-course dinner (including dessert and a cheese) for £26.50 (Mon-Sat); on Sunday they serve an all-day roast (£22.25 for three courses). They also open for breakfast.

For a cheaper night out try *The Bramber Dragon* (☎ 01903-812408; Sun & Tue-Thur 5.30-10.30pm, Fri-Sat 5.30-11pm), a Chinese restaurant that also serves Thai food. *Maharajah* (☎ 01903-814746, 🖳 maharajahgroup.co.uk; daily noon-2.30pm & 5-11.30pm) claims to be the 'largest and most famous Indian restaurant in Sussex'.

Moving into **Upper Beeding** there is more Indian food at *Khushbu* (☎ 01903-816646; daily 5.30-11pm), while *The King's Head* (☎ 01903-812196; food Mon-Fri noon-2.30pm, Sat & Sun till 3pm, daily 6-8.30pm; WI-FI; 🐾) does some fine pub grub. Note, the pub closes 3pm to 5.30pm Monday-Friday.

There is also pub food at *The Rising Sun* (see Where to stay; WI-FI; 🐾; food Mon & Wed-Sat noon-2.30pm & 6-9pm, Sun noon-3pm) at the far end of the village. On Tuesdays the pub is open from 5pm only and only serves drinks.

STEYNING TO PYECOMBE   MAPS 27a-32

The going is easy for most of this **10-mile (16km, 4-5½hrs)** section with a good track leading the way along the level escarpment of the Downs. There are, once again, great views in all directions but particularly to the north across the Weald.

Despite the ugly pub (see Poynings, p137) and car park at the top of the hill the highlight of this stretch has to be **Devil's Dyke** (Map 31, p139), a spectacular dry valley said to have been carved out by Satan himself in order to let the sea flood over the lowland Weald and destroy all the churches. Geologists have blown this theory out of the water by proving that it is in fact a result of folding of the chalk strata due to pressure building between the African and Eurasian plates.

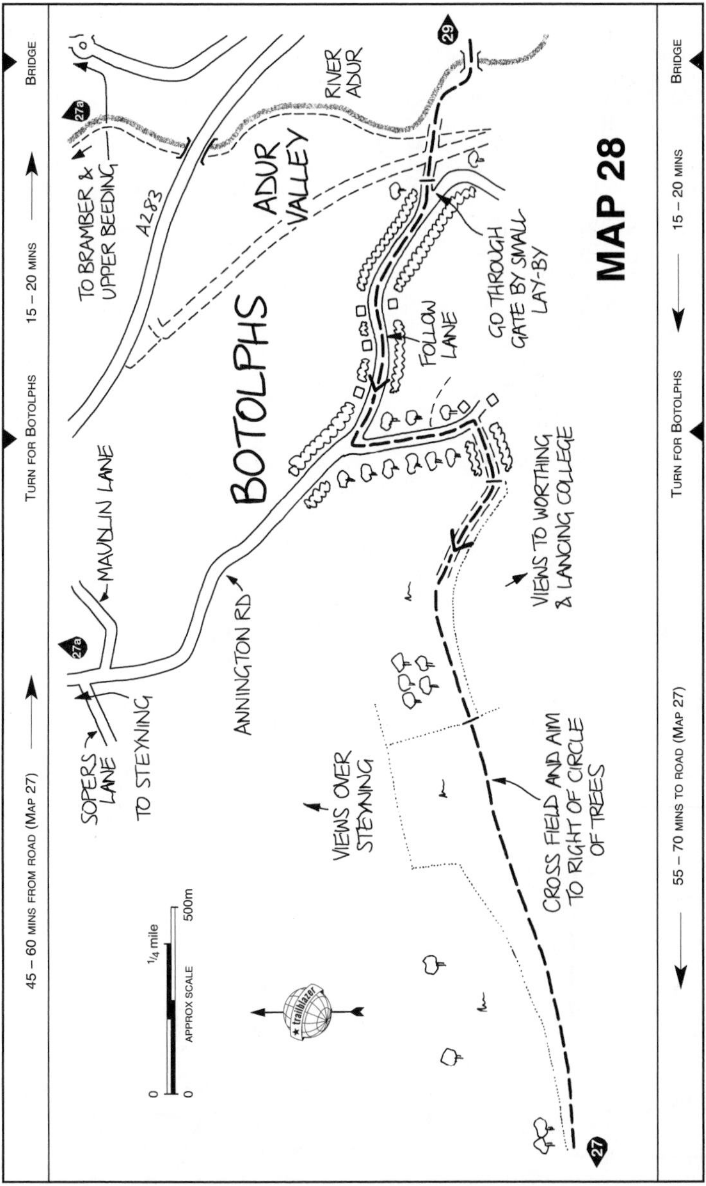

MAP 28

BRIDGE

15 – 20 MINS

TURN FOR BOTOLPHS

15 – 20 MINS

BRIDGE

TO BRAMBER & UPPER BEEDING

A283

RIVER ADUR

ADUR VALLEY

BOTOLPHS

GO THROUGH GATE BY SMALL LAY-BY

FOLLOW LANE

VIEWS TO WORTHING & LANCING COLLEGE

MAUDLIN LANE

TURN FOR BOTOLPHS

SOPERS LANE

TO STEYNING

ANNINGTON RD

VIEWS OVER STEYNING

CROSS FIELD AND AIM TO RIGHT OF CIRCLE OF TREES

45 – 60 MINS FROM ROAD (MAP 27)

55 – 70 MINS TO ROAD (MAP 27)

¼ mile

500m

APPROX SCALE

ROUTE GUIDE AND MAPS

ROUTE GUIDE AND MAPS

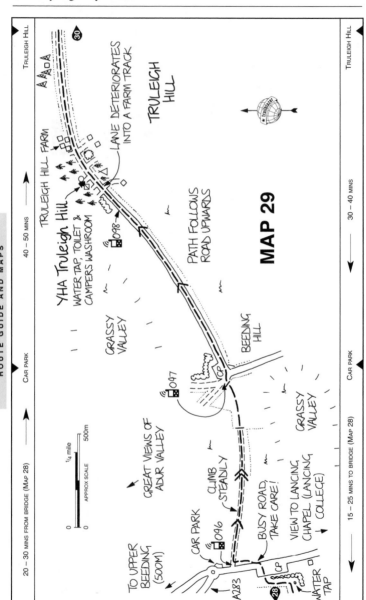

TRULEIGH HILL

20 – 30 MINS FROM BRIDGE (MAP 28)   CAR PARK   40 – 50 MINS

¼ mile
500m
APPROX SCALE
0
0

TO UPPER BEEDING (500m)

A283

WATER TAP

CP

CAR PARK 046

BUSY ROAD, TAKE CARE!

CLIMB STEADILY

GREAT VIEWS OF ADUR VALLEY

VIEW TO LANCING CHAPEL (LANCING COLLEGE)

047

GRASSY VALLEY

GRASSY VALLEY

BEEDING HILL

CP

PATH FOLLOWS ROAD UPWARDS

MAP 29

YHA Truleigh Hill
WATER TAP, TOILET & CAMPERS WASHROOM

048

Truleigh Hill

TRULEIGH HILL FARM

LANE DETERIORATES INTO A FARM TRACK

TRULEIGH HILL

30

trailblazer

15 – 25 MINS TO BRIDGE (MAP 28)   CAR PARK   30 – 40 MINS

TRULEIGH HILL

After leaving the Dyke the Way drops down to Saddlescombe Farm (where you can camp, see below) and then over the flanks of **Newtimber Hill**, owned by the National Trust and an oasis of calm after the crowds that flock to the Dyke.

TRULEIGH HILL   MAP 29

Right on the Way, *YHA Truleigh Hill* (reservations ☎ 0345-371 9047, or ☎ 01903-813419, 🖳 yha.org.uk/hostel/truleigh-hill; 6 x 2-, 1 x 4 -, 6 x 6-bed rooms: dorm bed £13-21pp; private rooms £30-100 for 2-6 sharing; shared facilities; WI-FI communal area; ⓛ; Mar-Oct) is a tree-shaded, purpose-built hostel with all the usual useful facilities including a day room and a drying room. The *café* (daily 8am-10pm, winter usually weekends only) serves meals, hot drinks, cold beer and ice-creams and is open to the public too. There's also a small **shop** and **kitchen** for those preferring to self-cater.

Camping (Mar-Oct; £13pp) is also available in the field opposite. There's a 24hr 'campers washroom' with toilet, shower and changing room beside the **water tap** outside the entrance to the hostel. They also have two **bell tents** (£50-100 for up to five sharing); each has a double bed, two single beds and a fold-out bed.

FULKING   MAP 30, p138

This tiny village has little of specific interest to the walker except for the delightful *Shepherd & Dog Inn* (☎ 01273-857382, 🖳 shepherdanddogpub.co.uk; food Mon-Sat noon-4pm & 6-9pm, Sun noon-6pm; limited WI-FI; 🐾 on lead). It's everything a proper country pub should be with plenty of real ales, good **food** (mains £14-20) and a beer garden with views of the Downs. The pub gets its name from Fulking's reputation for having a rather large population of sheep: in the early 19th century the village was home to ten times as many sheep as people and the pub was the place where the shepherds would meet after a hard day's shearing to spend their earnings on the local brew.

Next to the pub car park is the locally famous **Victorian fountain**, placed there in memory of John Ruskin, the man responsible for installing the village's water supply.

POYNINGS   MAP 31, p139

The hidden leafy village of Poynings sits at the foot of the escarpment away from the hustle and bustle high above at the beauty spot of Devil's Dyke. Poynings is a scenic two-mile walk from the Dyke.

Dyke Lane Cottage (☎ 01273-857335, 🖳 amberric@hotmail.com; 2D en suite/1T private bathroom; ☞; WI-FI; ⓛ) is both walker and cyclist friendly. B&B here costs from £40pp (sgl occ from £40). Note that the bathroom for the twin is downstairs. Set in the heart of the village, the *Royal Oak* (☎ 01273-857389, 🖳 royaloakpoynings.pub; food daily noon-9.30pm; WI-FI; 🐾) serves all the pub-grub classics (mains £12-14).

If descending to the Royal Oak does not appeal, the only other choice is the somewhat characterless *Devil's Dyke* (☎ 01273-857256, 🖳 vintageinn.co.uk/thedevilsdykebrighton; food Mon-Sat noon-10pm, Sun noon-9.30pm; WI-FI; 🐾), whose most redeeming feature is the fabulous views to be had from its benches outside. Main dishes cost £10-12 and sandwiches around £6.

NEWTIMBER HILL   MAP 31, p139

On the Way *Saddlescombe Farm* (☎ 01273-857712, 🖳 saddlescombefarmcampsite@nationaltrust.org.uk; Apr-end Sep; 🐾 on a lead) is a simple, vehicle-free **campsite** (£5pp) run by the National Trust. Facilities are basic – there are no showers, just washbasins, a toilet and a **water tap**. At the farm, there's *WildFlour Café* (summer Tue-Sun 10am-5pm, check 🖳 facebook.com/WildflourSouthDowns for their winter hours; cash only) serving cream teas, cakes and hot food, such as dhals, in a courtyard. Nearby is one of the last examples of a **donkey wheel** used to pump water from the well.

ROUTE GUIDE AND MAPS

70 – 100 MINS TO ROAD FROM TRULEIGH HILL (MAP 31)

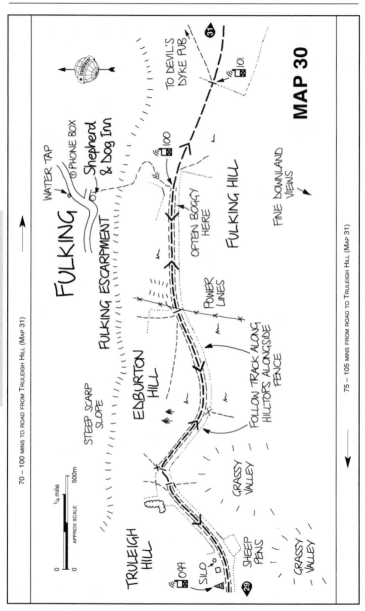

MAP 30

75 – 105 MINS FROM ROAD TO TRULEIGH HILL (MAP 31)

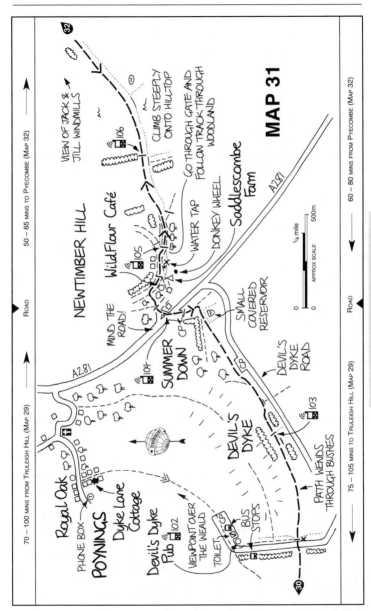

MAP 31

50 – 65 MINS TO PYECOMBE (MAP 32)

60 – 80 MINS FROM PYECOMBE (MAP 32)

70 – 100 MINS FROM TRULEIGH HILL (MAP 29)

75 – 105 MINS TO TRULEIGH HILL (MAP 29)

ROAD

ROAD

VIEW OF JACK & JILL WINDMILLS

CLIMB STEEPLY ONTO HILLTOP

GO THROUGH GATE AND FOLLOW TRACK THROUGH WOODLAND

106

WATER TAP

DONKEY WHEEL

Saddlescombe Farm

A281

WildFlor Café

105

Newtimber Hill

MIND THE ROAD!

104

SUMMER DOWN

CP

SMALL COVERED RESERVOIR

CP

DEVIL'S DYKE ROAD

103

DEVIL'S DYKE

PATH WENDS THROUGH BUSHES

¼ mile

500m

APPROX SCALE

0

0

A281

Royal Oak

PHONE BOX

POYNINGS

Dyke Lane Cottage

Devil's Dyke Pub

102

VIEWPOINT OVER THE WEALD

TOILET

CP

BUS STOPS

30

32

ROUTE GUIDE AND MAPS

PYECOMBE   MAP 32

Pyecombe, like many a downland village, has some very pretty ivy-clad flint houses but the peace and tranquillity that it evidently once had has been somewhat spoilt by the constant hum of traffic from the A23 which converges with the A273 just below the village. The trees hide the roads from view but struggle to do the same with the constant drone. Nevertheless, it's a convenient place to stay being right on the Way and with several B&Bs and a pub.

The Norman **church** (daily 9am-6pm, 4pm in winter) is very welcoming, allowing you to make yourself a cup of coffee or tea in their kitchen, or use the **toilet**. The former **forge** in the house opposite was once the source of some of the best shepherds' crooks in southern England.

If you're looking for a picnic lunch, the BP petrol station just south of the village has an **M&S food outlet** stocked with treats, as well as a **Wild Bean Café**.

Metrobus's No 270 (East Grinstead to Brighton) **bus** stops here as do their 271 and 273 (both Crawley to Brighton) services; see pp44-7.

Where to stay and eat

Camping is available at *Chantry Farm Campsite* (☎ 07540-350384, 🖳 chantry farm.org; 🐕 but on leads at certain times of the year), but it must be booked in advance; a phone call earlier that morning will usually suffice. It's a small eco-friendly place (hot-water tap-and-bucket 'showers'; compost toilets; no mains electricity) with room for half a dozen or so tents (£14pp) and a couple of cosy shepherd's huts (see the website for details).

You can also **camp** (£6pp) in the back field at *The White House* (☎ 01273-846563, 🖳 louloua@onetel.net; 1D or T private bathroom; 🐕; WI-FI; 🐕), a family-run **B&B**, which can sleep a group of up to five people (they also have 1S/1D) but then the bathroom would be shared. They charge from £40pp (sgl/sgl occ from £50/65). Campers can use a toilet and basin in the house for free but a shower costs £4; subject to prior arrangement they can pay extra and have breakfast. The owners have a drying area and offer a laundry service as well as a pick-up/drop off/baggage-transfer service subject to prior arrangement.

Next door *Tallai House* (☎ 01273-845848, 🖳 grahamsmudge@talk21.com; 2D or T, shared facilities; WI-FI) charges from £45pp (£75 sgl occ) for B&B and is equally welcoming.

The Plough (☎ 01273-842796, 🖳 the ploughpyecombe.co.uk; food Mon-Fri 11.30am-10pm, Sat & Sun from noon) commands unenviable views of the traffic hurtling down the A23 to and from Brighton. Despite this it is a good pub with tasty food; they also do takeaways.

PYECOMBE TO SOUTHEASE   MAPS 32-38

This reasonably long stretch, **14½ miles (23.5km, 5-7hrs)** provides sweeping views north. The high ground in the distance is the High Weald, a large area of sandstone incorporating Ashdown Forest, the home of Winnie the Pooh, while to the south is Brighton and the English Channel.

The high point of this section is **Ditchling Beacon** (Map 33). The name refers to the pyres that were burnt here and at other sites along the Downs such as the Beacon Hill (see p82) in Hampshire. The beacons were lit to warn of impending attack, most notably during the time of the Spanish Armada. More recently they were used for celebrating the Queen's Diamond Jubilee in 2012.

Ditchling Beacon is a National Nature Reserve and a popular tourist spot. Access is made easy by the road that winds in hairpins up the escarpment from Ditchling village. Brighton & Hove Buses operate a seasonal and weekend only **bus** service (No 79; see pp44-7) between the car park at the beacon and Brighton.

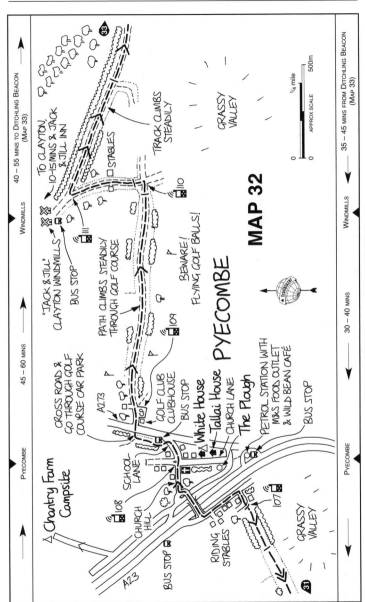

CLAYTON   off MAP 32, p141

The main attraction of Clayton is not the small village at the foot of the hill but the two windmills (see box below) just two minutes from the path.

There's no B&B in the village itself but out on the bend on the main road, about five minutes' walk away, is *Jack & Jill Inn* (☎ 01273-843595, 🖳 thejackandjillinn.co.uk; 3T/1D, all en suite; WI-FI; (L); 🐾 bar only), a family-run pub with good-value **food** (Mon-Fri noon-2pm & 6-9pm, Sat noon-9pm, Sun to 8pm), real ale (see box p22) and four rooms. **B&B** costs £42.50-47.50pp (sgl occ £60-70); room only £5pp less.

❑ **Jack and Jill windmills**   Map 32, p141

The twin windmills above Clayton, known as Jack and Jill, are famous local landmarks that can be seen for miles around. There is evidence that suggests the first windmill was erected way back in 1765. The names of the windmills are said to originate from the 1920s when tourists first came to visit. The post mill Jill, the white windmill, has been fully restored and occasionally grinds out some wholemeal flour. It is the only one of the two that is open to the public (🖳 jillwindmill.org.uk; May-Sep, most Sun & bank hols 2-5pm; free). There is a *tea shop* (same opening hours).

DITCHLING   MAP 33a

It is about a mile from the Downs to this village but if you are trying to decide on a place to spend the night this is a good choice and worth the short detour. Ditchling is among the prettiest of the pretty, perhaps bettered only by Alfriston and Amberley. There is a multitude of historic buildings centred around the crossroads but the oldest of all is the fine 13th-century Norman **St Margaret's Church**. Opposite the church you can see the house, **Wings Place**, bought by Henry VIII for his fourth wife, Anne of Cleves (see Plumpton p144 and Lewes p147), as part of a 'pay off' at the end of their marriage.

Not far from the church, in the old Victorian village school, is **Ditchling Museum of Art + Craft** (☎ 01273-844744, 🖳 ditchlingmuseumartcraft.org.uk; mid Jan to mid Dec Tue-Sat 10.30am-5pm, Sun 11am-5pm; £6.50). It's well worth visiting, with impressive collections by famous local artists and craftspeople such as the sculptor and engraver Eric Gill, the printer Hilary Pepler, the weaver Ethel Mairet and the painters David Jones and Sir Frank Brangwyn (see The Jointure Studios, p144).

Services

There are two small **village shops** with limited provisions. One, called **Parkers of Ditchling** (daily 7.30am-1pm) is a short way up the High St next to Church Lane while the other, incorporating the **post office** (☎ 01273-842736; shop and PO generally Mon-Sat 8am-1pm & 2.15-6pm, Sun 8am-2pm), is at the crossroads in the centre of the village. Close by is **Ditchling Pharmacy** (Mon-Thur 9am-1pm & 2-5.30pm, Fri 9am-1pm & 2-6.30pm).

Ditchling   MAP 33a

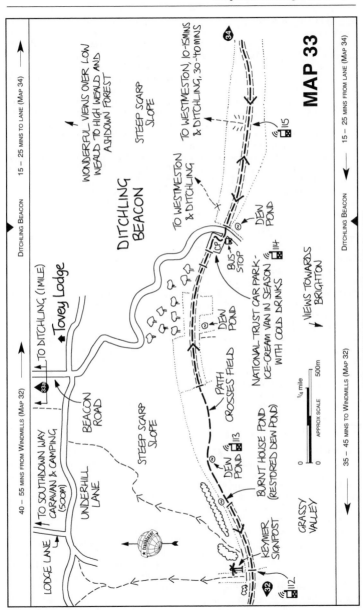

MAP 33

LODGE LANE

UNDERHILL LANE

BEACON ROAD

TO SOUTHDOWN WAY CARAVAN & CAMPING (500M)

40 – 55 MINS FROM WINDMILLS (MAP 32)

TO DITCHLING (1 MILE)

↑Tovey Lodge

DITCHLING BEACON

WONDERFUL VIEWS OVER LOW WEALD TO HIGH WEALD AND ASHDOWN FOREST

STEEP SCARP SLOPE

TO WESTMESTON, 10–15MINS & DITCHLING, 30–40 MINS

34

115

TO WESTMESTON & DITCHLING

DEW POND

CP

BUS STOP

114

VIEWS TOWARDS BRIGHTON

NATIONAL TRUST CAR PARK – ICE-CREAM VAN IN SEASON WITH COLD DRINKS

DEW POND

PATH CROSSES FIELD

DEW POND 113

BURNT HOUSE POND (RESTORED DEW POND)

STEEP SCARP SLOPE

Trailblazer

KEYMER SIGNPOST

GRASSY VALLEY

32

112

0   ¼ mile
APPROX SCALE
0   500m

DITCHLING BEACON

35 – 45 MINS TO WINDMILLS (MAP 32)

15 – 25 MINS TO LANE (MAP 34)

Where to stay and eat

Campers should head about a mile west along Clayton Rd to find *Southdown Way Caravan & Camping Park* (☎ 01273-841877 or ☎ 07483 251792, 🖳 www.southdown-caravancamping.org.uk; 🐾 on leads), which is exceptionally welcoming for a big caravan park. They charge £9pp for backpackers, the shower block is spotlessly clean and there's a laundry room and a small shop in reception (daily 9am-6pm). The campsite can also be reached from the Way, via a footpath from Keymer Signpost (Map 33); at the bottom of the path turn right onto Underhill Lane, left along Lodge Lane and the campsite is opposite the end of the road.

The Bull (☎ 01273-843147, 🖳 thebullditchling.com; 3D/1T, all en suite; WI-FI; 🐾 in bar area only), is a wonderful old pub on the High St. There's very comfortable **B&B** from £50 to £90pp (sgl occ full room rate); at weekends they also have a minimum two-night stay. It's a good place to eat (**food** Mon-Fri noon-2.30pm & 6-9.30pm, Sat noon-9.30pm, Sun noon-9pm), though you may have to book a table at weekends.

There's also *The White Horse* (☎ 01273-842006, 🖳 whitehorseditchling.com; 2D/1D or T all en suite, 2D/2D or T private bathroom; ☞; WI-FI; Ⓛ; 🐾 bar only), which charges £35-55pp (sgl occ from £60); note that the rooms with private bathroom are small. **Food** (Mon-Fri noon-3pm & 6-9pm, Sat noon-9pm, Sun noon-4pm & 6-9pm) is available in the pub or in their restaurant.

There's very comfortable B&B in the attractive studios once used by the artist Sir Frank Brangwyn: *The Jointure Studios* (☎ 01273-841244, 🖳 jointurestudiosbandb.co.uk; 1D or T in self-contained apartment; ☞; WI-FI) at 11 South St. B&B costs £60pp (sgl occ rates on request); minimum stay of two nights at weekends in May to September. The apartment has a bathroom and a living room with a kitchen area.

The most luxurious accommodation in the area is about a mile south of Ditchling, but is the closest to the Way. *Tovey Lodge* (Map 33; ☎ 01273-256156, 🖳 toveylodge.co.uk; 1D/4D or T, all en suite; ☞; WI-FI; Ⓛ) on Underhill Lane, has an indoor swimming-pool, spa hot tub and sauna. They charge according to the season and demand, with B&B rates ranging from £50-100pp (sgl occ £90-185). They do not accept advance bookings for less than a two-night stay on Fridays and Saturdays.

For breakfast or for lunch try the delightful *Ditchling Tea Rooms* (☎ 01273-842708, 🖳 ditchlingtearooms.com; Apr-Oct daily 8am-5pm, Oct-Mar Mon-Fri 8am-4pm, Sat & Sun 8am-5pm; WI-FI; 🐾 in garden), where you can have a cooked breakfast (from £5.50), a range of sandwiches or baguettes, or just a good old-fashioned cream tea (£4.95).

To make up a picnic visit *The Larder* (☎ 01273-845333; Mon-Sat 9am-6pm), a deli stocking local produce. You can also get hot drinks to take away.

PLUMPTON   MAP 34

Famous for its agricultural college, Plumpton is also the location for the privately owned **Plumpton Place**, a 16th-century mansion complete with moat, once owned by Anne of Cleves after it was given to her by Henry VIII. The best view of the mansion is from the Way on the top of the hill, so the only real reason for walkers to come down off the trail here is to visit The Half Moon pub.

The Half Moon (☎ 01273-890253, 🖳 www.halfmoonplumpton.com; food Mon-Sat noon-3pm & 6-9pm, Sun noon-4pm; WI-FI; 🐾) is an excellent local pub with a wide selection of interesting dishes and real ales on tap. The main kitchen is closed 3-6pm year-round but in the summer during the week they serve snacks such as filled ciabatta at that time.

Plumpton **railway station** (see box p43) is actually in Plumpton Green, 2½ miles due north of Plumpton; it's a stop on Southern's London to Eastbourne/Ore line. Compass's **bus** No 166 (see pp44-7) will take you to Lewes.

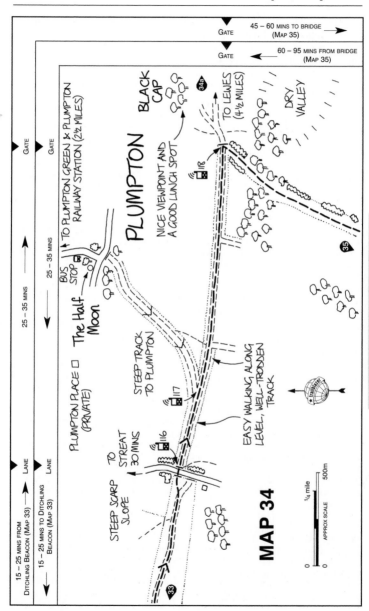

After leaving the hustle and bustle of the Beacon the route continues towards **Black Cap** (Map 34, p145) where the track takes a sharp right-hand turn. Those wishing to visit **Lewes** (see below) should head straight on at this point, but note it's at least an hour's walk from here. Also note, it is possible to take a side trip from Lewes to the isolated hill of Mount Caburn (see box p152), the only part of the South Downs that is not covered by the South Downs Way.

LEWES   MAP 34a, p149

'Lewes ... lying like a box of toys under a great amphitheatre of chalky hills ... on the whole it is set down better than any town I have seen in England'   **William Morris**

Lewes, the county town of East Sussex, is still an attractive place to visit and one of the most desirable places to live in the South-East. Like Totnes in Devon, it's a Transition Town (⌨ transitionnetwork.org) populated by a vibrant community of people, some of whom are dedicated to following this movement based on permaculture and sustainability. They've even issued their own currency (see box below). For the visitor it's interesting to see somewhere that's paying more than lip service to being green. It also means there's a profusion of places to buy and eat good healthy food; it's well worth spending the night here.

Lewes lies in a strategic position by the River Ouse with Mount Caburn (see box p152) rising steeply to the west. This did not go unnoticed by William the Conqueror who had William de Warrene fortify the town soon after the Battle of Hastings in 1066.

The town's focal point is **Lewes Castle** (☎ 01273-486290, ⌨ www.sussex past.co.uk; Mar-Oct Mon-Sat 10am-5.30pm & Sun from 11am, Nov-Dec & Feb 10am-3.45pm & Sun from 11am, Jan closed on Mon; £7.70, or combined ticket for Anne of Cleves House £12.30), which sits proudly at the very highest point on a grassy bluff. This Norman castle was built by Lieutenant William de Warenne shortly

---

❑ The Lewes Pound

In 2008, Lewes town took the unusual step of issuing its own currency, to be used alongside sterling. The idea behind the 'Lewes Pound' (⌨ thelewespound.org) is to encourage demand for local goods and services, and the logic behind it is simple: money spent in shops in the town that are merely another branch of a national chain does not stay in the local economy; but money spent in shops owned by locals or on local services does. So while the Lewes Pound would not be accepted in, for example, the local outlet of a nationwide superstore, of which there are several in Lewes, it would be accepted by a local trader – who would then spend it locally with another local trader, and so on and so on. Thus, by ensuring that money is spent locally and so stays within the community, the wealth of the locals is safeguarded.

People buy Lewes Pounds (with sterling) at one of the issuing points (including Lewes Town Hall, Mays General Store on Cliffe High St, and Richards & Son, Butchers, on Western Rd) – or from the website (see above) – then spend them with participating traders.

Whilst the establishing of a new currency may seem like a highly bizarre step to take, it isn't without precedent; indeed, Lewes itself had its own currency for over a century between 1789 and 1895. The issuers of the latest Lewes Pound, however, admit that their currency is not actually legal tender, in that there is no obligation on the part of retailers to accept the pound. Some residents, though, see the Lewes Pound as an unnecessary complication. They argue that they can support local traders by buying from them using good old-fashioned sterling. And it's true that the Lewes Pound doesn't seem to be quite as much in evidence as it was in the past.

ROUTE GUIDE AND MAPS

after the Battle of Hastings in 1066. The well-preserved castle gate and walls can be explored and the ticket also gives access to the **Barbican House Museum** opposite, which has artefacts from the castle, a scale model of 1880s Lewes and a 12-minute video on the history of the town.

Down the hill from the castle, **Anne of Cleves House** (☎ 01273-474610, 🖳 www .sussexpast.co.uk; Feb-Oct Tue-Sat 10am-5pm, Sun & Mon 11am-5pm; £5.90, or £12.30 with combined Lewes Castle ticket) is open to the public – unlike Plumpton Place (see p144) and Wing's Place (see p142) which were also given as a gift from Henry VIII to his fourth wife Anne of Cleves. This house is well worth visiting for its beautiful interior with timber beams and oak furnishings. There is a free-to-enter *café* here and a Tudor tea garden.

Lewes still has some excellent bookshops, the oldest of which, **The Fifteenth Century Bookshop** (from 11am Tue, Fri, Sat, Sun), can be found at the top of the High St near the castle entrance. The timber-framed building that houses the shop is worth a visit in itself.

At the same end of the High St is **Bull House** where Thomas Paine, the founder of American Independence, lived between 1768 and 1774. During his time in Lewes he acted as the local tobacconist and exciseman. A commemorative plaque can be seen on the outside wall, but the building isn't open to the public.

Priory Park (off Map 34a) and the ruins of the 11th-century **Priory of St Pancras** are worth visiting and the ruins are well labelled with interesting panels. There's also a little herb garden of medicinal herbs once grown by the monks. The park and the ruins are always open and there's no entry charge. Between here and the castle are the flower-filled **Southover Grange Gardens**, with a pleasant *tea garden* (Mon-Sat 9.30am-5pm, Sun 10.30am-5pm), a scattering of art sculptures, a 350-year-old mulberry tree and a tulip tree planted in 1951 by Princess Elizabeth before she became Queen Elizabeth II.

Real-ale drinkers cannot go to Lewes without visiting **Harvey's Brewery** (☎ 01273-480209, 🖳 harveys.org.uk) though with a waiting list of more than a year for guided tours most fans will get no further than the shop. Harvey's is the oldest brewery in Sussex and has been producing real ales (see box p22) for well over 200 years using hops from Sussex and Kent and water from their own spring. The company is still run by the same family that founded it seven generations ago. The **shop** (☎ 01273-480217; Mon-Sat 9.30am-5.30pm, Sun 11am-3pm) sells a vast array of Harvey's products and paraphernalia.

Services
The **tourist information centre** (☎ 01273-483448, 🖳 staylewes.org; all year Mon-Fri 9.30am-4.30pm, Apr-Sep Sat 9.30am-4pm, Sun & bank hols 10am-2pm, Oct-Mar Sat 10am-2pm) is on the corner of Fisher St and the High St at No 187. They can help find local accommodation (although they can't book it for you) and also sell maps, books and guides. The **post office** (Mon-Sat 9am-4.30pm, Sun 10am-2pm) has moved to the lower end of the High St where there is also a **chemist** and plenty of **banks** with **ATMs**. Waitrose **supermarket** is on Eastgate St while walking equipment and camping gear (including fuel for camping stoves) can be found at **The Outdoor Shop** (☎ 01273-487840; Mon-Sat 9am-5.30pm) just past the river. In the same area there's a **Waterstones bookshop** and *café* (Mon-Sat 9am-4.30pm, Sun 9am-3pm).

Public transport
Lewes is a stop on several of Southern's **train** services (see box p43); the **railway station** is on the southern side of town.

The **bus station** is on Eastgate St and there are several useful **bus** services (see pp44-7): Brighton and Hove Buses' No 28 runs to Brighton and their No 29/29B stop here en route between Brighton and Tunbridge Wells/Uckfield. For Rodmell, Southease or Newhaven take Compass's No 123; for Eastbourne take Compass's No 143 or Seaford & District's Nos 124 & 125 (the 125 route is shared with Cuckmere Community Bus); for Plumpton or Haywards Heath take Compass's No 166.

For a **taxi** try Lewes Taxis (☎ 01273-483232) or GM Taxis (☎ 01273-473737).

Where to stay

As with any other popular tourist town booking in advance is advised in Lewes.

At the bottom end of town, on quiet South St, *1 Garden Cottages* (☎ 01273-473343 or ☎ 07885-511109, 🖥 www.lewes room.co.uk; 1D/1T both en suite; ➤; WI-FI; Ⓛ), 59 South St, is an attractive B&B with a flower-filled front garden. You'll get a good breakfast and the friendly owner is a mine of information about the area. They charge £40-42.50pp (sgl occ from £55) and there is a two-night minimum stay on summer (May-Sep) weekends for advance bookings. The double room has its own entrance.

A short walk north are three more options: *Aleberry* (☎ 01273-480865, 🖥 ale berry.co.uk; 1S/1D or T shared bathroom; ➤; WI-FI) charges £42.50pp (sgl/sgl occ £42.50/65) with a healthy breakfast of cereal and toast. A cooked breakfast costs £5pp extra. There is a minimum two-night booking for bank holiday weekends and the bonfire festival (see box p14).

The Dorset (☎ 01273-474823, 🖥 the dorsetlewes.co.uk; 3D/2Qd, all en suite; ➤; WI-FI; Ⓛ) is a Harvey's Brewery pub which has rooms for £35-47.50pp (sgl occ £45-80). Breakfast costs £8.95pp extra.

Climbing the hill from the river towards the castle, you'll soon reach *Montys* (☎ 01273-476750, 🖥 montys accommodation.co.uk; 3D, all en suite; ➤; WI-FI; Ⓛ), Broughton House, 16 High St, which charges £37.50-80pp (sgl occ full room rate). Two of the rooms are self contained, all have a kitchenette (but no cooking facilities); one also has a four-poster bed and free-standing bath. The rate includes a continental breakfast with homemade muesli or granola.

Further up, *Pelham House* (☎ 01273-488600, 🖥 pelhamhouse.com; 2S/34D or T, all en suite; ➤; WI-FI; 🐾) is a classy hotel with B&B for £40-80pp (sgl/sgl occ from £79/85). However, rates vary all the time so it is always worth checking.

Felix House (off Map 34a; ☎ 01273-473250, 🖥 lewesbedandbreakfast.co.uk; 1S/2D, all en suite; ➤; WI-FI), 22 Gundreda Rd, is ideally placed for walkers being on the route between the Way and Lewes town centre. They charge from £45pp (sgl/sgl occ from £50/65) including a full cooked breakfast. There is a two-night minimum stay in summer for advance bookings at weekends. It's a half-mile walk from the centre of Lewes; walk along West St then turn left down The Avenue. At the end of the road negotiate the staggered junction into Gundreda Rd.

See p152 for additional options between Lewes and Kingston-near-Lewes.

Where to eat and drink

Cafés At the bottom end of town, over the river, *Café du Jardin* (☎ 01273-480777, 🖥 cafedujardin.co.uk; Tue-Sat 9am-5pm, also open some summer Sundays and Fri & Sat 6-9pm; WI-FI; 🐾) is a quirky little courtyard café serving breakfasts, lunches and teas. Set amongst an antique shop and a studio it's right at home here in Lewes.

Overlooking the river, *Riverside* (🖥 riverside-lewes.co.uk) is a small, market-like food hall with a *café* (☎ 01273-487888; daily 8am-7pm; WI-FI; 🐾), a delicatessen, an ice-cream parlour and fruit and veg stalls on the ground floor, and a good-value *brasserie* (☎ 01273-472247; Mon-Sat 9.30am-5pm, Sun 10.30am-4pm; WI-FI; 🐾) upstairs. Next door, *Bake Out* (🖥 bakeout.uk; Mon-Sat 7.30am-5.30pm, Sun 10am-4pm) is a small bakery with some seating for coffee drinkers. Further up the hill, *Flint Owl Bakery* (🖥 flintowlbakery .com; Mon-Sat 9am-5pm) is a lovely bakery-cum-café, with more comfortable seating including some in a small back garden. Across the road, *Robson's of Lewes* (☎ 01273-480654; Mon-Sat 9am-5pm, Sun 10am-5pm; WI-FI; 🐾 garden only) is a coffee shop and takeaway that serves breakfasts, light lunches, teas and ice-cream.

For sandwiches, try *Castle Sandwich Bar* (☎ 01273-478080; Mon-Fri 9.30am-3pm) or nearby *Beckworths* (☎ 01273-474502; Mon-Sat 9am-4pm) which is set in a tiny timber-framed house at 67 High St and is also a deli serving a variety of cold meats.

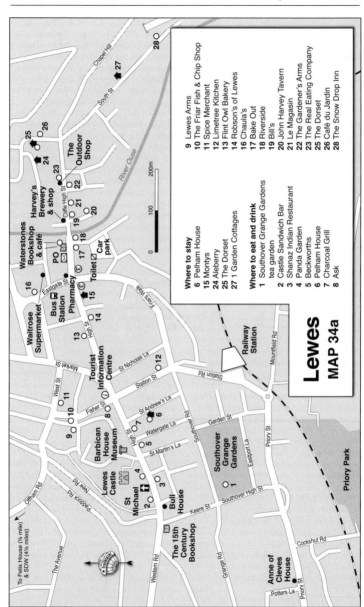

Lewes
MAP 34a

Where to stay
6 Pelham House
15 Montys
24 Aleberry
25 The Dorset
27 1 Garden Cottages

Where to eat and drink
1 Southover Grange Gardens tea garden
2 Castle Sandwich Bar
3 Shanaz Indian Restaurant
4 Panda Garden
5 Beckworths
6 Pelham House
7 Charcoal Grill
8 Ask
9 Lewes Arms
10 The Friar Fish & Chip Shop
11 Spice Merchant
12 Limetree Kitchen
13 Flint Owl Bakery
14 Robson's of Lewes
16 Chaula's
17 Bake Out
18 Riverside
19 Bill's
20 John Harvey Tavern
21 Le Magasin
22 The Gardener's Arms
23 The Real Eating Company
25 The Dorset
26 Café du Jardin
28 The Snow Drop Inn

Pubs With a brewery in town it's not surprising that there's a wide choice of pubs with a cracking selection of real ales. Harvey's owns several pubs in town, including *The Dorset* (see Where to Stay; food served Mon-Sat noon-9pm, Sun noon-6pm; WI-FI; 🐕 bar only), on Mailing St, and *John Harvey Tavern* (☎ 01273-479880, 🖥 johnharveytavern.co.uk; food Mon-Sat noon-3pm & 5-9pm, Sun noon-4.30pm; WI-FI; 🐕), opposite the brewery. Both serve food and Harvey's ales. Another good spot for a pint of the local brew, and many others since it's a real ale pub is *The Gardener's Arms* (☎ 01273-474808; bar Mon-Sat 11am-11.30pm, Sun noon-11pm; WI-FI; 🐕) which is conveniently situated a short way down the High St; it is a popular place with locals wanting a quiet drink.

Tucked away in the side streets behind the castle, *Lewes Arms* (☎ 01273-473152, 🖥 lewesarms.co.uk; food Mon-Fri noon-8.30pm, Sat noon-9pm, Sun noon-8pm; WI-FI; 🐕) is a lovely traditional pub with snugs and quiet corners where you can enjoy a beer; they offer good pub fare too.

Perhaps best of the lot, though, is *The Snow Drop Inn* (☎ 01273-471018, 🖥 the snowdropinn.pub; food Mon-Sat noon-9pm, Sun noon-8pm; WI-FI; 🐕), situated under the chalk cliffs that tower above the quiet end of South St, and named to commemorate the eight people who were killed here in the 1836 avalanche; the deadliest avalanche in British history. The community ties are strong, and it's a very friendly place with good food, fine ale and some courtyard seating. It also has live music some evenings.

Restaurants & takeaways There are several decent restaurants down by the river. *Bill's* (☎ 01273-476918, 🖥 bills-website.co.uk/restaurants/lewes; Mon-Thur 8am-10.30pm, Fri & Sat 8am-11pm, Sun 8am-3pm) is a popular place with tables outside on the cobbled street. It's become a nationwide club, but the original was here in Lewes (albeit at different premises before they were destroyed in a flood). Wholesome offerings range from shepherd's pie and hamburgers to halloumi salad and Thai green curry.

Almost next door is *Le Magasin* (☎ 01273-474720, 🖥 www.le-magasin.co.uk; Mon-Wed 8am-5pm, Thur-Sat 8am-5pm & 6-9pm, Sun 9am-4pm), serving restaurant food for bistro prices in a café atmosphere. It's highly recommended. Opposite is *The Real Eating Company* (☎ 01273-402650, 🖥 www.real-eating.co.uk/lewes; food Mon-Sat 8.30am-6pm, Sun 10am-5pm), another pleasant café-restaurant that serves drinks and light meals and grills, including burgers, flat-iron steaks and lobster rolls.

Further up the hill, just off the High St, is *Limetree Kitchen* (☎ 01273-478636, 🖥 limetreekitchen.co.uk; Wed-Sat noon-2.30pm & 6-9.30pm, Sun noon-2.30pm), at 14 Station St. It's an excellent restaurant (one of the best places to eat in Lewes) and a café. Main dishes for dinner may include saltmarsh lamb with parma ham, and sea bass with orzo and clams. They have tapas-style small plates (£5) at lunchtime.

There's also a good restaurant at *Pelham House* (see Where to stay; daily noon-2.30pm & 6-9pm). Two courses cost £25. Booking recommended. For Italian food you could try *Ask* (☎ 01273-479330; Mon-Thur & Sun 11am-10pm, Fri & Sat 11am-10pm), a reliable chain serving the usual pizza and pasta dishes.

There are several Indian restaurants. The best of the lot is *Spice Merchant* (☎ 01273-470707, 🖥 www.spice-merchant.biz; daily 5-11pm) at 18 West St. There's also *Chaula's* (☎ 01273-476707, 🖥 chaulas.co.uk; Sun-Thur noon-3pm & 5-10.30pm, Fri & Sat noon-3pm & 5-11pm), at 6 Eastgate St near the bus station, and *Shanaz Indian Restaurant* (☎ 01273-488028, 🖥 shanazoflewes.com; daily from 6pm) up at the top end of the High St.

For Chinese, there's *Panda Garden* (☎ 01273-473235, 🖥 pandagarden.uk; Tue-Fri noon-2pm & daily 6-10pm, Mon & Sat 6-10pm) near the castle, which is a takeaway and a sit-down restaurant, while for takeaway only there's *Charcoal Grill* (☎ 01273-471126; Sun-Thur noon-midnight, Fri & Sat noon-1am), with kebabs and burgers, and *The Friar Fish and Chip Shop* (☎ 01273-472016; Tue-Thur noon-1.45pm & 5-9.30pm, Fri-Sat noon-2pm & 5-9.30pm) on the aptly named Fisher St.

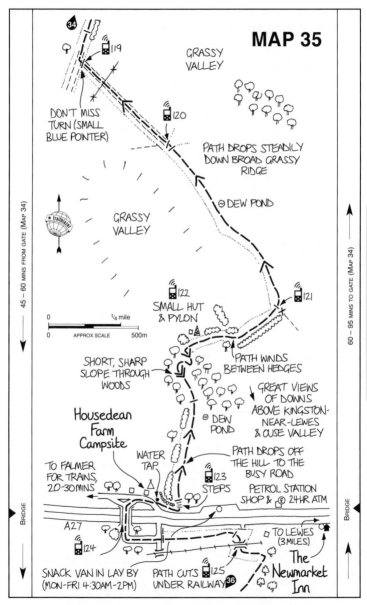

MAP 35

🔵34

📱119

GRASSY VALLEY

DON'T MISS TURN (SMALL BLUE POINTER)

📱120

PATH DROPS STEADILY DOWN BROAD GRASSY RIDGE

⊙ DEW POND

GRASSY VALLEY

★ trailblazer

0 ¼ mile
0 500m
APPROX SCALE

📱122
SMALL HUT & PYLON

📱121

PATH WINDS BETWEEN HEDGES

SHORT, SHARP SLOPE THROUGH WOODS

GREAT VIEWS OF DOWNS ABOVE KINGSTON-NEAR-LEWES & OUSE VALLEY

Housedean Farm Campsite

WATER TAP

⊙ DEW POND

PATH DROPS OFF THE HILL TO THE BUSY ROAD

TO FALMER FOR TRAINS, 20-30 MINS

📱123 STEPS

PETROL STATION SHOP & £ 24HR ATM

A27

📱124

TO LEWES (3 MILES)

The Newmarket Inn

SNACK VAN IN LAY BY (MON-FRI 4:30AM-2PM)

PATH CUTS UNDER RAILWAY 📱125 🔵36

45 – 60 MINS FROM GATE (MAP 34)

60 – 95 MINS TO GATE (MAP 34)

BRIDGE

BRIDGE

ROUTE GUIDE AND MAPS

❑ **Side trip (from Lewes) to Mount Caburn**

The only part of the South Downs that is not covered by the South Downs Way is the isolated hill near Lewes, known rather grandly as Mount Caburn. It is something of an anomaly, being the only part of the Downs separated from the main spine of chalk hills. The hill's unique position makes it an excellent vantage point for admiring the rest of the Downs stretched out to the south, as well as the Ouse Valley and the county town of Lewes. The top of the hill is a National Nature Reserve renowned for its butterflies as well as its paragliders.

The hill is best approached from the village of **Glynde** where there is a railway station (trains leave hourly from Lewes; 5 mins). From Glynde station, Mount Caburn (152m/498ft) looms above. Head towards the hill by walking up the road for five minutes. Just past the old village smithy (blacksmith), which is still being used, is a junction that marks the centre of Glynde village. Turn left and look for the stile in the hedgerow opposite the village shop. The path to the top of Mount Caburn follows the obvious route through the fields from the stile and takes about 30-45 minutes. The return is by the same route or via a path further to the north which drops through a small copse to emerge on the lane north of Glynde village.

BETWEEN LEWES & KINGSTON-NEAR-LEWES   MAP 35, p151

Accommodation and food options between Lewes and Kingston-near-Lewes are: *Housedean Farm Campsite* (☎ 07919-668816, 🖳 housedean.co.uk; 🐾; Mar-Oct) which is right on the SDW. In addition to its 28 **pitches** (£12pp) they also have three **camping pods**, two of which sleep two people (£50), and one which sleeps four (£65); bedding is not provided. There's also a fully furnished **shepherd's hut** (sleeps two; £160 for two nights). There's sometimes a 2-night minimum stay at weekends, during June to August. There are toilets, showers and a fire pit at each pitch. The stop for buses to Lewes and Brighton is nearby.

Half a mile up the A27 from here and also convenient for the SDW (though being right by the road it's hardly the most beautiful location) *The Newmarket Inn* (☎ 01273-470021, 🖳 newmarketinn.relaxinnz.co.uk; 2S/7D/5T/1Tr, all en suite; ●; WI-FI; Ⓛ) has **B&B** from £34.50pp (sgl from £44, sgl occ from £66), although rates can be a lot higher when there are events in the area. The cheap **pub grub** (summer daily noon-9pm, winter hours vary) served here is good, although walkers who pass through this way before 2pm might prefer eating at the excellent **snack van** (Mon-Fri 4.30am-2pm) that parks in a layby on the A27 on weekdays. It does huge cooked breakfasts as well as jacket potatoes, bacon baps and hot drinks, and has some tables and chairs on the grass verge beside it.

Once over the A27 dual carriageway (Map 35) the path returns to the ridge of the Downs before crossing the Greenwich Meridian to reach the villages of **Rodmell** and **Southease** (Map 38, p156) where the smell of the sea will probably be prevalent and the chalk cliffs of Seaford Head can be seen in the distance.

KINGSTON-NEAR-LEWES   MAP 36

This is one of the larger downland villages. From the top of the hill the rather out-of-place housing estate is all too obvious but once you're down in the village it is well hidden. The main street, lined with pretty cottages, comes as a pleasant surprise.

Compass Travel's No 123 **bus** service (Lewes–Newhaven) calls here; see pp44-7.

There's a **campsite** half a mile from here, although it was closed in 2017, so make sure you check if it has re-opened before you turn up. When it is open, *Spring*

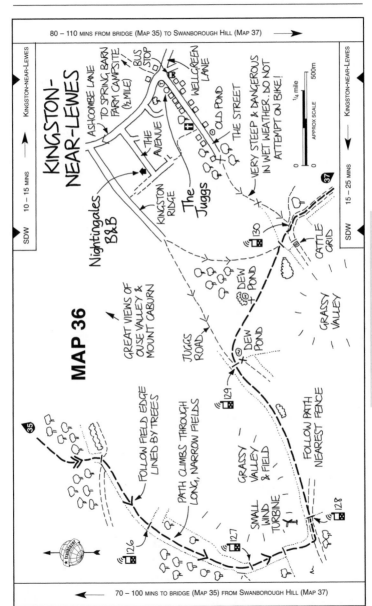

ROUTE GUIDE AND MAPS

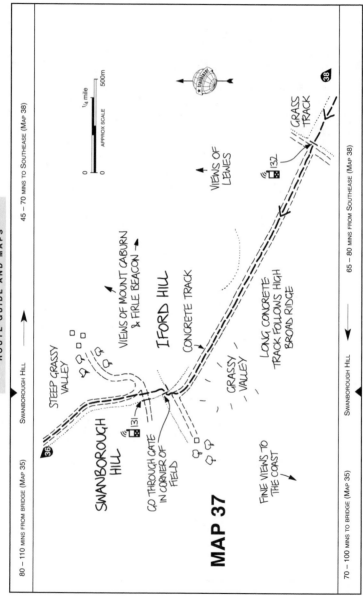

MAP 37

SWANBOROUGH HILL →

45 – 70 MINS TO SOUTHEASE (MAP 38)

80 – 110 MINS FROM BRIDGE (MAP 35)

65 – 80 MINS FROM SOUTHEASE (MAP 38)

70 – 100 MINS TO BRIDGE (MAP 35)

← SWANBOROUGH HILL

STEEP GRASSY VALLEY

VIEWS OF MOUNT CABURN & FIRLE BEACON

IFORD HILL

CONCRETE TRACK

SWANBOROUGH HILL

GO THROUGH GATE IN CORNER OF FIELD

GRASSY VALLEY

LONG CONCRETE TRACK FOLLOWS HIGH BROAD RIDGE

FINE VIEWS TO THE COAST

VIEWS OF LEWES

GRASS TRACK

¼ mile

500m

APPROX SCALE

Barn Farm (☎ 01273-488450, 🖳 spring barnfarm.com; £12pp) has showers and toilets, plus a **farm shop** (summer daily 9am-5.30pm) selling baked goods and hot pies as well as groceries.

On The Avenue *Nightingales* (☎ 01273-475673, 🖳 nightingalesbandb.co .uk; 1D/1T, both en suite; ➶; WI-FI) offers

B&B for £45-47.50pp (sgl occ from £75). *The Juggs* (☎ 01273-472523, 🖳 thejuggs .co.uk; WI-FI; 🐕; food daily noon-9pm) is an excellent pub with a pretty front garden. The unusual name refers to the baskets once used for carrying fish from Brighton to the market in Lewes. Opens for coffee at 10am.

RODMELL   MAP 38, p156

Rodmell is famous for having been home to Virginia Woolf (see box below) and her husband Leonard. **Monk's House** (☎ 01273-474760, 🖳 nationaltrust.org.uk/ monks-house; Apr-Oct Wed-Sun 1-5pm; £5.75, free to NT members), where they once lived, is now open to the public.

For general information about Rodmell visit 🖳 rodmell.net.

Compass Travel's No 123 **bus** service also calls here; see pp44-7.

Where to stay, eat and drink

Opposite the pub is the friendly *Sunnyside Cottage B&B* (☎ 01273-476876; 1T or Tr, en suite; ⓛ; 🐕) with B&B from £36pp (sgl occ also £36) including a good cooked breakfast. The accommodation is like a

separate flat though the entrance is through the main house. The sitting room has a single sofa bed so three can sleep here but access to the shower and toilet is through the main bedroom. Nearby, *Rodmell House* (☎ 01273-479620, 🖳 lornaamelia@gmail .com; 1S shared bathroom/1D en suite; ➶; WI-FI; ⓛ; 🐕) offers B&B from £42.50pp (sgl £45, sgl occ £55).

The Abergavenny Arms (☎ 01273-472416, 🖳 abergavennyarms.com; food Apr-Oct Mon-Sat noon-2.30pm & 6-9pm, Sun noon-3.30pm; WI-FI; 🐕) is a great place to take a break and sit by the log fire if it's cold. The filled baguettes (£4.50-5.50) make a perfect light lunch. The well inside the pub was once the main source of water for the entire village.

❏ Virginia Woolf and the Bloomsbury Group

Born in 1882 in London, Virginia Woolf was a highly accomplished novelist, writing such titles as *The Voyage Out*, *Night and Day*, and *Jacob's Room*. In 1912 she married Leonard Woolf. Their links with Sussex began in 1919 when they moved to the 18th-century **Monk's House** in Rodmell. Their friends included a number of famous artists and writers of the time, not least Virginia's sister the artist Vanessa Bell. Along with the poet TS Eliot and the artists Duncan Grant, Roger Fry and Clive Bell they were known collectively as the Bloomsbury Group.

Many of the paintings from the Bloomsbury Group can be seen in the gallery at the former home of Vanessa Bell and Duncan Grant, **Charleston** (see p158), and also in the small church of St Michael and All Angels at **Berwick** (see p161).

Woolf's life was beset by frequent and sometimes enduring spells of mental breakdown. She tried to kill herself through defenestration (ie throwing herself from a window) before finally, on 18 March 1941, filling her pockets with stones and drowning herself in the nearby River Ouse. Her husband was left with a suicide note in which she spelt out the depths of her love for him: 'If anybody could have saved me it would have been you. Everything has gone from me but the certainty of your goodness'.

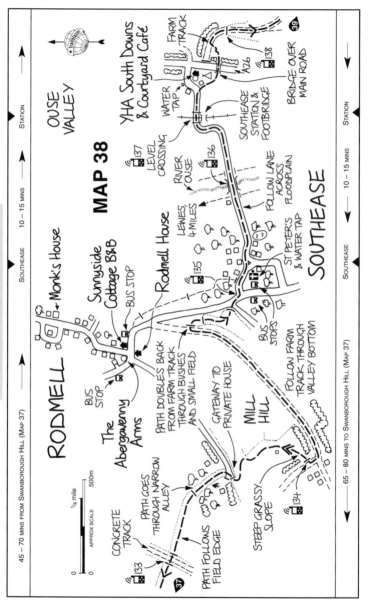

ROUTE GUIDE AND MAPS

45 – 70 MINS FROM SWANBOROUGH HILL (MAP 37)

SOUTHEASE ◄— 10 – 15 MINS —► STATION

¼ mile
APPROX SCALE
0   500m
0

RODMELL

Monk's House

Sunnyside Cottage B&B

BUS STOP

The Abergavenny Arms

BUS STOP

CR

PATH GOES THROUGH NARROW ALLEY

CONCRETE TRACK

PATH FOLLOWS FIELD EDGE

📷 133

37

STEEP GRASSY SLOPE

PATH DOUBLES BACK FROM FARM TRACK THROUGH BUSHES AND SMALL FIELD

GATEWAY TO PRIVATE HOUSE

MILL HILL

FOLLOW FARM TRACK THROUGH VALLEY BOTTOM

📷 134

Rodmell House

📷 135

BUS STOPS

St Peter's & Water Tap

SOUTHEASE

OUSE VALLEY

MAP 38

YHA South Downs & Courtyard Café

WATER TAP

📷 137 LEVEL CROSSING

📷 136

RIVER OUSE

LEWES, 4 MILES

FOLLOW LANE ACROSS FLOODPLAIN

SOUTHEASE STATION & FOOTBRIDGE

📷 138

A26

FARM TRACK

39

BRIDGE OVER MAIN ROAD

◄— 65 – 80 MINS TO SWANBOROUGH HILL (MAP 37)

SOUTHEASE ◄— 10 – 15 MINS —► STATION

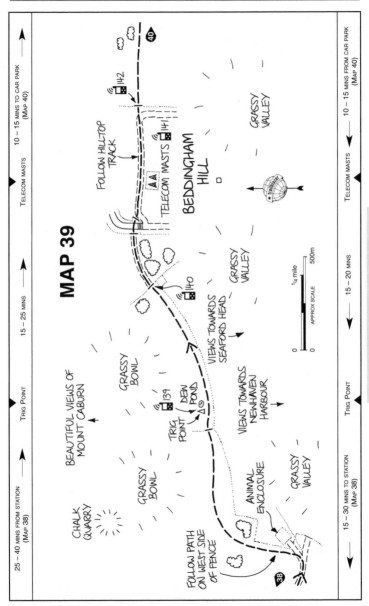

MAP 39

Beautiful views of Mount Caburn

Chalk Quarry

Grassy Bowl

Grassy Bowl

Grassy Bowl

Trig Point

Den Pond

Trig Point

Views towards Newhaven Harbour

Views towards Seaford Head

Grassy Valley

Animal Enclosure

Follow path on west side of fence

Follow hilltop track

Telecom masts

Beddingham Hill

Grassy Valley

Grassy Valley

Grassy Valley

APPROX SCALE

0   ¼ mile

0   500m

25 – 40 MINS FROM STATION (MAP 38)   →   TRIG POINT   →   15 – 25 MINS   →   TELECOM MASTS   ◄   10 – 15 MINS TO CAR PARK (MAP 40)

15 – 30 MINS TO STATION (MAP 38)   ◄   TRIG POINT   ◄   15 – 20 MINS   ◄   TELECOM MASTS   ◄   10 – 15 MINS FROM CAR PARK (MAP 40)

SOUTHEASE   MAP 38, p156

Pretty little Southease is tucked away from any main roads, with a tiny Saxon church, **St Peter's**, incorporating an unusual Norman round tower. This round tower is one of three in Sussex, all in the Ouse Valley and all built in the first half of the 12th century. Inside the church are the remains of some 13th-century wall paintings which once covered the whole church; they were revealed again in the 1930s.

Because Southease is a stop on Southern's **train** service (see box p43) between Brighton and Seaford it's an ideal place to start or end a day walk. Compass Travel's **bus** No 123 (Lewes–Newhaven) stops here; see pp44-7.

The excellent **YHA South Downs** (☎ 0345-371 9574, 🖳 www.yha.org.uk/hostel/ south-downs; 4 x 2-, 2 x 3-, 3 x 4-, 2 x 5-, 2 x 6-bed rooms, 1 x 8-bed male dorm, some

en suite, some have double beds; Ⓛ) is housed in a converted farmhouse near Southease railway station. A dorm bed costs from £15pp, and a private room from £29 but rates can vary a lot so check the website for details. There's **camping** (£15pp; 🐾), although only room for two tent pitches so booking is recommended, plus four heated **camping pods** (from £35/50 for 2/4 people; 🐾) and two **bell tents** (up to four people; £50-100; 🐾; Easter to end Sep). Bedding is provided for the pods and bell tents. Other facilities include a self-catering kitchen, drying room, bike shed and laundry facilities. The on-site *Courtyard Café* (daily 10am-6pm) is licensed and is open to the public (10am-4pm) unless the hostel is booked for sole occupancy.

SOUTHEASE TO ALFRISTON   MAPS 38-42

Continuing along the crest of the escarpment, with the high point at **Firle Beacon** (Map 40), this stretch affords easy walking for **7¾ miles (12.5km, 2½-3½hrs)** with fine views to the coast and across the lowlands to **Mount Caburn** (see box p152), probably the most grandiose name for any hill of 150 metres' altitude.

WEST FIRLE   off MAP 40

This small village among the trees lies at the foot of the Downs escarpment. **Firle Stores & Post Office** (☎ 01273-858219; Mon-Fri 9am-1pm & 2-5.30pm, Sat 9am-1pm and also June-Aug Sun 11am-4pm), offers plenty of choice for your lunchbox.

The Ram Inn (☎ 01273-858222, 🖳 raminn.co.uk; 2D/3D or T, some en suite, some private bathroom; 🛏; 🐾; WI-FI; Ⓛ) charges £50-100pp (sgl occ £90-200) for luxurious B&B rooms. **Food** (main dishes £11-21) is served in what was formerly the Court Room where judges once passed sentence on misbehaving villagers. The real ales are worth the detour and the kitchen is open daily from 9am to 9.30pm.

About a 2½-mile walk from the pub is **Charleston** (☎ 01323-811626, 🖳 charleston

.org.uk; guided tours Mar-June & Sep to late Oct Wed-Sat noon-5pm, July & Aug Wed-Sat 11.30am-5.30pm, Sun & Bank hol Mon timed entry noon-5pm; note these days and times can change so it is best to double check; £12.50) which houses a gallery of work by the Bloomsbury group of artists (see box p155), and hosts a festival each May (see p14). The guided tours (1hr) operate regularly but it is worth booking if you want to be sure of a place.

Charleston is a stop on Seaford & District's Travel's No 125 **bus** service (Lewes to Eastbourne) as well as their seasonal No 124; Cuckmere Community Bus operates the No 125 route on Saturdays and the limited-frequency No 40 service. See pp44-7.

There's **B&B** at *Bo-Peep Farmhouse* (off Map 40; ☎ 01323-871299, 🖳 bopeepfarmhouse.co.uk; 2D/1T, all en suite; 🛏; WI-FI; Ⓛ), about half a mile from the trail, on your right; they charge £52.50-57.50pp (sgl occ full room rate).

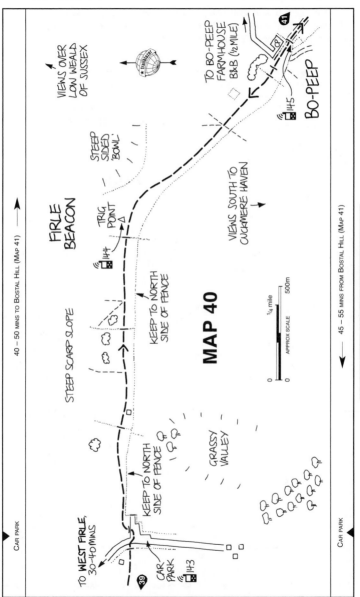

Once past **Bostal Hill** (Map 41) the Way passes pathways that lead to **Alciston** (see opposite) and **Berwick** (see opposite) before it drops steadily down to pretty, wee **Alfriston** (see opposite).

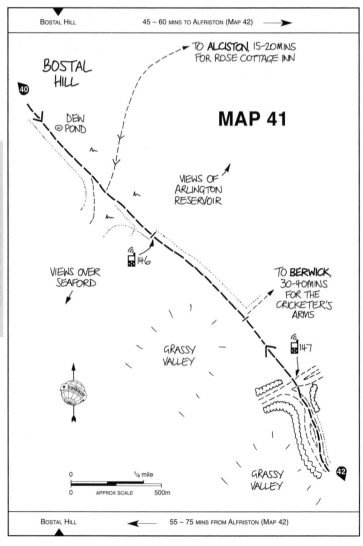

BOSTAL HILL   45 – 60 MINS TO ALFRISTON (MAP 42) ⟶

TO **ALCISTON**, 15-20MINS FOR ROSE COTTAGE INN

BOSTAL HILL

40

DEW POND

MAP 41

VIEWS OF ARLINGTON RESERVOIR

146

VIEWS OVER SEAFORD

TO **BERWICK**, 30-40MINS FOR THE CRICKETER'S ARMS

147

★ trailblazer

GRASSY VALLEY

0   ¼ mile
0   APPROX SCALE   500m

GRASSY VALLEY

42

BOSTAL HILL   ⟵ 55 – 75 MINS FROM ALFRISTON (MAP 42)

ROUTE GUIDE AND MAPS

ALCISTON   off MAP 41

Alciston is yet another beautiful but tiny downland village with little to draw the walker here apart from *The Rose Cottage Inn* (☎ 01323-870377, 🖳 therosecottage inn.com; 2D in self-contained flats; ✦; WI-FI and 🐾 bar area only; Ⓛ), a genuine country pub that has been around for over 350 years. Timber framing and open fires add to the charm and there is also a good choice of locally brewed ales. There is a mouth-watering menu (**food** Tue-Sat noon-2pm & 6.30-9.30pm, Sun noon-3pm) based

on locally sourced produce: the restaurant menu contains a wide selection of fish dishes as well as standard pub fare. The self-contained flats (with kitchen/lounge diner, toilet & shower room) cost £37.50-40pp (sgl occ full room rate); note that there is a **two-night** minimum stay. The rate includes a welcome pack with ingredients to make breakfast.

Alciston is a stop on Cuckmere Community Buses' infrequent Nos 40, 42 and 44 **bus** services; see pp44-7.

BERWICK   off MAP 41

Berwick is famous for the Bloomsbury Group of Victorian artists which included Vanessa Bell, Roger Fry and Duncan Grant. Some of Vanessa Bell's work can be seen in the small **church** (St Michael and All Angels) on the edge of the village.

Berwick is a stop on Southern's Ore/Eastbourne to Brighton **railway** line (see box p43) as well as on the Ashford International to Brighton line on Sundays.

Seaford & District's No 125 (Eastbourne–Lewes) **bus** service calls here; on Saturdays this is operated by Cuckmere Community Bus (CCB). CCB's No 126, No

47 (Cuckmere Valley Rambler; seasonal weekend) and their limited frequency Nos 40, 42 & 44 services also call here. Many of these connect with train arrivals, making it a good place to start or end a day walk. See pp44-7.

For food head to *The Cricketer's Arms* (☎ 01323-870469, 🖳 cricketersber wick.co.uk; food Mon-Sat noon-8.30pm, Sun noon-8pm; WI-FI; 🐾). Their menu generally includes sharing platters (£12-13) and pub favourites such as ham, eggs & chips (£12).

ALFRISTON   MAP 42, p163

Alfriston is another candidate for 'prettiest village on the South Downs Way'. However, this small collection of Tudor wood-beamed buildings slung higgledy-piggledy along a narrow main street is far from a well-kept secret. In high season coachloads of tourists come to 'ooh' and 'ahh' at the sights and have cream teas. Nevertheless, it is worth planning on

spending a few hours to take it all in at a leisurely pace. Whilst here make sure you take a look around the **church** and the **Clergy House** (see box below) by the church and the village green.

Services

The **post office** (Mon-Fri 1.30-5.30pm, Sat 9am-12.30pm), on The Square, doubles as

---

❏ **Alfriston Church and Clergy House**
The **14th-century flint church** by the river sits in the middle of a well-groomed lawn and is worth a look, as is **Clergy House** (☎ 01323-871961, 🖳 nationaltrust.org.uk/ alfriston-clergy-house; mid Mar-end Oct Sat-Wed 10.30am-5pm, late Feb-mid Mar & Nov-mid Dec Sat & Sun 11am-4pm; £5.35, guided tour £1.50 extra) nearby. This beautiful 14th-century, timber-framed thatched house was the first property the National Trust bought thanks to the local vicar who, in 1896, suggested the building be safeguarded for the nation. Apart from anything else it's a good spot for a picnic lunch.

the village **shop/deli** (Mon-Sat 8am-7pm, Sun 10am-5pm). It is worth a visit just to take in its almost authentic 'Olde Worlde' atmosphere. The now-forgotten 'Lamson' system of moving cash to a single cashier, whereby cannisters containing the money were shot along wires and tubes, is still in place though no longer used. The deli here is a great place to pick up the ingredients for a top-class picnic. There's an excellent independent bookshop, **Much Ado Books** (☎ 01323-871222, 🖳 muchadobooks.com; Sun-Fri 11am-5pm, Sat 10am-5.30pm) with an interesting stock of old and new books, maps and guides. Another good place to browse is **Music Memorabilia**, a record and CD shop.

Compass's Nos 119 & 126 **bus** services (to Seaford) call here as do Seaford & District's Nos 124 & 125, though on Saturdays the latter is operated by Cuckmere Community Bus (CCB). CCB's 126 also calls here and their No 47 (seasonal, weekends only) and the limited frequency No 42. See pp44-7.

Where to stay

For the latest information on accommodation it's worth checking the village website: 🖳 alfriston-village.co.uk

Campers will find plenty of room at the family-friendly *Alfriston Camping Park* (☎ 07591 880129, ☎ 07920 879098, 🖳 alfristoncamping.com; 🐾; open all year), situated in a large field surrounded by woods, a couple of minutes' walk from the village centre. There's a laidback atmosphere, so it can get noisy, but it's a fun place to camp. They charge £7pp, including use of the toilets and showers.

There are numerous **B&B** options, but it's advisable to book ahead. *Chestnuts* (☎ 01323-870959, 🖳 chestnutsalfriston.co.uk; 1D or T, en suite, 1D/1T shared bathroom; ✎; WI-FI; Ⓛ; 🐾) is a cute *café* (see Where to eat) with rooms costing £37.50-42.50pp (sgl occ £50-65).

Down near Alfriston Camping Park, *Dacres* (☎ 01323-870447, 🖳 patsyembry @gmail.com; 1Tr en suite; WI-FI) charges from £45pp (sgl occ from £55) for B&B. The room has its own entrance, is open plan and is more of a studio apartment; the excellent organic cooked breakfasts are served here and the hospitable owner is more than happy to provide a vegetarian or vegan breakfast if preferred. There's also a lovely garden to relax in.

Riverdale House (☎ 01323-871038, 🖳 riverdalehouse.co.uk; 3D/1D or T/1Tr, all en suite; ✎; WI-FI; 🐾) is peacefully located on the edge of the village, off Seaford Rd. It's a very comfortable B&B with lots of options for sleeping as they can put aerobeds in most rooms so they can accommodate families with up to three children. Rates range from £45 to £72.50pp (sgl occ rates on request). Luggage transfer is available by prior arrangement: to/from Lewes and Eastbourne (£20 per trip). *Wingrove House* (☎ 01323-870276, 🖳 wingrove housealfriston.com; 12D, all en suite; ✎; WI-FI) is a restaurant with rooms in a 19th-century colonial-style building. The rooms are luxurious and the food good. B&B costs £62.50-97.50pp (sgl occ rates on request).

❏ **Smuggling**

Smuggling of wool, brandy and gin was rife along the Sussex coast with Cuckmere Haven and Birling Gap being favourite places for gangs of smugglers to load and unload their contraband in the late 18th and early 19th centuries. One of the most infamous groups was the Alfriston Gang who would smuggle goods to and from Cuckmere Haven along the Cuckmere River.

The leader of the Alfriston Gang was Stanton Collins who owned the now aptly named Ye Olde Smugglers Inne from where the group plotted their exploits. These included a raid on a Dutch ship wrecked at Cuckmere Haven. The figurehead of the ship, a red lion's head, still stands next to the Star Inn in the village. Stanton Collins was eventually arrested in 1831 for sheep rustling and was shipped off to Australia.

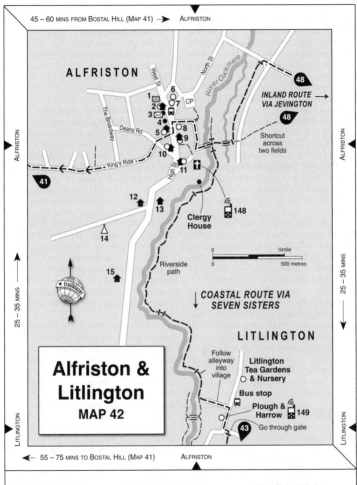

ALFRISTON

Where to stay
2 Ye Olde Smugglers Inne (Market Inn)
5 The Star Inn
9 The George Inn
10 Chestnuts B&B
11 Wingrove House
12 Dacres

13 Deans Place Hotel
14 Alfriston Camping Park
15 Riverdale House

Where to eat and drink
2 Ye Olde Smugglers Inne (Market Inn)
3 Deli (in Village Shop)
5 The Star Inn
6 Badgers Tea House
7 The Singing Kettle
8 The Apiary
9 The George Inn
10 Chestnuts Tearoom
11 Wingrove House

Other
1 Much Ado Books
3 Village Shop/Deli & PO
4 Music Memorabilia

Three of the villages' historic **pubs** also have rooms. *The Star Inn* (☎ 01323-870495, 🖳 thestaralfriston.co.uk; 2S/21D/14T, all en suite; ☞; WI-FI; (L); 🐾) is one of the oldest inns in England, said to date back to 1345. Prices for B&B vary considerably depending on the season but expect to pay £45-70pp (sgl/sgl occ £70-140). *The George Inn* (☎ 01323-870319, 🖳 the george-alfriston.co.uk; 5D, all en suite; ☞; WI-FI; (L); 🐾) is a magnificent old building with oak beams. B&B costs £50-70pp (sgl occ £75-95). There is a minimum two-night booking policy at the weekend in the summer. *Ye Olde Smugglers Inne* (aka **The Market Inn**; 🖳 smugglersalfriston.co.uk; 1T/1D shared bathroom, 1D or T private bathroom, 1D en suite shower; ☞; WI-FI; 🐾) charges from £35pp plus £7pp for breakfast. The name is derived from a famous gang of smugglers (see box p162) who once used the pub to plan smuggling ventures at Cuckmere Haven. Note, they only take accommodation bookings through the website 🖳 booking.com.

At the southern end of the village is the large *Deans Place Hotel* (☎ 01323-870248, 🖳 deansplacehotel.co.uk; 3S/29D or T/4Tr, all en suite; ☞; WI-FI; (L); 🐾), a smart 14th-century country house hotel set in a big garden with manicured lawns and an open-air (unheated) swimming-pool (May-Sep). B&B costs £50-80pp (sgl £80, sgl occ from £90); contact them also to enquire if they have any special deals.

Where to eat and drink

For such a small village Alfriston does well for pubs and cafés, many of which have long histories.

Badgers Tea House (☎ 01323-871336, 🖳 badgersteahouse.com; Mon-Fri 9.30am-4pm, Sat & Sun 10am-4.30pm; food served until 3pm every day; 🐾 garden only) is a traditional English tearoom with a little walled garden to sit in. Housed in a building dating back to 1510, they serve breakfasts (from £8.95), a selection of home-made cakes, soups served with chunky bread (£6), light lunches and cream teas (£7).

Of a similar ilk, though less twee, *The Singing Kettle* (☎ 01323-870723; daily 10am-5pm; 🐾) does a good range of breakfasts, plus sandwiches, cakes and good strong coffee. Down the road, *Chestnuts Tearoom* (see Where to stay; Tue-Sat 10.30am-5pm, Sun 10.30am-4.30pm) does good-value breakfasts, including numerous egg options, plus soups, toasties and cream teas (£3.75).

The Apiary (☎ 01323-870730) is a coffee shop (Apr-Sep daily 10am-5pm, winter hours variable; WI-FI; 🐾 garden only) one side and a dress shop the other. There's a nice garden and they also serve soups, paninis and cream teas (£6).

One of the best **pubs** is undoubtedly *The George Inn* (see Where to stay; food daily noon-9pm), which was first licensed way back in 1397. The menu changes seasonally but mains tend to start from £13. Also serves some cracking real ales.

Ye Olde Smugglers Inne (☎ 01323-870241; see also Where to stay; food Mon-Fri noon-2.30pm & 6-8.30pm, Sat noon-3pm & 6-9pm, Sun noon-9pm; WI-FI; 🐾) has friendly staff and an attractive conservatory at the back. They serve good-value pub grub (most mains cost around £11), Harvey's ales and Long Man Brewery beer (see box p22).

Like its two main rivals, *The Star Inn* (see Where to stay; food Mon-Thur noon-2pm & 6-9pm, Fri-Sun noon-9pm) also has plenty of wooden beams throughout its aged interior, as well as two lovely old fireplaces, and it's a freehouse so is allowed to stock a variety of local Sussex ales, such as Long Man and Harvey's. Mains are quite pricey (£14-22), but there are lunchtime sandwiches (£7) and set menus (2-course/3-course £18/22) too.

Wingrove House (see Where to stay; breakfast daily 8am-10am, Thur-Sun noon-2pm, Mon-Sat 6-9.30pm, Sun 6-8pm) is a stylish **restaurant** with guest rooms. The building is 19th-century colonial, but the restaurant is modern and the contemporary British menu top notch. A two- or three-course lunch costs £18.95 or £25. Dinner will set you back £29/35 for two/three courses respectively. The wine list is extensive, and there's garden and terrace seating. Non-residents can eat here but booking is recommended.

ALFRISTON TO EASTBOURNE (COASTAL ROUTE VIA CUCKMERE)
MAPS 42-47

These **10½ miles (17km, 4¼-5¾hrs** – plus another 1½ miles to Eastbourne; see Map 52, p181) are arguably the highlight of the whole walk, including a stretch through the beautiful **Cuckmere Valley** (Map 43, p167) which culminates in wide meanders leading to what is one of the few undeveloped river mouths in the South-East. Before that, though, you'll pass through the cute little villages of **Litlington** (below) and **Westdean** (p166).

The final assault on Eastbourne is a spectacular roller-coaster ride over the **Seven Sisters** (see Map 44, p168 & Map 45, p169), a line of chalk cliffs that are less famous than The White Cliffs of Dover, but far more spectacular and, ironically, given the names, far whiter due to more constant erosion.

If that was not enough the path continues, past the popular shingle beach at **Birling Gap** (p170), to reach the final high point of the whole walk: **Beachy Head** (see p170), a spectacular chalk cliff jutting into the English Channel with 360° views (Map 47, p173). Even the sprawling mess of Eastbourne is worth admiring from here.

The path finishes at the foot of the hill where it meets abruptly with Eastbourne's suburbs. There is accommodation and refreshments in the neighbourhood of **Meads Village** (see p170), but if you want to go into Eastbourne there is a bus from there or a half-hour coastal walk along pavements to the town centre.

LITLINGTON   MAP 42, p163

Sitting on the eastern bank of the Cuckmere River, Litlington is yet another oh-so-charming downland village complete with flint cottages. On the other side of the valley is a chalk-horse figure carved into the hillside in 1924.

Litlington is a stop on Cuckmere Community Bus's No 47 **bus** service (Mar-Oct weekends only) and their limited No 40 service. See pp44-7.

The local pub is *The Plough and Harrow* (☎ 01323-870632, 🖳 ploughand harrowlitlington.co.uk; food Mon-Fri noon-3pm & 6-9pm, Sat noon-9pm, Sun noon-6pm; WI-FI; 🐾) which serves a variety of bar meals ranging from sandwiches

(£7.75) and specialist cheese salads (£9.50) to classic pub-grub mains (£10.50) as well as finer fare such as salmon on chilli and coriander noodles (£15.50). The bar is open all day, and there's a beer garden at the back. See also box p22.

The village is also home to the delightful *Litlington Tea Gardens & Nursery* (☎ 01323-870222; Apr-end Oct Tue-Sun & bank hols 11am-5pm; 🐾), which claims to have been around since 1870. Their lovely tree-shaded garden is the perfect spot for a cream tea (£4-9). They also do sandwiches (£4), jacket potatoes (£6.50) and soups (£5). Note they accept cash only.

ROUTE GUIDE AND MAPS

❏ **Important note – walking times**
Unless otherwise specified, **all times in this book refer only to the time spent walking**. You will need to add 20-30% to allow for rests, photography, checking the map, drinking water etc. When planning the day's hike count on 5-7 hours' actual walking.

WESTDEAN & EXCEAT   MAP 43

On the north side of the small wooded ridge of chalk is the wonderfully secluded and secret **Westdean**, a tiny collection of beautiful cottages complete with duck pond, nestled in a wooded fold. On the other side of the ridge is **Exceat**, more a collection of tourist facilities than a village but with a very good information centre. This is the gateway to **Seven Sisters Country Park** (see box below) and the spectacular Cuckmere Valley and beach. If Exceat is an overnight stop on your walk, try to arrive here early in the day to give yourself time to enjoy the area around the beach.

Services

The excellent **Seven Sisters Country Park Visitors Centre** (🖳 www.sevensisters.org.uk; Easter-Oct daily 10.30am-4.30pm, Nov & Feb-Easter weekends & school hols only) sells souvenirs, cold drinks and snacks, and has information on wildlife and conservation efforts in Seven Sisters Country Park. There's a **water tap** by the toilet block behind the visitors centre.

Brighton & Hove Buses' Nos 12A and 13X **bus** services provide regular links to Brighton and Eastbourne. Cuckmere Community Bus's No 47 stops at Seven Sisters Country Park at weekends (Mar-Oct) and their No 40 (Tue & Fri only) calls at both Westdean and Exceat; see pp44-7.

Where to stay and eat

Saltmarsh Farmhouse (☎ 01323-870218, 🖳 saltmarshfarmhouse.co.uk; 2D/2T/1Qd, all en suite; ✆; WI-FI) is an upmarket *café* (daily 9am-5pm) with some courtyard seating. They also have extremely smart rooms (including a £350-a-night, two-bedroom suite), with **B&B** ranging from £60pp to £90pp (sgl occ full room rate).

By the bridge, the large **Cuckmere Inn** (☎ 01323-892247, 🖳 vintageinn.co.uk/the cuckmereinnseaford; food daily noon-9pm but in summer sometimes start at 11.30am and serve food till 9.30pm; WI-FI; 🐾 designated area only) has a big garden overlooking the River Cuckmere. Their menu includes standard pub fare (mains £9-12). It gets very busy during the summer due to its great location. If staying at Saltmarsh and visiting the pub in the evening, take a torch as the road between the two is unlit.

❑ Seven Sisters Country Park

This extensive country park of rolling coastal downland includes the spectacular Seven Sisters chalk cliffs over which the South Downs Way passes. There is an excellent visitor centre at Exceat where you can glean all sorts of information from the displays and exhibitions.

Apart from the obvious attraction of the chalk cliffs and downland the park also includes Cuckmere Haven and estuary, one of the only river mouths in the south-east of England that has not been spoilt by development. That is not to say that the estuary is untouched. The natural meanders of the river, seen so spectacularly from the ridge above Exceat, have been left to sit as idle ponds thanks to the man-made channel that diverts the flow of the river more swiftly to the sea. Plans were underway to restore the Cuckmere Estuary to its natural state by filling in the man-made channel and allowing the blockade to gradually deteriorate. This would have restored the flow of the river through the meanders and encouraged the natural restoration of the saltmarsh and mudflats. However, by 2006 this plan had been suspended after a 'modelling miscalculation' by the project's environmental consultant was found.

The country park covers an area steeped in history. Some of the most fascinating stories involve the numerous shipwrecks that litter the seabed below the Seven Sisters' cliffs. The most significant of these is that of the Spanish ship *Nympha Americana* which, in 1747, ran aground halfway along the line of chalk cliffs, resulting in the deaths of 30 crewmen.

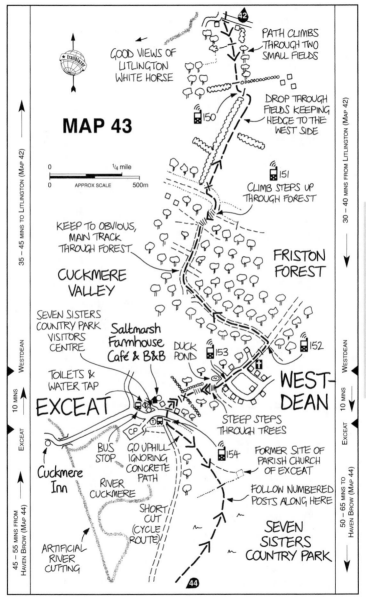

MAP 43

GOOD VIEWS OF LITLINGTON WHITE HORSE

PATH CLIMBS THROUGH TWO SMALL FIELDS

150

DROP THROUGH FIELDS KEEPING HEDGE TO THE WEST SIDE

151

CLIMB STEPS UP THROUGH FOREST

KEEP TO OBVIOUS, MAIN TRACK THROUGH FOREST

CUCKMERE VALLEY

FRISTON FOREST

SEVEN SISTERS COUNTRY PARK VISITORS CENTRE

Saltmarsh Farmhouse Café & B&B

DUCK POND

152

153

TOILETS & WATER TAP

WEST-DEAN

EXCEAT

STEEP STEPS THROUGH TREES

BUS STOP

GO UPHILL IGNORING CONCRETE PATH

154

FORMER SITE OF PARISH CHURCH OF EXCEAT

Cuckmere Inn

RIVER CUCKMERE

FOLLOW NUMBERED POSTS ALONG HERE

SHORT CUT (CYCLE ROUTE)

SEVEN SISTERS COUNTRY PARK

ARTIFICIAL RIVER CUTTING

0   1/4 mile
0   APPROX SCALE   500m

trailblazer

35 – 45 MINS TO LITLINGTON (MAP 42)
45 – 55 MINS FROM HAVEN BROW (MAP 44)
WESTDEAN
EXCEAT
30 – 40 MINS FROM LITLINGTON (MAP 42)
WESTDEAN
EXCEAT
10 MINS
10 MINS
50 – 65 MINS TO HAVEN BROW (MAP 44)

ROUTE GUIDE AND MAPS

42

44

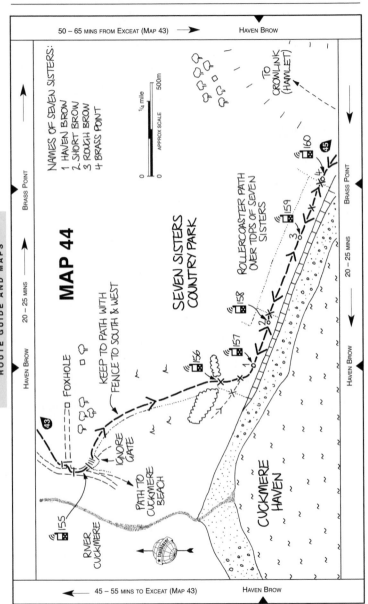

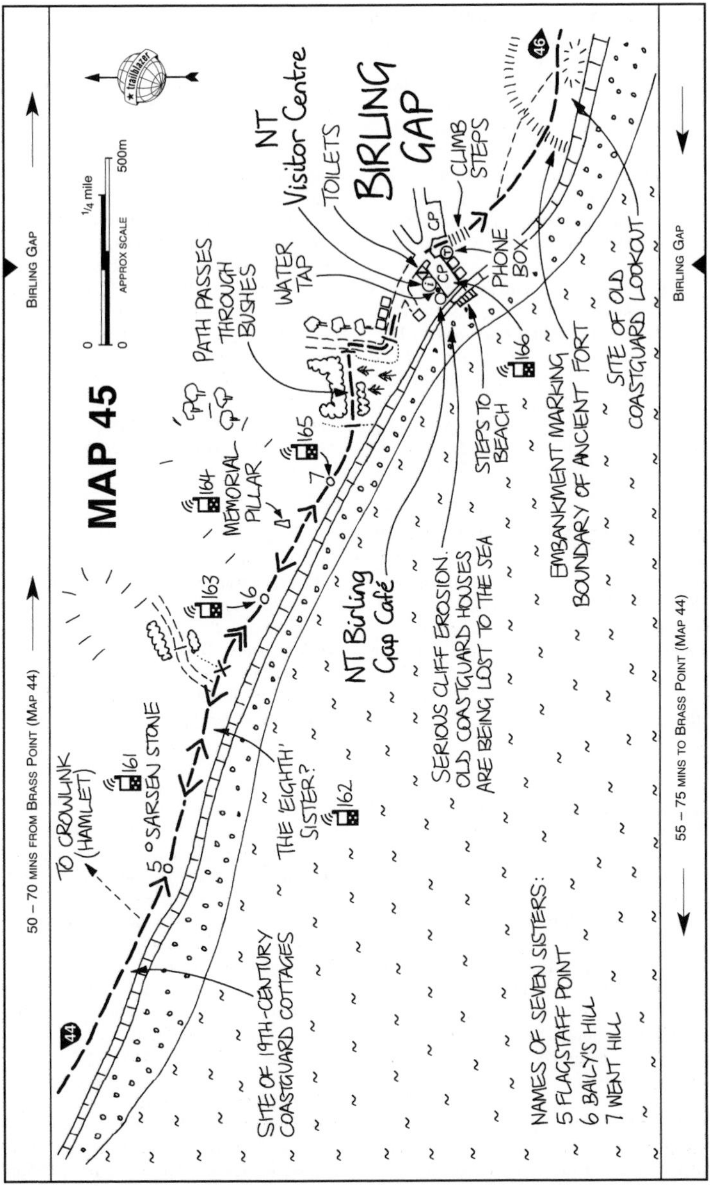
MAP 45
BIRLING GAP
50 – 70 MINS FROM BRASS POINT (MAP 44)
55 – 75 MINS TO BRASS POINT (MAP 44)
APPROX SCALE
0
0
1/4 mile
500m
44
46
TO CROWLINK (HAMLET)
161
5 SARSEN STONE
162
THE 'EIGHTH' SISTER?
163
6
164
MEMORIAL PILLAR
165
7
166
PATH PASSES THROUGH BUSHES
WATER TAP
NT Visitor Centre
TOILETS
BIRLING GAP
CP
CP
CLIMB STEPS
PHONE BOX
NT Birling Gap Café
SERIOUS CLIFF EROSION. OLD COASTGUARD HOUSES ARE BEING LOST TO THE SEA
STEPS TO BEACH
EMBANKMENT MARKING BOUNDARY OF ANCIENT FORT
SITE OF OLD COASTGUARD LOOKOUT
SITE OF 19TH-CENTURY COASTGUARD COTTAGES
NAMES OF SEVEN SISTERS:
5 FLAGSTAFF POINT
6 BAILY'S HILL
7 WENT HILL

BIRLING GAP   MAP 45, p169

All that's in this gap is a small line of terraced houses that are falling into the sea, plus a visitor centre and café of sorts. Considering the beautiful position of the hamlet on a low saddle along the line of chalk cliffs, it's a shame that some of the buildings are so ugly and out of place. The huge steel staircase leading down to the stony beach is also an eyesore, although the beach is a popular spot on sunny summer days.

Birling Gap is a stop on the 13X **bus service** (weekends only) operated by Brighton and Hove Buses; see pp44-70.

National Trust Birling Gap Café (☎ 01323-423197, 🖳 www.nationaltrust.org .uk; food daily 10am-5pm, often closes earlier in winter) has seating both inside and outside, but doesn't serve meals. They sell sandwiches and hot paninis from around

10.30am to 2.30pm, but the rest of the time it's just snacks, drinks, cakes and ice-creams. There's an attached **visitor centre** and **souvenir shop**, and a **water tap** outside.

A 15- to 20-minute walk from Birling Gap, *Belle Tout Lighthouse* (Map 46; ☎ 01323-423185, 🖳 belletout.co.uk; 6D, all en suite; ✆; WI-FI; mid Jan to mid Dec) is now a luxury B&B with incredible coastal views. They charge £80-120pp (sgl occ £112-204). They don't accept children aged under 15 years old and there's a two-night minimum-stay policy but it's worth contacting them at short notice for a single-night stay.

Outside the lighthouse there's a *snack shop* (mid Feb-Oct 11am-5pm, or until the ice-cream runs out) serving drinks and ice-creams.

BEACHY HEAD   MAP 47, p173

Beachy Head is, thankfully, relatively unspoilt with just one large chain pub near the top: *The Beachy Head* (☎ 01323-728060, 🖳 vintageinn.co.uk/thebeachy headeastbourne; food summer Mon-Sat noon-10pm, Sun noon-9.30pm, winter daily noon-9pm; WI-FI; 🐾 lounge area and garden only) isn't really the best place to celebrate the walk's end but is useful if you

need to shelter from the weather, and does have a sun-trap beer garden. The food is good value too.

Brighton & Hove Buses' No 13X weekend-only **bus** service calls here; Stagecoach's Nos 3 & 3A services call at the foot of Beachy Head (end of South Downs Way); see pp44-7.

MEADS VILLAGE   MAP 47, p173

Meads Village is actually the most westerly suburb of Eastbourne. It is a quiet, well-to-do part of town with a genuine village feel. More importantly for South Downs Way walkers, it is positioned right at the official end of the walk, making a stop here a more appealing prospect than the half-hour walk into the more hectic centre of Eastbourne.

To reach Meads Village head straight on where the South Downs Way reaches the kiosk at the bottom of the hill and turn left at Holywell Rd.

Services

Everything you might need here is centred along one short stretch of Meads St. There

is a **Co-op** (daily 7am-10pm) on the corner of Matlock Rd which also incorporates the **post office** (Mon-Fri 9am-5.30pm, Sat 9am-12.30pm), and has an **ATM** outside it. There's also a **Tesco Express** (daily 6am-11pm) and a **pharmacy** (Mon-Fri 9am-5.30pm, Sat 9am-noon).

Stagecoach's No 3 & 3A **bus services** (see pp44-7) go to central Eastbourne from here as well as from the foot of the hill at the end of the South Downs Way.

Where to stay and eat

Beachy Rise (☎ 01323-639171, 🖳 beachy rise.com; 2D/1T/1Tr, all en suite; ✆; WI-FI; Ⓛ), on Meads Rd, has B&B from £35pp

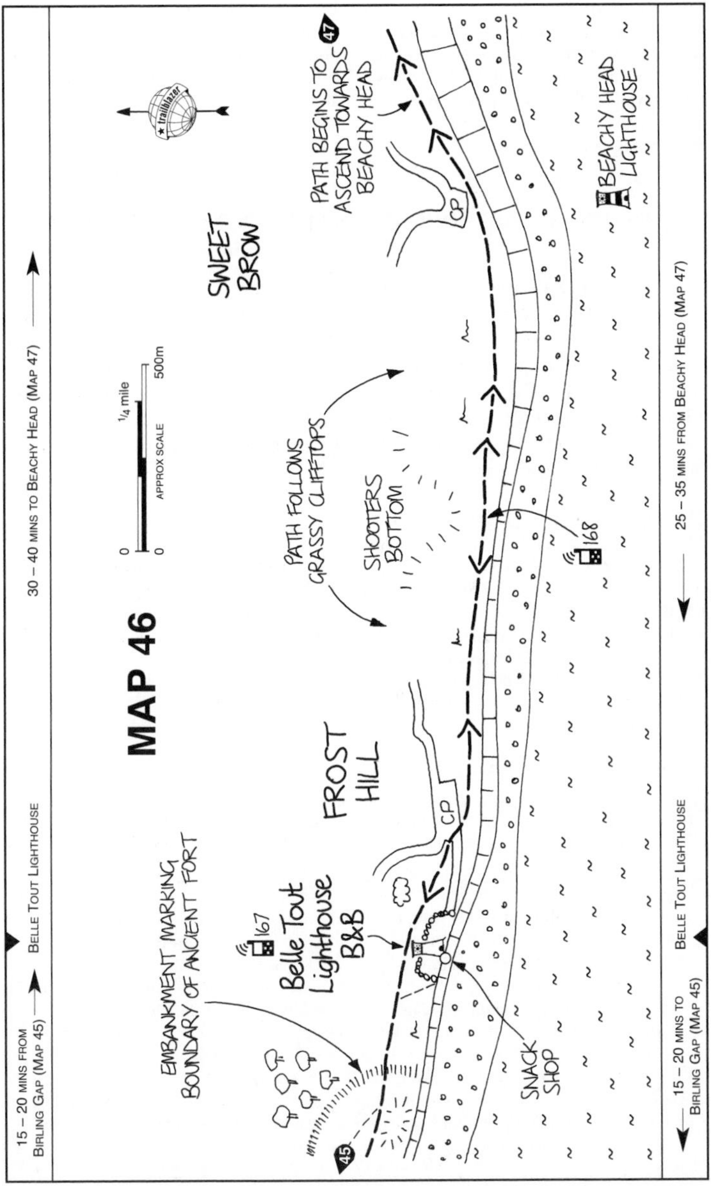
15 – 20 MINS FROM BIRLING GAP (MAP 45)
BELLE TOUT LIGHTHOUSE
30 – 40 MINS TO BEACHY HEAD (MAP 47)
MAP 46
0
1/4 mile
0
APPROX SCALE
500m
trailblazer
SWEET BROW
FROST HILL
PATH FOLLOWS GRASSY CLIFFTOPS
SHOOTERS BOTTOM
PATH BEGINS TO ASCEND TOWARDS BEACHY HEAD
47
CP
CP
168
BEACHY HEAD LIGHTHOUSE
EMBANKMENT MARKING BOUNDARY OF ANCIENT FORT
167
Belle Tout Lighthouse B&B
SNACK SHOP
45
15 – 20 MINS TO BIRLING GAP (MAP 45)
BELLE TOUT LIGHTHOUSE
25 – 35 MINS FROM BEACHY HEAD (MAP 47)

(sgl occ from £55). *The Pilot Inn* (☎ 01323-723440, 🖳 pilot-inn.co.uk; 3D, all en suite; WI-FI; 🐾 bar only), on a bend on Meads St, is the first pub reached after leaving the end of the South Downs Way. The bar is open all day (from 11am), which makes it convenient for a celebration drink. And the **food** (daily noon-9pm) is well-priced (mains £10-13, sandwiches £6). **B&B** costs from £45pp (sgl occ from £65).

EASTBOURNE
For the guide to Eastbourne turn to p178.

ALFRISTON TO EASTBOURNE (INLAND ROUTE VIA JEVINGTON)
MAP 42 & MAPS 48-51

This inland **alternative route** is geared towards horse-riders and cyclists but walkers are welcome to use the bridleway too. Although these **7½ miles (12km, 2¾-3½hrs** – plus another 1½ miles to Eastbourne centre) are not as spectacular as the coastal route there are still plenty of fine downland views to enjoy high up on **Windover Hill** (Map 48, p175) while a detour to see the famous **Long Man of Wilmington** (see box below) is strongly recommended.

It is a good idea to keep an extra day spare for this section even if you have already walked the coastal route.

MILTON STREET   MAP 48, p175
Milton Street is nothing more than a small collection of scattered houses. There is, however, a good pub here; *The Sussex Ox* (☎ 01323-870840, 🖳 thesussexox.co.uk; food served Mon-Sat noon-2.30pm & 6-9pm, Sun noon-3pm & 6-9pm; WI-FI; 🐾). Note the pub is closed between 3pm and 5.30pm during the week between late October and late March.

The menu is varied and changes daily but it usually features a selection of sandwiches and ploughman's (£6-10.50), plus mains such as beer-battered pollock & chips (£13.95) and mussels in cider (£13.95). Ales include Long Man and Harvey's, plus South Downs cider, which is brewed in nearby Wilmington.

WILMINGTON   off MAP 48, p175
Wilmington is best known for the **Long Man**, a huge chalk figure adorning Windover Hill above the village.

A short distance from the South Downs Way and on the main road north of the village is *Crossways Hotel* (☎ 01323-482455,

---

❑ The Long Man of Wilmington   **Map 48, p175**
No-one is quite sure when or why this large chalk figure appeared on the side of Windover Hill above Wilmington.

Best viewed from the lane leading out of the village, he stands 70m tall and holds a vertical rod in each hand. Although it was only in 1969 that the white blocks were placed along the lines of the figure, suggestions as to when the original was made range from the prehistoric era or the Roman age to just a few hundred years ago.

As for the question of why, well that is even harder to answer. Some say he is a fertility symbol robbed of his genitalia; others claim he was carved out for fun by monks from the nearby Wilmington Priory. Or could it be that a real giant collapsed and died on that very spot?

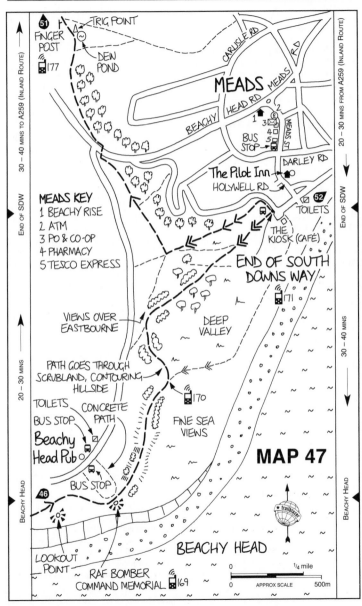

MEADS KEY
1 BEACHY RISE
2 ATM
3 PO & CO-OP
4 PHARMACY
5 TESCO EXPRESS

TRIG POINT
51
FINGER POST
177
DEW POND

CARLISLE RD

MEADS RD

MEADS

BEACHY HEAD RD

MEADS ST

BUS STOP

DARLEY RD

The Pilot Inn

HOLYWELL RD

52 TOILETS

THE KIOSK (CAFÉ)

END OF SOUTH DOWNS WAY

171

VIEWS OVER EASTBOURNE

DEEP VALLEY

PATH GOES THROUGH SCRUBLAND, CONTOURING HILLSIDE

170

TOILETS
BUS STOP
CONCRETE PATH
Beachy Head Pub

BUS STOP

FINE SEA VIEWS

MAP 47

46

LOOKOUT POINT

RAF BOMBER COMMAND MEMORIAL
169

BEACHY HEAD

0   1/4 mile
0   APPROX SCALE   500m

trailblazer

30 – 40 MINS TO A259 (INLAND ROUTE)

20 – 30 MINS FROM A259 (INLAND ROUTE)

END OF SDW

END OF SDW

20 – 30 MINS

30 – 40 MINS

BEACHY HEAD

BEACHY HEAD

ROUTE GUIDE AND MAPS

crosswayshotel.co.uk; 1S/5D/2D or T, all en suite; ☛; WI-FI; Ⓛ) which is actually a restaurant with rooms. They offer **B&B** from £72.50pp (sgl/sgl occ from £80/99). From Tuesday to Saturday (7.30-8.30pm) they serve a four-course set meal including coffee and petits fours for £41pp; booking is recommended.

Wilmington is a stop on Seaford & District's Nos 124 & 125 **bus** services. On Saturdays the 125 is operated by Cuckmere Community Bus (CCB). CCB also run the No 126; the No 47 seasonal (weekend only) service; and the limited frequency Nos 40 & 44; see pp44-7.

JEVINGTON   MAP 49, p176

Jevington, sitting comfortably in the Cuckmere valley, is another beautiful village that provides a potential alternative stop to the somewhat exploited streets of Alfriston.

In the centre of the village is a plaque commemorating the former Hungry Monk Restaurant, which claimed to be the birthplace in 1971 of banoffi pie.

Jevington is a stop on Cuckmere Community Buses' No 41 (Tue & Thur) service; see pp44-7.

Where to stay and eat

For accommodation in the village there is *The Paddocks* (☎ 01323-482499, 🖳 www .thepaddockstables.co.uk; 1D/1T, both en suite; ☛; WI-FI; Ⓛ; 🐴), a comfortable B&B

charging from £37.50pp (sgl occ from £50). They welcome dogs and there is also stabling to keep your horse, should you require it.

The only place to eat is at the village pub, *The Eight Bells* (☎ 01323-484442, 🖳 theeightbellsjevington.co.uk; food Mon-Fri noon-3pm & 6-9pm, Sat noon-9pm, Sun noon-6pm; 🐕 on lead). It's a 5-minute walk up the lane; note the blind bend on the road is very dangerous as there is no pavement for pedestrians – it is safer to use the path by the church. The bar is open all day, every day, and they have a wide range of pub meals as well as a pleasant garden, with views over the Downs. It's a freehouse, so has a variety of ales, and is proud not to have wi-fi.

❑ **Lullington Heath**
This hidden National Nature Reserve near Jevington (see Map 49) is a short detour from the South Downs Way and is a good place to escape the crowds who tend to congregate around the tourist traps of Alfriston, Jevington and Wilmington.

The rough chalk grassland is a fine place to see a variety of species of butterfly including the chalkhill blue. In summer the shallow valley is often ablaze with the yellow flowers of gorse and broom. To the south of Lullington Heath is the expansive cover of **Friston Forest**, another good place to get lost and explore countless forest tracks.

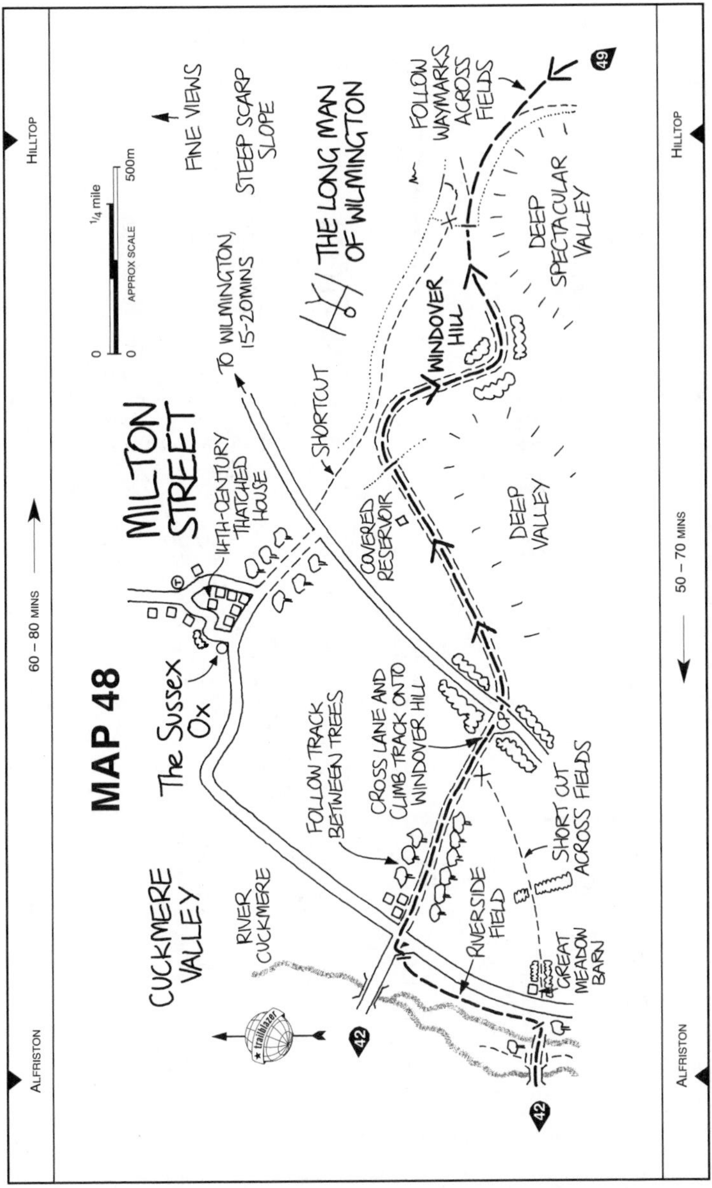

MAP 48

CUCKMERE VALLEY

RIVER CUCKMERE

The Sussex Ox

MILTON STREET

FIFTH-CENTURY THATCHED HOUSE

FINE VIEWS

STEEP SCARP SLOPE

TO WILMINGTON, 15–20 MINS

¼ mile

500m

0

0 APPROX SCALE

THE LONG MAN OF WILMINGTON

FOLLOW WAYMARKS ACROSS FIELDS

FOLLOW TRACK BETWEEN TREES

CROSS LANE AND CLIMB TRACK ONTO WINDOVER HILL

COVERED RESERVOIR

SHORTCUT

WINDOVER HILL

DEEP SPECTACULAR VALLEY

DEEP VALLEY

RIVERSIDE FIELD

SHORT CUT ACROSS FIELDS

GREAT MEADOW BARN

trailblazer

42

42

49

60 – 80 MINS

50 – 70 MINS

HILLTOP

ALFRISTON

ROUTE GUIDE AND MAPS

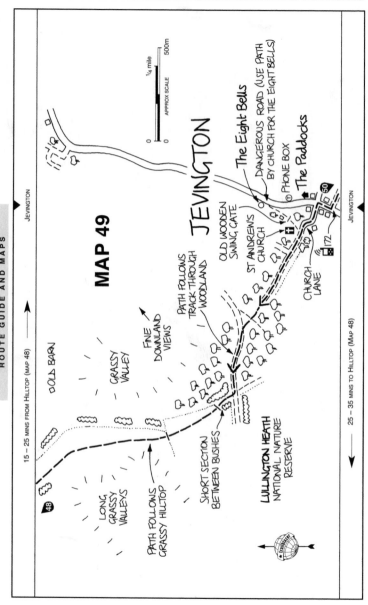

MAP 49

JEVINGTON

The Eight Bells

DANGEROUS ROAD (USE PATH BY CHURCH FOR THE EIGHT BELLS)

PHONE BOX

The Paddocks

50

172

OLD WOODEN SWING GATE

ST ANDREW'S CHURCH

CHURCH LANE

PATH FOLLOWS TRACK THROUGH WOODLAND

FINE DOWNLAND VIEWS

OLD BARN

GRASSY VALLEY

LONG GRASSY VALLEYS

PATH FOLLOWS GRASSY HILLTOP

SHORT SECTION BETWEEN BUSHES

LULLINGTON HEATH NATIONAL NATURE RESERVE

48

¼ mile

500m

APPROX SCALE

JEVINGTON

15 – 25 MINS FROM HILLTOP (MAP 48)

JEVINGTON

25 – 35 MINS TO HILLTOP (MAP 48)

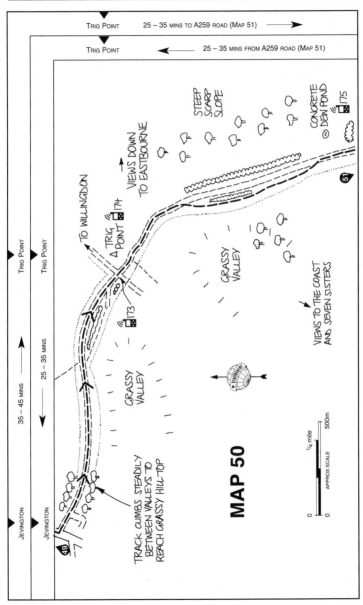

TRIG POINT ▼   25 – 35 MINS TO A259 ROAD (MAP 51) ⟶

TRIG POINT   ⟵ 25 – 35 MINS FROM A259 ROAD (MAP 51)

STEEP SCARP SLOPE

CONCRETE DEW POND

175

VIEWS DOWN TO EASTBOURNE

TO WILLINGDON

TRIG POINT 174

173

51

GRASSY VALLEY

VIEWS TO THE COAST AND SEVEN SISTERS

GRASSY VALLEY

MAP 50

¼ mile
500m
APPROX SCALE

TRACK CLIMBS STEADILY BETWEEN VALLEYS TO REACH GRASSY HILL-TOP

JEVINGTON

49

TRIG POINT ▼

TRIG POINT

35 – 45 MINS

25 – 35 MINS

JEVINGTON ▼

JEVINGTON

ROUTE GUIDE AND MAPS

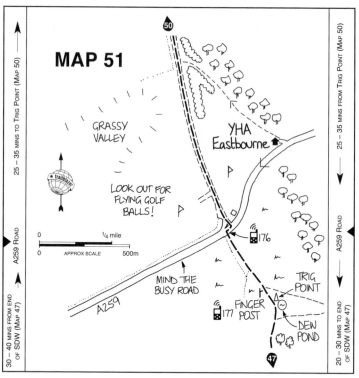

MAP 51

GRASSY VALLEY

LOOK OUT FOR FLYING GOLF BALLS!

YHA Eastbourne

176

MIND THE BUSY ROAD

A259

177 FINGER POST

TRIG POINT

DEW POND

25 – 35 MINS TO TRIG POINT (MAP 50)

A259 ROAD

30 – 40 MINS FROM END OF SDW (MAP 47)

ROUTE GUIDE AND MAPS

25 – 35 MINS FROM TRIG POINT (MAP 50)

A259 ROAD

20 – 30 MINS TO END OF SDW (MAP 47)

EASTBOURNE   MAP 52, p181

Eastbourne is a typical English seaside resort, complete with a grand Victorian pier (despite the fire in 2014), though it does have something of a reputation as a retirement town.

Having received a lot of criticism over the years as being one of the least adventurous resorts, particularly when compared to its upbeat neighbour Brighton, Eastbourne has undergone something of a revival. The signs on the edge of town shout out 'Welcome to the Sunshine Coast' and certainly this is one of the sunnier corners of the UK. However, parts of the centre, particularly the area around the railway station, are far from appealing, and not the sort of places to linger. It certainly doesn't

have the history and charm of Winchester at the other end of the South Downs Way, although Beachy Head, at least, makes for a fitting end to a long walk.

You can walk along the long, stony **beach** on either side of the 300m-long **pier** which was built between 1866 and 1872 on stilts sitting in cups on the sea-bed allowing it to shift a little in stormy weather. In July 2014 the central domed building was destroyed by fire, but the pier is open again and is a good spot for arcades, fish & chips, coffee and ice-cream. It's also a great place from which to watch the annual airshow, **Airbourne** (see box p14), which takes place over several days in the middle of August.

Towner (☎ 01323-434670, 🖳 towner
eastbourne.org.uk; Tue-Sun & Bank Hol
Mons 10am-5pm; free) is an interesting
contemporary art gallery on College Rd.

Wish Tower is a Martello Tower, one
of a number built along the coast to count-
er an invasion threat from Napoleon.

Services

Terminus Rd is both the commercial and
tourist centre, with most of the shops up at
the railway station end of the road, and the
restaurants, cafés and souvenir shops at the
beach end. It's about 30 minutes' walk from
the foot of the South Downs and the end of
the Way.

The **tourist information centre** (TIC;
☎ 01323-415415, 🖳 visiteastbourne.com;
end May to end Sep Mon-Fri 9am-5.30pm,
Sat to 5pm, Sun 10am-1pm, bank hols
10am-4pm, Mar-May & Oct Mon-Fri 9am-
5.30pm, Sat to 4pm, Nov-Feb Mon-Fri
9am-4.30pm, Sat to 1pm; WI-FI) is off the
northern end of Terminus Rd on Cornfield
Rd. There is plenty of free information
here, not only for Eastbourne but also the
rest of South-East England and London too.
They also do accommodation booking for
Eastbourne (£3 booking fee 10% deposit).

The **post office** (Mon-Sat 9am-
5.30pm) is inside WH Smith, on Terminus
Rd, where you'll also find a **pharmacy**
(Boots, Mon-Sat 8.30am-6pm & Sun
10.30am-4.30pm) and several **banks**.

Rainbows Launderette (Mon-Fri
8.30am-5.30pm, Sat 9am-5.30pm, Sun
9am-3pm) is on Seaside Rd.

Outdoor shops, **Millets** and **Blacks**,
are also on Terminus Rd (both open Mon-
Sat 9am-5.30pm, Sun 10.30am-4.30pm).
Also here is **Waterstones** bookshop (Mon-
Sat 9am-5.30pm, Sun 10.30am-4.30pm),
department stores **Debenhams** and **M&S**,
and a **Curzon cinema**.

There is a big **Sainsbury's supermarket** in Arndale Shopping Centre, a **Premier**
and **Tesco Express** on Seaside Rd, a **Co-op**
on Cornfield Rd and **Spar** on Terminus Rd.
Most open daily from around 7am to 11pm.
Hudson's (Tue-Fri 8am-5.30pm, Sat 8am-
2pm) is a quality **deli** with great-value
made-to-order sandwiches for around £3.

For sticks of rock, jars of humbug
mints, boxes of Eastbourne fudge and other
traditional teeth-rotting souvenirs, head to
Ye Olde Fashioned Humbugge Shoppe
(Mon-Sat 9am-6pm, Sun 10am-4pm), a
family-run business that's been here for
more than 50 years.

Public transport

Eastbourne is connected by **train** (see box
p43) to places along the south coast as well
as to Gatwick Airport and London Victoria.
National Express's No 24 **coach** (see box
p44) also goes to Gatwick and London
Victoria and their 315 service runs west
along the coast to Helston in Cornwall.

Stagecoach's **bus** No 3/3A runs to
Meads Village at the end of the South
Downs Way. Brighton & Hove Buses go to
Brighton (12A, 12X & 13X; the weekend
only 13X calls at Birling Gap and Beachy
Head). Compass Travel's No 143 service
goes to Lewes. Seaford & District's Nos
124 & 125 go to Lewes; Cuckmere
Community Bus (CCB) operates the No
125 on Saturdays and the No 126 at weekends to Seaford. CCB also run Nos 41 & 44
which call here on certain days of the week;
see pp44-7.

Try Eastbourne Taxis (☎ 01323-
720720) if you need a **taxi**.

Where to stay

As a major seaside resort Eastbourne is
overflowing with hotels and guesthouses.
Note that for most hotels rates vary depending on whether there are any events on and
also for places on the seafront whether you
have a seaview or inland room.

YHA Eastbourne (Map 51, p178; ☎
0345-371 9316, 🖳 www.yha.org.uk/hostel/
eastbourne; 1 x 2-, 1 x 3-, 2 x 4-, 1 x 5-bed
room, 1 x 6-bed female dorm, 1 x 7-bed
male dorm, all en suite; WI-FI communal
areas only; Mar/Apr to end Oct) is self-
catering only but has a drying room, laundry facilities and a bike shed. A dorm bed
starts from £15 and private rooms cost from
£59 but the rates can vary a lot so check the
website for details. The hostel is housed in
a modern building by the A259 near the
golf course on the western edge of

Eastbourne, about a mile from the town centre. The next closest thing to a hostel is *The Big Sleep Hotel* (☎ 01323-722676, 🖳 thebigsleephotel.com; 10S/14D/12T/1Tr/ 2Qd and two studio rooms sleeping up to six and with a kitchenette; all en suite; ☛; WI-FI; 🐾), a stylish, modern place on the seafront. Curiously pitched somewhere between a hostel and a boutique hotel, it's packed with facilities including pool and table tennis tables, 12-channel TVs in the rooms and even a bar serving snack food. Prices are reasonable: £22.50-47.50pp (sgl/sgl occ £29-75; three/four/six sharing £79-125) including continental breakfast (cooked breakfast additional £4pp or £6pp for a large breakfast).

Near here you'll find three good B&Bs. *Cherry Tree Guesthouse* (☎ 01323-722406, 🖳 cherrytree-eastbourne.co.uk; 3S/2T/3D/1Tr, all en suite; ☛; WI-FI; ⓛ; 🐾) is at 15 Silverdale Rd; it's an Edwardian townhouse with B&B for £40-42pp (sgl/sgl occ from £42/60). Just around the corner is *Brayscroft House* (☎ 01323-647005, 🖳 brayscrofthouse.co.uk; 1S/2T/ 3D, all en suite; ☛; WI-FI; ⓛ), at 13 South Cliff Ave, another Edwardian house with lots of antique furniture and beds for £27.50-47.50pp (sgl/sgl occ £45-70); dinner from £18 (book in advance). Next door at No 15 is *Southcroft* (☎ 01323-729071, 🖳 southcrofthotel.co.uk; 1S/2D or T/2D/ 1Tr, all en suite; ☛; WI-FI; ⓛ), a guesthouse which charges £40pp (sgl/sgl occ £45/60-80) for B&B.

Along the seafront and King Edward's Parade there's also *Alexandra Hotel* (☎ 01323-720131, 🖳 alexandrahoteleastbour ne.co.uk; 11S/10D/17T, all en suite; ☛; WI-FI) where B&B costs £35-60pp (sgl £35-52, sgl occ £60-85) and *Oban Hotel* (☎ 01323-731581, 🖳 oban-hotel.co.uk; 7S/9D/8D or T/3T, all en suite; ☛; WI-FI), a large establishment with B&B for £42.50-47.50pp (sgl from £50, sgl occ full room rate).

Nearby, *da Vinci* (☎ 01323-727173, 🖳 davinci.uk.com; 4S/8D/5D or T/1Tr/1Qd, all en suite; ☛; WI-FI), on Howard Sq, has an **art gallery** downstairs and 'art-themed' rooms. It's a friendly, comfortable place and B&B costs from around £35-55pp

(sgl/sgl occ £35-60). Phone them for the best prices.

The chain *Premier Inn* (☎ 0871-527 9448, 🖳 www.premierinn.com; 65D, all en suite; ☛; WI-FI), has a hotel on Terminus Rd. Book online rather than calling the high-rate phone number. Saver rates can be as low as £55 for the room (two people; a sofabed is available if you need separate beds) if booked well in advance or more than twice that if booked last minute. The rooms have very comfortable beds and 40" flat-screen TVs. There's a restaurant: a continental/ cooked breakfast costs £6.99/8.99pp.

Right opposite the pier is the appropriately named *The Pier Hotel* (☎ 01323-649544, 🖳 pierhotel.relaxinnz.co.uk; 13S/11D/8T, all en suite; ☛; WI-FI), a place that's not without its charms and is in a great location. Rooms are fair value at around £55-79pp (sgl £39-72, sgl occ rates on request) but do vary all the time so contact them for a precise rate. Also on the seafront are *Hotel Iverna* (☎ 01323-730768, 🖳 www.hoteliverna.com; 1S/2D/ 2T/1Tr, en suite or private facilities; ☛; 🐾), 32 Marine Parade, with B&B for £27.50-38pp (sgl occ rates on request but full room rate in summer); and *Cromwell House* (☎ 01323-725288, 🖳 cromwell-house.co.uk; 2S/2T/1D/3D or T, all en suite; WI-FI; ⓛ), at 23 Cavendish Place, a Victorian townhouse with B&B for £25-40pp (sgl £30-40, sgl occ £50-60).

Sea Beach House (☎ 01323-410458, 🖳 seabeachhouse.com; 5D/4T, all en suite; ☛; WI-FI; 🐾), is at 40 Marine Parade. B&B costs £36.50-41pp (sgl occ £50-60); some rooms have sea views. Princess (later to become Queen) Victoria is said to have stayed here. If it's luxury you require after your walk, try *Waterside Boutique Hotel* (off Map 52; ☎ 01323-646566, 🖳 water sidehoteleastbourne.co.uk; 2D or T/16D, all en suite; WI-FI), 11-12 Royal Parade; B&B costs £40-75pp (sgl occ rates on request). Some rooms have Jacuzzis.

Where to eat and drink

You'll find a surprisingly eclectic mix of restaurants and cafés on or around busy **Seaside Rd** and **Terminus Rd**.

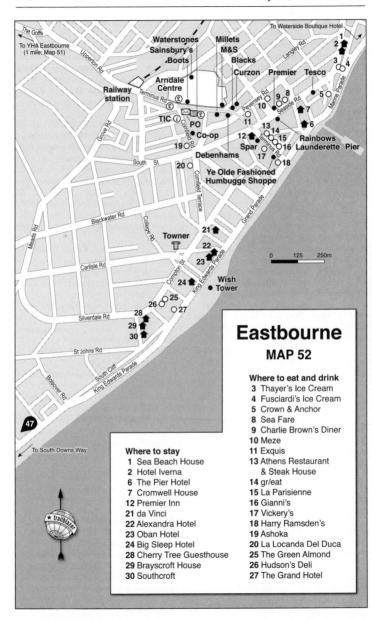

ROUTE GUIDE AND MAPS

The Goffs

To YHA Eastbourne
(1 mile; Map 51)

To Waterside Boutique Hotel

Upperton Rd

Langley Rd

Marine Parade

Waterstones **Millets**
Sainsbury's **M&S**
Boots **Blacks**
Curzon **Premier** **Tesco**

Arndale
Centre

Railway
station

Terminus Rd

Pevensey Rd

Seaside Rd

TIC ℹ

PO

Co-op

19 ○

Grove Rd

Cornfield Rd

South St

20 ○

Cornfield Terrace

Debenhams

Ye Olde Fashioned
Humbugge Shoppe

Spar

Terminus Rd

12 ▲

13

14

15

16

17

18

Grand Parade

Rainbows
Launderette **Pier**

Blackwater Rd

College Rd

Meads Rd

Towner

21 ▲

22

23

Carlisle Rd

Compton St

King Edwards Parade

24 ○

Wish
● **Tower**

26 ○ 25 ○

Silverdale Rd

28 ▲

29 ▲

30 ▲

27 ○

St Johns Rd

Belsover Rd

South Cliff

King Edwards Parade

47

To South Downs Way

★ trailblazer

0   125   250m

Eastbourne
MAP 52

Where to eat and drink
3 Thayer's Ice Cream
4 Fusciardi's Ice Cream
5 Crown & Anchor
8 Sea Fare
9 Charlie Brown's Diner
10 Meze
11 Exquis
13 Athens Restaurant
   & Steak House
14 gr/eat
15 La Parisienne
16 Gianni's
17 Vickery's
18 Harry Ramsden's
19 Ashoka
20 La Locanda Del Duca
25 The Green Almond
26 Hudson's Deli
27 The Grand Hotel

Where to stay
1 Sea Beach House
2 Hotel Iverna
6 The Pier Hotel
7 Cromwell House
12 Premier Inn
21 da Vinci
22 Alexandra Hotel
23 Oban Hotel
24 Big Sleep Hotel
28 Cherry Tree Guesthouse
29 Brayscroft House
30 Southcroft

Cafés & pubs On Terminus Rd, *Vickery's* (daily 9am-5pm) is a good-value café with all-day breakfasts. Opposite, *La Parisienne* (daily 10am-10pm) is a French-style café-bistro with some road-side seating. Next door, the Greek café and deli *gr/eat* (Wed-Mon noon-10pm) has a terrible name, but a good selection of Mediterranean fare. On Seaside Rd, at No 54, *Charlie Brown's Diner* (☎ 01323-726588, ⌨ charliebrownsdiner.co.uk; Tue-Sat 6-10.30/11pm; WI-FI) is good for burgers and the like. For something more refined, and away from the holiday-maker hordes, *The Green Almond* (☎ 01323-734470, ⌨ thegreenalmond.com; Mon-Thur noon-4pm, Fri & Sat noon-4pm & 7-11pm), 12 Grand Hotel Buildings, Compton St, is an award-winning vegetarian bistro that does popular lunchtime buffets (£7-8.50) as well as a three-course evening dinner (£20). Booking is recommended.

There are numerous **pubs**, some a lot rougher than others. *Crown & Anchor* (☎ 01323-642500, ⌨ crownandanchoreastbourne.co.uk; food daily 11am-9pm; WI-FI; 🐾), on the seafront at 15 Marine Parade, often has live music at weekends and is one of the more welcoming places.

As with any British seaside town, **ice-cream** is a big seller in Eastbourne. You can get it pretty much anywhere, but between Marine Parade and Seaside Rd are two particularly popular competing outlets; both very good. The cheaper of the two, *Thayer's Ice Cream*, is a small family-run business with dozens of different flavours. Bigger, brasher *Fusciardi's* (daily 9am-7pm), on the seafront, also has a sit-down café area.

Restaurants & takeaways At the seafront end of Terminus Rd, *Gianni's* (Sun-Thur noon-9pm, Fri-Sat noon-10pm) is a friendly pizzeria that also sells Italian ice-cream, and there are various pizza chains around town. For something a bit classier, *La Locana Del Duca* (☎ 01323-737177, ⌨ la-locanda-del-duca.com; daily noon-2.30pm & 5.30-11pm, Sun to 10.30pm), 26 Cornfield Terrace, is an authentic Italian place offering set menus for £18.95/20.95 for two/three courses and traditional favourites à la carte.

Back on Terminus Rd there's *Athens Restaurant & Steak House* (☎ 01323-733278; daily 11.30am-2.30pm & 6-10.30pm), at No 195. It's efficiently run by three generations of a hospitable Greek-Cypriot family and their moussaka is particularly good.

At 1 Pevensey Rd, *Exquis* (☎ 01323-430885; Tue-Sat 6-11pm, also from noon Fri), is shabby outside but actually a delightful French bistro with a simple menu that's good value. Nearby *Meze* (☎ 01323-731893, ⌨ www.meze-restaurant.com; daily noon-midnight), at 15 Pevensey Rd, is a good Turkish restaurant. For decent Indian cuisine, head to *Ashoka* (daily noon-2pm & 6-11.30pm), on Cornfield Rd. It's been in business nearly 30 years.

But for something more traditionally English, it has to be fish & chips. There are plenty of options here, including a branch of the *Harry Ramsden's* chain (☎ 01323-417454; summer Sun-Thur 11.30am-9pm Fri & Sat to 10pm, winter to 8pm/9pm), on the seafront at the end of Terminus Rd. For a more down-to-earth chippie, try *Sea Fare* (☎ 01323-641893; daily 11.30am-3.30pm & 4.30-9pm), at 66 Seaside Rd.

❏ **Afternoon tea at The Grand**
If your walk ends at about tea-time and you wish to celebrate in style there can be no better place for a top-of-the-range cream tea than *The Grand Hotel* (☎ 01323-412345, ⌨ grandeastbourne.com). You should phone ahead to book. It's served daily from 2.45pm to 6.30pm when for £26-28.50 you get a full spread including sandwiches, scones and cakes. You can push the boat out even further with the Grand Champagne Tea (£34.50-37). The hotel is easy to find: you walk right past it on the way into Eastbourne from the end of the South Downs Way. Splash out – you deserve it!

APPENDIX A: GPS WAYPOINTS

Each waypoint was taken on the route at the reference number marked on the map as below.

MAP	REF	GPS WAYPOINT		DESCRIPTION
Map 2	001	N51° 03.228'	W01° 16.749'	Join road
Map 2	002	N51° 02.862'	W01° 16.146'	Turn left onto track
Map 2	003	N51° 03.006'	W01° 15.865'	Leave track
Map 3	004	N51° 02.813'	W01° 14.842'	Road crossing
Map 3	005	N51° 02.997'	W01° 14.437'	Through gate on track
Map 3	006	N51° 03.433'	W01° 14.089'	Track junction at farmyard
Map 3	007	N51° 02.955'	W01° 12.769'	Crossroads
Map 4	008	N51° 02.727'	W01° 12.399'	Gate into field
Map 4	009	N51° 02.346'	W01° 12.081'	Cross A272 road
Map 4	010	N51° 01.586'	W01° 11.793'	Join lane leading uphill
Map 5	011	N51° 01.041'	W01° 11.358'	The Milbury's
Map 5	012	N51° 00.821'	W01° 10.521'	Gate to Wind Farm
Map 5	013	N51° 00.580'	W01° 09.631'	Track passes houses
Map 6	014	N51° 00.059'	W01° 08.913'	Beacon Hill car park
Map 6	015	N50° 59.555'	W01° 08.413'	Stile to cross fields
Map 6	016	N50° 59.342'	W01° 08.227'	Stile to cross track
Map 7	017	N50° 59.040'	W01° 07.728'	The Shoe Inn, Exton
Map 7	018	N50° 59.252'	W01° 07.208'	Bridge over River Meon
Map 7	019	N50° 59.196'	W01° 06.725'	Cross disused railway
Map 7	020	N50° 58.854'	W01° 05.328'	Hill fort, Old Winchester Hill
Map 8	021	N50° 59.009'	W01° 04.712'	Turn off track
Map 8	022	N50° 59.279'	W01° 04.827'	Car park
Map 8	023	N50° 59.443'	W01° 04.934'	Gate at fork in road
Map 8	024	N50° 59.238'	W01° 04.546'	Join track
Map 8	025	N50° 59.296'	W01° 04.200'	Left turn at farmyard
Map 8	026	N50° 59.446'	W01° 03.153'	Turn onto tree-lined avenue
Map 8	027	N50° 59.066'	W01° 03.085'	Crossroads
Map 9	028	N50° 58.079'	W01° 02.373'	Wetherdown Lodge
Map 9	029	N50° 57.939'	W01° 01.698'	Road junction
Map 10	030	N50° 58.051'	W01° 00.110'	Homelands Farm
Map 10	031	N50° 58.026'	W00° 59.794'	Junction with Hogs Lodge Lane
Map 10	032	N50° 58.465'	W00° 59.274'	Butser Hill car park
Map 10	033	N50° 57.891'	W00° 58.866'	Gate before A3 road crossing
Map 11	034	N50° 57.450'	W00° 58.658'	Turn off track into woods
Map 11	035	N50° 58.095'	W00° 57.775'	Join other track
Map 12	036	N50° 58.372'	W00° 57.375'	Car park and road crossing
Map 12	037	N50° 58.206'	W00° 56.456'	Track junction
Map 12	038	N50° 58.153'	W00° 55.787'	Road junction
Map 13	039	N50° 57.980'	W00° 54.137'	Road crossing
Map 13	040	N50° 57.611'	W00° 53.213'	Car park, B2146 road crossing
Map 13	041	N50° 57.435'	W00° 52.672'	Car park, B2141 road crossing
Map 14	042	N50° 57.659'	W00° 51.469'	Turn-off to East Harting
Map 14	043	N50° 57.547'	W00° 51.119'	Trig point, Beacon Hill
Map 14	044	N50° 57.535'	W00° 50.447'	Path, not farm track!
Map 14	045	N50° 57.267'	W00° 49.981'	Track junction
Map 15	046	N50° 56.760'	W00° 49.665'	Track crossroads
Map 15	047	N50° 56.999'	W00° 48.587'	Track crossroads

(waypoints continued on p186)

	START Winchester	Chilcomb	(Cheriton +1.5)	Exton	(East Meon + 1)	(Buriton + 0.5)	(South Harting + 0.5)	(Cocking + 0.5)	(Heyshott + 0.5)	(Graffham + 1)	(Sutton/Bignor + 1)	(Bury + 1)	Houghton Bridge	Amberley	(Storrington + 1.5)	(Washington + 0.5)	(Steyning/Bramber/Upper Beeding + 1)
START Winchester	0																
Chilcomb	2																
(Cheriton +1.5)	6½	4½															
Exton	12	10	5½														
(East Meon + 1)	17	15	10½	5													
(Buriton + 0.5)	24½	22½	18	12½	7½												
(Sth Harting + 0.5)	28	26	21½	16	11	3½											
(Cocking + 0.5)	35	33	28½	23	18	10½	7										
(Heyshott + 0.5)	37	35	30½	25	20	12½	9	2									
(Graffham + 1)	38½	36½	32	26½	21½	14	10½	3½	1½								
(Sutton/Bignor + 1)	42½	40½	36	30½	25½	18	14½	7½	5½	4							
(Bury + 1)	45	43	38½	33	28	20½	17	10	8	6½	2½						
Houghton Bridge	46	44	39½	34	29	21½	18	11	9	7½	3½	1					
Amberley	47½	45½	41	35½	30½	23	19½	12½	10½	9	5	2½	1½				
(Storrington + 1.5)	50½	48½	44	38½	33½	26	22½	15½	13½	12	8	5½	4½	3			
(Washington + 0.5)	53½	51½	47	41½	36½	29	25½	18½	16½	15	11	8½	7½	6	3		
(Steyning/U Bd + 1)	57½	55½	51	45½	40½	33	29½	22½	20½	19	15	12½	11½	10	7	4	
(Fulking + 0.5)	64	62	57½	52	47	39½	36	29	27	25½	21½	19	18	16½	13½	10½	6½
(Poynings + 0.5)	66	64	59½	54	49	41½	38	31	29	27½	23½	21	20	18½	15½	12½	8½
Pyecombe	68	66	61½	56	51	43½	40	33	31	29½	25½	23	22	20½	17½	14½	10½
(Clayton + 0.5)	69	67	62½	57	52	44½	41	34	32	30½	26½	24	23	21½	18½	15½	11½
(Ditchling + 1.5)	70½	68½	64	58½	53½	46	42½	35½	33½	32	28	25½	24½	23	20	17	13
(Plumpton + 0.5)	72½	70½	66	60½	55½	48	44½	37½	35½	34	30	27½	26½	25	22	19	15
(Lewes + 3)	73½	71½	67	61½	56½	49	45½	38½	36½	35	31	28½	27½	26	23	20	16
(Kingston + 1)	78½	76½	72	66½	61½	54	50½	43½	41½	40	36	33½	32½	31	28	25	21
Rodmell/Southease	82½	80½	76	70½	65½	58	54½	47½	45½	44	40	37½	36½	35	32	29	25
(West Firle + 1)	86	84	79½	74	69	61½	58	51	49	47½	43½	41	40	38½	35½	32½	28½
(Alciston/Bwk + 1)	88½	86½	82	76½	71½	64	60½	53½	51½	50	46	43½	42½	41	38	35	31
Alfriston	90½	88½	84	78½	73½	66	62½	55½	53½	52	48	45½	44½	43	40	37	33
[via AR] Jevington*	93	91	86½	81	76	68½	65	58	56	54½	50½	48	47	45½	42½	39½	35½
[via AR] End (E + 1)*	97	95	90½	85	80	72½	69	62	60	58½	54½	52	51	49½	46½	43½	39½
Litlington	91½	89½	85	79½	74½	67	63½	56½	54½	53	49	46½	45½	44	41	38	34
Exceat/Seven Sstrs	93	91	86½	81	76	68½	65	58	56	54½	50½	48	47	45½	42½	39½	35½
Birling Gap	96	94	89½	84	79	71½	68	61	59	57½	53½	51	50	48½	45½	42½	38½
Beachy Head	99	97	92½	87	82	74½	71	64	62	60½	56½	54	53	51½	48½	45½	41½
END (Eastbrn + 1)	100	98	93½	88	83	75½	72	65	63	61½	57½	55	54	52½	49½	46½	42½

* ALTERNATIVE (INLAND) ROUTE FROM ALFRISTON

South Downs Way
DISTANCE CHART

Winchester to Eastbourne

miles (approx) – 1 mile = 1.6km

Note: Where a place name is shown in (brackets) on this chart the distance to the turnoff to this place is shown. Add the (+) number in the brackets to calculate the total distance to that place. Most villages lie below the South Downs.

(Fulking + 0.5)	(Poynings + 0.5)	Pyecombe	(Clayton + 0.5)	(Ditchling + 1.5)	(Plumpton + 0.5)	(Lewes + 3)	(Kingston near Lewes + 1)	Rodmell/Southease	(West Firle + 1)	(Alciston/Berwick + 1)	Alfriston	[via inland route*] Jevington	[via inland route*] End (Eastbourne + 1)	Litlington	Exceat/Seven Sisters	Birling Gap	Beachy Head	END (Eastbourne + 1)
2																		
4	2																	
5	3	1																
6½	4½	2½	1½															
8½	6½	4½	3½	2														
9½	7½	5½	4½	3	1													
14½	12½	10½	9½	8	6	5												
18½	16½	14½	13½	12	10	9	4											
22	20	18	17	15½	13½	12½	7½	3½										
24½	22½	20½	19½	18	16	15	10	6	2½									
26½	24½	22½	21½	20	18	17	12	8	4½	2								
29	*27*	*25*	*24*	*22½*	*20½*	*19½*	*14½*	*10½*	*7*	*4½*	*2½*							
33	*31*	*29*	*28*	*26½*	*24½*	*23½*	*18½*	*14½*	*11*	*8½*	*6½*	*4*						
27½	25½	23½	22½	21	19	18	13	9	5½	3	1							
29	27	25	24	22½	20½	19½	14½	10½	7	4½	2½			1½				
32	30	28	27	25½	23½	22½	17½	13½	10	7½	5½			4½	3			
35	33	31	30	28½	26½	25½	20½	16½	13	10½	8½			7½	6	3		
36	34	32	31	29½	27½	26½	21½	17½	14	11½	9½			8½	7	4	1	

MAP	REF	GPS WAYPOINT		DESCRIPTION *(cont'd from p183)*
Map 15	048	N50° 56.873'	W00° 47.494'	Path junction, Cocking Down
Map 16	049	N50° 56.759'	W00° 47.002'	Track crossroads
Map 16	050	N50° 56.660'	W00° 46.360'	Junction near chalk boulder
Map 16	051	N50° 56.571'	W00° 45.338'	Car park at A268 crossing
Map 16	052	N50° 56.544'	W00° 45.002'	Water tap
Map 17	053	N50° 56.440'	W00° 44.226'	Fork in track
Map 17	054	N50° 56.463'	W00° 43.706'	Path junction
Map 17	055	N50° 56.466'	W00° 43.258'	Turn-off to Heyshott
Map 18	056	N50° 56.457'	W00° 42.857'	Path junction
Map 18	057	N50° 56.378'	W00° 42.375'	Track junction
Map 18	058	N50° 56.353'	W00° 42.128'	Track junction
Map 18	059	N50° 56.239'	W00° 40.938'	Signpost with memorials
Map 18	060	N50° 56.016'	W00° 39.082'	Track junction
Map 19	061	N50° 55.902'	W00° 39.598'	Track crossroads
Map 19	062	N50° 55.307'	W00° 38.925'	Cross A285 road
Map 19	063	N50° 54.803'	W00° 38.488'	Track junction
Map 20	064	N50° 54.441'	W00° 37.926'	Track junction
Map 20	065	N50° 54.402'	W00° 37.319'	Track junction
Map 20	066	N50° 54.464'	W00° 36.968'	Bignor Hill car park
Map 20	067	N50° 54.587'	W00° 36.157'	Memorial to Toby 1888-1955
Map 21	068	N50° 54.470'	W00° 35.814'	Track junction
Map 21	069	N50° 53.884'	W00° 34.403'	Cross A29 road
Map 21	070	N50° 53.837'	W00° 33.310'	Cross country lane
Map 22	071	N50° 53.952'	W00° 32.927'	Bridge over River Arun
Map 22	072	N50° 54.025'	W00° 32.358'	Leave B2139 road
Map 22	073	N50° 54.195'	W00° 31.927'	Road junction
Map 22	074	N50° 54.188'	W00° 31.839'	Leave road
Map 22	075	N50° 54.158'	W00° 31.215'	Gate & stile
Map 23	076	N50° 54.190'	W00° 30.413'	Join track
Map 23	077	N50° 54.145'	W00° 29.540'	Track junction
Map 23	078	N50° 54.111'	W00° 28.747'	Track junction
Map 23	079	N50° 54.051'	W00° 28.347'	Turn-off to Storrington
Map 25	080	N50° 53.656'	W00° 26.641'	Barn
Map 25	081	N50° 53.755'	W00° 26.032'	Gate on track
Map 25	082	N50° 53.791'	W00° 25.812'	Turn-off to Washington
Map 25	083	N50° 54.262'	W00° 25.039'	Join track
Map 25	084	N50° 54.251'	W00° 24.885'	Join road into Washington
Map 25	085	N50° 54.304'	W00° 24.306'	Frankland Arms, Washington
Map 25	086	N50° 54.189'	W00° 24.382'	Road junction, Washington
Map 25	087	N50° 53.807'	W00° 24.344'	Steep section of track
Map 26	088	N50° 53.617'	W00° 23.643'	Track junction
Map 26	089	N50° 53.757'	W00° 23.351'	Gate on track
Map 26	090	N50° 53.779'	W00° 22.928'	Chanctonbury Ring
Map 26	091	N50° 53.637'	W00° 22.612'	Gate on track
Map 26	092	N50° 53.409'	W00° 22.421'	Track junction
Map 26	093	N50° 53.269'	W00° 22.001'	Track junction
Map 27	094	N50° 53.219'	W00° 21.675'	Turn-off to Steyning
Map 27	095	N50° 52.669'	W00° 20.972'	Track junction
Map 29	096	N50° 52.403'	W00° 17.958'	Turn-off A283 road
Map 29	097	N50° 52.430'	W00° 17.094'	Car park
Map 29	098	N50° 52.881'	W00° 15.991'	Road to YHA Truleigh Hill
Map 30	099	N50° 52.919'	W00° 15.461'	Communications tower

MAP	REF	GPS WAYPOINT		DESCRIPTION
Map 30	100	N50° 53.063'	W00° 13.763'	Turn-off to Fulking
Map 30	101	N50° 52.937'	W00° 13.213'	Gate
Map 31	102	N50° 53.092'	W00° 12.744'	Devil's Dyke pub
Map 31	103	N50° 52.978'	W00° 12.254'	Gate on path
Map 31	104	N50° 53.309'	W00° 11.663'	Road crossing (A281)
Map 31	105	N50° 53.349'	W00° 11.466'	Gate into woodland
Map 31	106	N50° 53.410'	W00° 10.968'	Gate on path
Map 32	107	N50° 53.743'	W00° 10.001'	Join road
Map 32	108	N50° 53.923'	W00° 09.837'	Crossroads, Pyecombe
Map 32	109	N50° 54.056'	W00° 09.593'	Car park at golf club
Map 32	110	N50° 54.026'	W00° 08.687'	Track crossroads
Map 32	111	N50° 54.227'	W00° 08.718'	Track junction
Map 33	112	N50° 54.027'	W00° 07.845'	Gate by Keymer signpost
Map 33	113	N50° 54.146'	W00° 07.327'	Dew pond
Map 33	114	N50° 54.046'	W00° 06.278'	Car park, Ditchling Beacon
Map 33	115	N50° 53.940'	W00° 05.814'	Turn-off to Ditchling
Map 34	116	N50° 53.910'	W00° 04.709'	Gate after crossing road
Map 34	117	N50° 53.876'	W00° 04.387'	Turn-off to Plumpton
Map 34	118	N50° 53.759'	W00° 03.198'	Path turns sharp right; stay on track for Lewes
Map 35	119	N50° 53.259'	W00° 03.666'	Gate at track junction
Map 35	120	N50° 53.000'	W00° 03.295'	Leave track through gate
Map 35	121	N50° 52.505'	W00° 02.808'	Through gate by stile
Map 35	122	N50° 52.426'	W00° 03.190'	Small hut and pylon
Map 35	123	N50° 51.977'	W00° 03.268'	Steps
Map 35	124	N50° 51.977'	W00° 03.487'	Bridge over A27 road
Map 35	125	N50° 51.872'	W00° 02.952'	Path cuts under railway
Map 36	126	N50° 51.548'	W00° 03.227'	Through gate
Map 36	127	N50° 51.224'	W00° 03.463'	Through gate
Map 36	128	N50° 51.025'	W00° 03.266'	Through gate, follow fence
Map 36	129	N50° 51.278'	W00° 02.526'	Through gate by dew pond
Map 36	130	N50° 51.032'	W00° 01.876'	Join track
Map 37	131	N50° 50.673'	W00° 01.557'	Track, Swanborough Hill
Map 37	132	N50° 50.086'	E00° 00.479'	Leave track through gate
Map 38	133	N50° 50.009'	E00° 00.149'	Through gate, cross track
Map 38	134	N50° 49.566'	E00° 00.315'	Through gate onto track
Map 38	135	N50° 49.795'	E00° 01.061'	Road junction, Southease
Map 38	136	N50° 49.805'	E00° 01.562'	Bridge over River Ouse
Map 38	137	N50° 49.888'	E00° 01.849'	Level crossing
Map 38	138	N50° 49.804'	E00° 02.228'	Gate after bridge over A26
Map 39	139	N50° 49.875'	E00° 03.090'	Trig point & dew pond
Map 39	140	N50° 50.092'	E00° 03.667'	Gate onto track
Map 39	141	N50° 50.063'	E00° 04.114'	Telecom masts, Beddingham Hill
Map 39	142	N50° 50.069'	E00° 04.468'	Gate on path
Map 40	143	N50° 50.018'	E00° 04.987'	Car park, Firle Beacon
Map 40	144	N50° 50.029'	E00° 06.497'	Trig point, Firle Beacon
Map 40	145	N50° 49.527'	E00° 07.208'	Gate, Bo-Peep
Map 41	146	N50° 49.108'	E00° 07.823'	Gate on path
Map 41	147	N50° 48.659'	E00° 08.550'	Track junction
Map 42	148	N50° 48.405'	E00° 09.581'	Church, Alfriston
Map 42	149	N50° 48.689'	E00° 09.581'	Plough & Harrow, Litlington
Map 43	150	N50° 47.440'	E00° 09.628'	Path goes to the east of the hedge

MAP	REF	GPS WAYPOINT		DESCRIPTION
Map 43	151	N50° 47.098'	E00° 09.471'	Climb steps up through forest
Map 43	152	N50° 46.707'	E00° 09.699'	Track junction
Map 43	153	N50° 46.398'	E00° 09.559'	Crossroads, Westdean
Map 43	154	N50° 46.499'	E00° 09.244'	Road crossing, Exceat
Map 44	155	N50° 45.905'	E00° 09.085'	Turn off track
Map 44	156	N50° 45.909'	E00° 09.508'	Stile on path
Map 44	157	N50° 45.376'	E00° 09.578'	Haven Brow
Map 44	158	N50° 45.310'	E00° 09.793'	Short Brow
Map 44	159	N50° 45.198'	E00° 10.139'	Rough Brow
Map 44	160	N50° 45.143'	E00° 10.376'	Brass Point
Map 45	161	N50° 44.995'	E00° 10.792'	Sarsen stone
Map 45	162	N50° 44.957'	E00° 11.020'	The 'Eighth' Sister
Map 45	163	N50° 44.910'	E00° 11.284'	Baily's Hill
Map 45	164	N50° 44.570'	E00° 11.462'	Memorial pillar
Map 45	165	N50° 44.766'	E00° 11.667'	Went Hill
Map 45	166	N50° 44.585'	E00° 12.075'	Car park, Birling Gap
Map 46	167	N50° 44.302'	E00° 12.901'	Belle Tout Lighthouse
Map 46	168	N50° 44.112'	E00° 13.870'	Path near Shooters Bottom
Map 47	169	N50° 44.335'	E00° 15.220'	RAF Bomber Command Memorial
Map 47	170	N50° 44.634'	E00° 15.478'	Fork in path
Map 47	171	N50° 45.113'	E00° 16.027'	End of SDW (coastal route)
Map 49	172	N50° 47.518'	E00° 12.825'	Turn left off main road
Map 50	173	N50° 47.222'	E00° 14.083'	Turn-off to Willingdon
Map 50	174	N50° 47.196'	E00° 14.162'	Trig point
Map 50	175	N50° 46.658'	E00° 14.575'	Concrete dew pond
Map 51	176	N50° 45.901'	E00° 14.776'	Road crossing
Map 51	177	N50° 45.729'	E00° 15.000'	Finger post
Map 47	171	N50° 45.113'	E00° 16.027'	End of SDW (inland route)

APPENDIX C: TAKING A DOG

TAKING DOGS ALONG THE WAY

Many are the rewards that await those prepared to make the extra effort required to bring their best friend along the trail. However, because the South Downs is a prime sheep-farming area your dog may have to be on a lead for much of the walk.

And you shouldn't underestimate the amount of work involved. Indeed, just about every decision you make will be influenced by the fact that you've got a dog: how you plan to travel to the start of the trail, where you're going to stay, how far you're going to walk each day, where you're going to rest and where you're going to eat in the evening etc.

If you're sure your dog can cope with (and will enjoy) walking 10 miles or more a day for several days in a row, you need to start preparing accordingly. Extra thought needs to go into your itinerary. The best starting point is to study the town & village facilities table on pp30-1 (and the advice below), and plan where to stop and where to buy food.

Looking after your dog

To begin with, you need to make sure that your dog is fully **inoculated** against the usual doggy illnesses, and also up to date with regard to **worm pills** (eg Drontal) and **flea preventatives** such as Frontline – they are, after all, following in the pawprints of many a dog before them, some of whom may well have left fleas or other parasites on the trail that now lie in wait for their next meal to arrive. **Pet insurance** is also a very good idea; if you've already got insurance, do check that it will cover a trip such as this. On the subject of looking after your dog's health, perhaps the most important implement you can take with you is the **plastic tick remover**, available from vets for a couple of quid. These removers, while fiddly, help you to remove the tick safely (ie without leaving its head behind buried under the dog's skin). Being in unfamiliar territory also makes it more likely that you and your dog could become separated. All dogs now have to be **microchipped** but make sure your dog also has a **tag with your contact details on it** (a mobile phone number would be best if you are carrying one with you).

When to keep your dog on a lead

● **On cliff tops** It's a sad fact that, every year, a few dogs lose their lives falling over the edge of the cliffs. It usually occurs when they are chasing rabbits (which know where the cliff-edge is and are able, unlike your poor pooch, to stop in time).

● **When crossing farmland**, particularly in the lambing season (March to May) when your dog can scare the sheep, causing them to lose their young. Farmers are allowed by law to shoot at and kill any dogs that they consider are worrying their sheep. During lambing, most farmers would prefer it if you didn't bring your dog at all. The exception is if your dog is being attacked by cows. Some years ago there were three deaths in the UK caused by walkers being trampled as they tried to rescue their dogs from the attentions of cattle. The advice in this instance is to let go of the lead, head speedily to a position of safety (usually the other side of the field gate or stile) and call your dog to you.

● **On National Trust land**, where it is compulsory to keep your dog on a lead.

● **Around ground-nesting birds** It's important to keep your dog under control when crossing an area where certain species of birds nest on the ground. Most dogs love foraging around in the woods but make sure you have permission to do so; some woods are used as 'nurseries' for game birds and dogs are only allowed through them if they are on a lead.

What to pack

You've probably already got a good idea of what to bring to keep your dog alive and happy, but the following is a checklist:

● **Food/water bowl** Foldable cloth bowls are popular with walkers, being light and taking up little room in the rucksack. You can get also get a water-bottle-and-bowl combination, where the bottle folds into a 'trough' from which the dog can drink.

● **Lead and collar** An extendable one is probably preferable for this sort of trip. Make sure both lead and collar are in good condition – you don't want either to snap on the trail, or you may end up carrying your dog through sheep fields until a replacement can be found.

● **Medication** You'll know if you need to bring any lotions or potions.

● **Bedding** A simple blanket may suffice, or you can opt for something more elaborate if you aren't carrying your own luggage.

● **Tick remover** See above.

● **Poo bags** Essential.

● **Hygiene wipes** For cleaning your dog after it's rolled in stuff.

● **A favourite toy** Helps prevent your dog from pining for the entire walk.

● **Food/water** Remember to bring treats as well as regular food to keep up the mutt's morale. That said, if your dog is anything like mine the chances are they'll spend most of the walk dining on rabbit droppings and sheep poo anyway.

● **Corkscrew stake** Available from camping or pet shops, this will help you to keep your dog secure in one place while you set up camp/doze.

● **Raingear** It can rain!

● **Old towels** For drying your dog.

When it comes to packing, I always leave an exterior pocket of my rucksack empty so I can put used poo bags in there (for deposit at the first bin reached). I always like to keep all the dog's kit together and separate from the other luggage (usually inside a plastic bag inside my rucksack). I have also seen several dogs sporting their own 'doggy rucksack', so they can carry their own food, water, poo etc – which certainly reduces the burden on their owner!

Cleaning up after your dog

It is extremely important that dog owners behave in a responsible way when walking the path. Dog excrement should be cleaned up. In towns, villages and fields where animals graze or which will be cut for silage, hay etc, you need to pick up and bag the excrement.

Staying (and eating) with your dog

In this guide we have used the symbol 🐾 to denote where a place welcomes dogs. However, this always needs to be arranged in advance and some places may charge extra. Many B&B-style places have only one or two rooms suitable for people with dogs; hostels (both YHA and independent) do not permit them unless they are an assistance (guide) dog; smaller campsites tend to accept them, but some of the larger holiday parks do not – however, in either case it is likely the dog will have to be on a lead. Before you turn up always double check whether the place you would like to stay accepts dogs and whether there is space for them. When it comes to eating, some cafés accept dogs and most landlords allow dogs in at least a section of their pubs, though few restaurants do. Make sure you always ask first and ensure your dog is on a lead and secured to your table or a radiator so it doesn't run around.

Henry Stedman

Map key

🛏	Where to stay	📖	Library/bookstore	●	Other	
O	Where to eat and drink	@	Internet	CP	Car park	
Δ	Campsite	🏛	Museum/gallery	🚌	Bus station/stop	
⊠	Post Office	✝	Church/cathedral	━⊏━	Rail line & station	
ⓔ	Bank/ATM	☎	Phone box	▭	Park	
ⓘ	Tourist Information	☑	Public toilet	📟 082	GPS waypoint	
		▢	Building			

/	South Downs Way	⊁	Stile	~ ~ ~	Water
/	Other path	⊁	Gate	⌇	Stream/river
//	4 x 4 track	⌒	Cliffs	♣	Trees/woodland
//	Tarmac road	⊁	Bridge	∴	Beach
/ᴍ	Steps	⋯	Fence	🗼	Lighthouse
↗	Slope	⌒⌒	Wall	4	Golf course
↗	Steep slope	⌀⌀	Hedge	32	Map continuation

INDEX

Page references in bold type refer to maps; NR = Nature Reserve; NP = National Park

TRAILBLAZER
British Walking Guides
SEE p203 FOR FULL TITLE LIST

Great Glen WAY

Dales Way

Norfolk Coast Path AND PEDDARS WAY

Dorset & South Devon COAST PATH

Thames Path

North Downs WAY

Scottish Highlands Hillwalking Guide

Great Glen Way

West Highland Way

Pennine Way

Hadrian's Wall Path

Coast to Coast

Dales Way

Pennine Way

Cleveland Way

Peddars Way & Norfolk Coast Path

Offa's Dyke Path

Cotswold Way

The Ridgeway

Pembrokeshire Coast Path

Thames Path

Exmoor & N Devon Coast Path

North Downs Way

Cornwall Coast Path

South Downs Way

Dorset & S Devon Coast Path

SCOTLAND

N. IRELAND

REP. OF IRELAND

ENGLAND

WALES

IRISH SEA

ENGLISH CHANNEL

Orkney
Thurso
Stornoway
Skye
Inverness
Aberdeen
Mull
Fort William
Milngavie
Glasgow
Edinburgh
Arran
Berwick upon Tweed
Kirk Yetholm
Bowness-on-Solway
Carlisle
Wallsend
Newcastle upon Tyne
Belfast
St Bees
Bowness-on-Windermere
Robin Hood's Bay
Filey
Helmsley
Ilkley
York
Dublin
Hull
Isle of Man
Liverpool
Manchester
Leeds
Edale
Prestatyn
Crewe
Lincoln
Anglesey
Bangor
Nottingham
Cromer
Norwich
Knettishall Heath
Cardigan
Birmingham
Cambridge
Amroth
Chipping Campden
Kemble
Ivinghoe Beacon
Chepstow
London
Cardiff
Bristol
Bath
Overton Hill
Canterbury
Dover
Minehead
Winchester
Farnham
Salisbury
Bude
Portsmouth
Brighton
Eastbourne
Exeter
Poole
Plymouth
Isle of Wight
Isles of Scilly

0   50   100km
0   25   50 miles

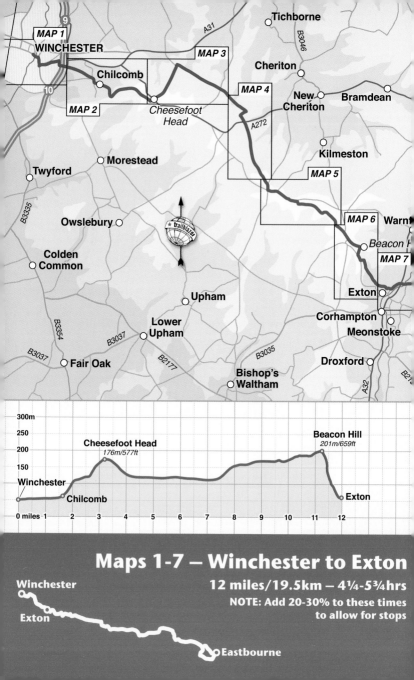

MAP 1
WINCHESTER

MAP 3

MAP 2

Cheesefoot Head

Chilcomb

Tichborne

B3046

Cheriton

MAP 4

New Cheriton

Bramdean

A272

Kilmeston

MAP 5

MAP 6

Warn

Beacon H

MAP 7

Morestead

Twyford

B3335

Owslebury

Colden Common

Upham

Lower Upham

Exton

Corhampton

Meonstoke

B3354

B3037

Fair Oak

B3037

B2177

B3035

Droxford

A32

B2

Bishop's Waltham

300m
250
200
150

Cheesefoot Head
176m/577ft

Beacon Hill
201m/659ft

Winchester

Chilcomb

Exton

0 miles 1   2   3   4   5   6   7   8   9   10   11   12

Maps 1-7 – Winchester to Exton

12 miles/19.5km – 4¼-5¾hrs

NOTE: Add 20-30% to these times to allow for stops

Winchester

Exton

Eastbourne

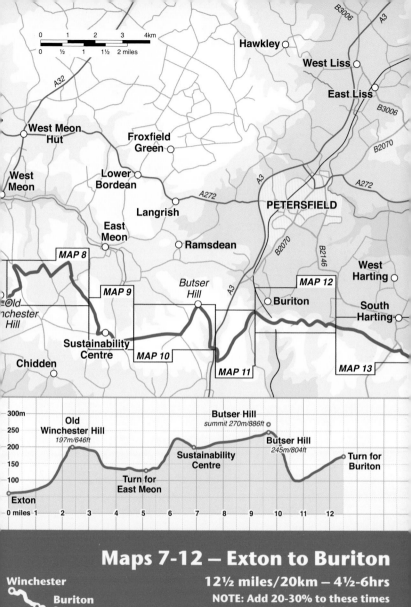

Maps 7–12 – Exton to Buriton

12½ miles/20km – 4½-6hrs

NOTE: Add 20-30% to these times to allow for stops

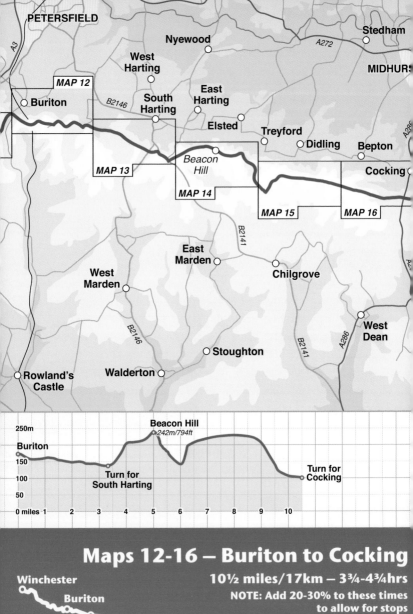

PETERSFIELD

Stedham

Nyewood

A272

MIDHURS

West
Harting

MAP 12

B2146

East
Harting

Buriton

South
Harting

Elsted

Treyford

Bepton

*Beacon
Hill*

Didling

MAP 13

Cocking

A286

MAP 14

MAP 15

MAP 16

B2141

East
Marden

Chilgrove

West
Marden

West
Dean

B2146

A286

B2141

Stoughton

A2

Walderton

Rowland's
Castle

250m

Beacon Hill
242m/794ft

Buriton

150

Turn for
South Harting

Turn for
Cocking

100

50

0 miles 1   2   3   4   5   6   7   8   9   10

Maps 12–16 – Buriton to Cocking

10½ miles/17km – 3¾-4¾hrs

NOTE: Add 20-30% to these times
to allow for stops

Winchester

Buriton

Cocking

Eastbourne

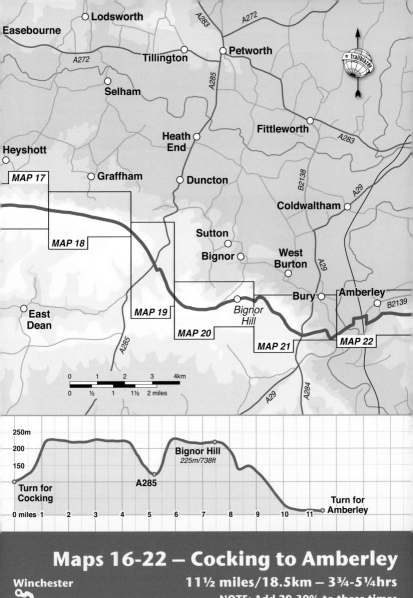

MAP 17

MAP 18

MAP 19

MAP 20

MAP 21

MAP 22

Lodsworth

Easebourne

A272

Tillington

Petworth

A283

A272

Selham

A285

Fittleworth

A283

Heyshott

Heath
End

B2138

A29

Graffham

Duncton

Coldwaltham

Sutton

Bignor

West
Burton

A29

East
Dean

Bignor
Hill

Bury

Amberley

B2139

A285

A29

A284

0   1   2   3   4km
0   ½   1   1½   2 miles

250m

200

150

Bignor Hill
225m/738ft

Turn for
Cocking

A285

Turn for
Amberley

0 miles 1   2   3   4   5   6   7   8   9   10   11

Maps 16-22 – Cocking to Amberley

11½ miles/18.5km – 3¾-5¼hrs

**NOTE: Add 20-30% to these times
to allow for stops**

Winchester

Cocking

Amberley

Eastbourne

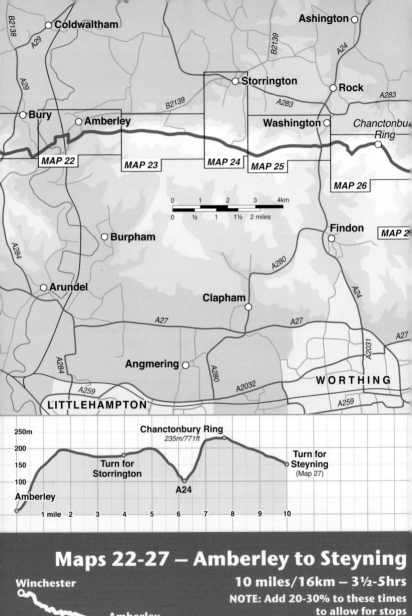

MAP 22

MAP 23

MAP 24

MAP 25

MAP 26

MAP 2

Coldwaltham

Ashington

Storrington

Rock

Bury

Amberley

Washington

Chanctonbu
Ring

Burpham

Findon

Arundel

Clapham

Angmering

WORTHING

LITTLEHAMPTON

Chanctonbury Ring
235m/771ft

Turn for
Storrington

Turn for
Steyning
(Map 27)

Amberley

A24

Maps 22-27 – Amberley to Steyning

10 miles/16km – 3½-5hrs

**NOTE: Add 20-30% to these times
to allow for stops**

Winchester

Amberley

Steyning

Eastbourne

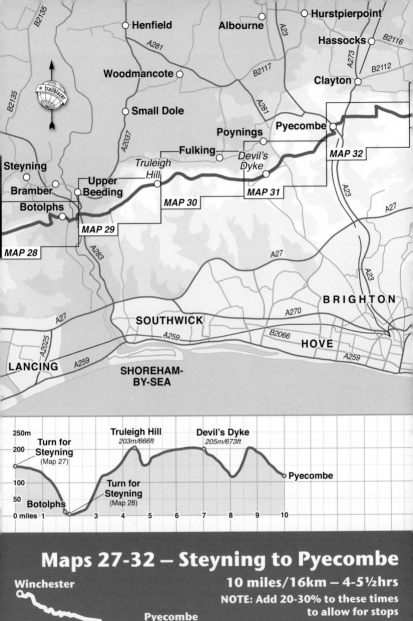

Maps 27-32 – Steyning to Pyecombe

10 miles/16km – 4-5½hrs

NOTE: Add 20-30% to these times
to allow for stops

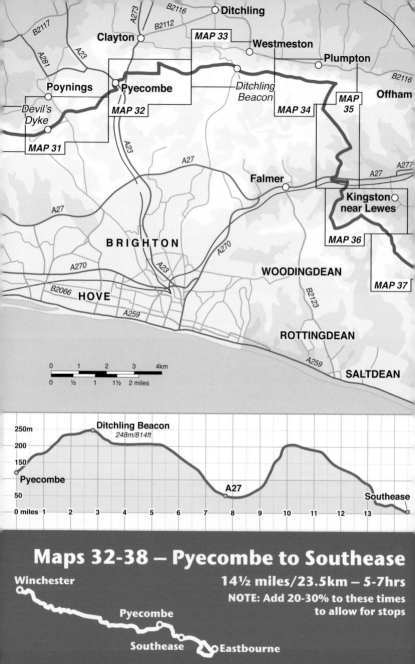

B2117
B2116
Ditchling
B2112
A273
Clayton
A23
Westmeston
MAP 33
Plumpton
B2116
A281
Poynings
Pyecombe
Offham
Ditchling
Beacon
MAP 35
Devil's
Dyke
MAP 32
MAP 34
A277
MAP 31
A23
A27
A27
Falmer
Kingston
near Lewes
A27
A270
MAP 36
BRIGHTON
A270
A23
A270
WOODINGDEAN
MAP 37
B2066
HOVE
B2123
A259
ROTTINGDEAN
A259
SALTDEAN

0   1   2   3   4km
0   ½   1   1½   2 miles

250m
Ditchling Beacon
248m/814ft
200
150
Pyecombe
A27
Southease
50
0 miles 1   2   3   4   5   6   7   8   9   10   11   12   13

Maps 32-38 – Pyecombe to Southease

Winchester

14½ miles/23.5km – 5-7hrs
**NOTE: Add 20-30% to these times
to allow for stops**

Pyecombe

Southease   Eastbourne

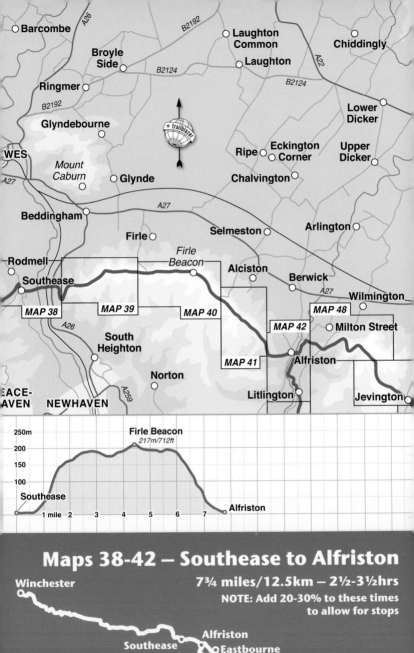

Barcombe

Broyle Side

Ringmer

Glyndebourne

WES

Mount Caburn

Beddingham

Firle

Rodmell

Southease

MAP 38

A26

Laughton Common

Laughton

Chiddingly

A22

B2124

B2124

Lower Dicker

★ trailblazer

Ripe

Eckington Corner

Upper Dicker

Glynde

Chalvington

A27

Selmeston

Arlington

Firle Beacon

Alciston

Berwick

A27

Wilmington

MAP 39

MAP 40

MAP 48

MAP 42

Milton Street

South Heighton

MAP 41

Alfriston

A26

Norton

Litlington

Jevington

A259

PEACE-HAVEN

NEWHAVEN

250m

Firle Beacon
217m/712ft

200

150

100

Southease

1 mile 2   3   4   5   6   7

Alfriston

Maps 38-42 – Southease to Alfriston

7¾ miles/12.5km – 2½-3½hrs
NOTE: Add 20-30% to these times to allow for stops

Winchester

Alfriston

Southease

Eastbourne

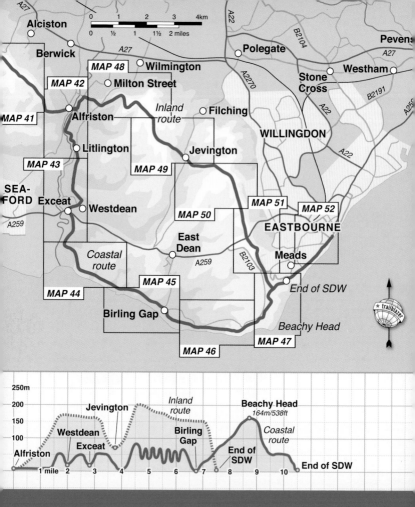

Maps 42-52 – Alfriston to end of SDW

COASTAL ROUTE – 10½ miles/17km – 4¼-5¾hrs
INLAND ROUTE – 7½ miles/12km – 2¾-3½hrs
NOTE: Add 20-30% to these times to allow for stops
Add 1½ miles for end of SDW to Eastbourne centre